the PROGRESSIVE ERA

Arthur Mann
University of Chicago

Major Issues of Interpretation
Second Edition

The Dryden Press
901 North Elm Street
Hinsdale, Illinois 60521

Library of Congress Catalog Card Number: 74-2802
ISBN: 0-03-013291-6
Printed in the United States of America
456 006 987654321

Cover Credit:
Illustration, "From the Depths" in John A. Mitchell's *The Silent War* (1906). General Research and Humanities Division, The New York Public Library, Astor, Lenox and Tilden Foundations.

Contents

Introduction

Eleven years have passed since the publication of the first edition of *The Progressive Era* in 1963. Many of the original selections are now out of date, not only because of newly gathered information, but also because of the emergence of new ideological and methodological differences among historians. The purpose of this second and enlarged edition, which includes only two readings from the first edition, is to acquaint students with the latest views of the Progressive movement.

But not even the best contemporary scholarship has resolved the major issues of interpretation concerning the first expression of twentieth-century liberalism in the United States. On the contrary, historians are still arguing over why the Progressive movement began and ended when it did; who led and supported it; what it stood for; whether it changed America for the good; and how it is related to reform movements that came both before and after it. Like the first edition of *The Progressive Era*, this second is about that ongoing historiographical debate.

With regard to this much however, there is general agreement. The foundations of the society we live in today were laid by industrialization, urbanization, and immigration between 1880 and 1920. That trinity of forces, while beneficial, also created massive problems. Like every country before or since, America paid a high price for modernization in the form of social dislocation, moral confusion, and human suffering. Why, asked an observer, must abysmal poverty accompany economic growth? The response to that and other paradoxes deriving from the rapid transformation of a commercial-agricultural society was the Progressive movement.

The central paradox was the unequal distribution of wealth, power, rights, and prestige in a country that claimed to stand for equal opportunity. It explains why reformers were concerned with the deprivations suffered by women, children, blacks, and immigrants, and why they were alarmed by the slum problem and the farm problem, the trust problem and the labor problem, and the problem of political corruption and governmental irresponsibility. To the Progressive way of thinking, all such problems were moral problems. The big question was whether democracy, whose values descended from earlier and less complicated times in America, could survive in the twentieth century.

Thanks to an impressive body of scholarship, we know that a pre-Progressive generation in the 1880s and 1890s anticipated the Progressives of 1900-1920 in their social concern. A minority in the population, they won few legislative victories but succeeded in prodding the democratic conscience. By the twentieth century, for example, three million copies had been sold of Henry George's *Progress and Poverty* (1879) and Edward Bellamy's *Looking Backward* (1888). It mattered little that only a handful of readers were converted to the single tax or socialism; George and Bellamy made the best-seller lists because each was saying, in his own way, that something must be done to solve The Social Question.

By the 1910s a consensus for reform defined the goals for many areas of American life. That decade was the high noon of the Progressive era. In the 1912 presidential election—to cite the most dramatic example—the Democratic Wilson, the Progressive (party) Roosevelt, the Socialist Debs, and the Republican Taft stood to the left of every president from the Civil War to 1900. The same was true, and had been true for a decade and more, of many political leaders in the cities and the states. Americans other than politicians moved toward Progressive reform between 1900 and World War I: businessmen and trade unionists; women as well as men; black and white ethnic groups; Protestant, Catholic, and Jewish clergymen; writers, artists, professors, journalists, publishers, social workers, doctors, lawyers; above all, the electorate.

And here we touch on a semantic difficulty that involves a major question of substance. With so many different kinds of people called Progressive, can it be said that they constituted a single movement? Peter G. Filene has argued that they did not and that the Progressive movement ought to be discarded as a fiction. Most historians disagree, partly because the Progressive movement is an established term in scholarly discourse, but more importantly because they think it makes sense.

They use it as an umbrella term to cover a variety of reform thrusts that set the tone of American life early in this century.

But if the Progressive movement was a many-sided affair—and what movement isn't—it also rested on unifying "tendencies." The word is Benjamin Parke De Witt's, the first historian of the Progressive movement. In 1915 he wrote that Progressivism was moving in the direction of three related goals: the regulation of big business, political reform, and the welfare state. This book of readings opens with De Witt's statement.

Although published more than a half-century ago, De Witt's history is still the fullest account of what he and his contemporaries were trying to do in the name of Progressivism. But De Witt was too close to his times to raise questions that historians have since raised. Concerned only with "the movement," he did not ask what kinds of people went into it. Just who were the Progressives? Further, because he wrote before the full record was in, De Witt could not evaluate the results of Progressive reforms in politics, the economy, and welfare. What were the achievements and failures of the Progressive movement? Finally, believing in Progressive values as an unmixed good when so many other Americans did, De Witt felt no need to justify those values. Were they as worthy as he assumed them to be?

One would think that, by now, there would be definitive answers to those questions. The fact is no aspect of the American past is more controversial than the Progressive movement. Besides, it is uncharacteristic of students of the past to believe for long in definitive answers. An interpretation no sooner succeeds with one generation than it is rejected by a succeeding generation. One reason is the discovery of new evidence, but different historians often interpret the same evidence in different ways. The reasons for that stem not only from historians themselves—their respective values, methods, times, and skill in handling evidence—but also from the intrinsic difficulties of establishing the "truth" in history.

Take the problem of causation, the subject of Part One. The most intriguing problem in historical analysis, it is also the most baffling and the most treacherous. No one has ever seen a cause; it is not a thing but an idea of how things are connected. Causation is an abstraction, a human construct, a mental contrivance designed to give order and meaning to experience. A cause can be an event or an idea, a push or a pull, a social force or a personal motive, a long tradition or a chance happening. All that and much more an historian must consider when he tries to figure out why human beings once behaved the way they did.

When the first edition of *The Progressive Era* was published in 1963, many textbooks traced the roots of Progressivism to Populism. That idea had been popular earlier in the century; the Progressives "caught the Populists in swimming," quipped William Allen White, a 1912 Bull Mooser, "and stole all their clothing except the frayed underdrawers of free silver." But that view of cause and effect did not fully catch on in the academy until, in 1931, Professor John D. Hicks documented it in a fact-filled volume. His *Populist Revolt* called attention to so many similarities between Populist objectives of the 1890s and Progressive programs of the early 1900s that many historians accepted Hicks' thesis that the one social movement had led to the other.

The belief that Progressivism was Populism with the hayseed removed (to paraphrase still another quip by William Allen White) remained the conventional wisdom until questioned by a post-World-War-II generation of scholars. Some historians, in monographs on urban reform in the 1880s and 1890s, concluded that the late-nineteenth century origins of Progressivism lay in the cities as well as in the farms. Other writers went so far as to read Populism out of the liberal fraternity altogether, claiming that Populist provincialism, nativism, isolationism, and paranoia prepared the ground for subsequent right-wing organizations. Still other writers noted that most Progressive leaders had opposed Populist and other reforms in the 1890s, that their family histories went way back in American history, and that as members of an established middle class they generated their own programs for reform in the early 1900s.

The latter interpretation, as expounded by George E. Mowry, reappears in this second edition of *The Progressive Era*. Professor Mowry was the first to formulate it, in the late 1940s, while preparing a monograph on the California Progressives. At about the same time, on the basis of evidence from many states, Alfred D. Chandler, Jr., arrived at the same conclusion as Mowry's—namely, that the driving force behind Progressivism was the old-stock, Protestant, urban middle class. It fell to the late Richard Hofstadter, perhaps the boldest synthesizer among post-World-War-II historians, to pull the new findings together in his strikingly named "status-revolution" theory. It boiled down to this: resentful of robber barons, political bosses, and immigrants for displacing them, the urban gentry proposed Progressive reform in order to restore both themselves and their standards of conduct and morality to public life.

The status-revolution theory was well received (Hofstadter's *Age of Reform* won a Pulitzer Prize in 1955), but like the Populist interpretation it was eventually challenged by younger historians. The revisionism began in the 1960s. One line of attack—initiated by J. Joseph Huthmacher and represented in this book of readings by Michael Rogin and John L. Shover—argues that the reform thrust came not merely from the urban gentry on the defensive, but also from the urban masses on the move. Another line of attack, while agreeing with the Hofstadter-Mowry school that Progressivism emanated from above, contends that it was free of status anxieties. Robert H. Wiebe, for example, has located the driving force behind Progressivism in a new, confident, rising class of bureaucratic-minded professional men and women who wanted to impose order on a chaotic society. Similarly, but in more extreme form and from a political position far to the left of Wiebe's, James Weinstein and Gabriel Kolko isolate the Progressive impulse in the desire of aggressive businessmen to rationalize the economy.

The debate launched in the 1960s over the status-revolution theory is still going on, but as David P. Thelen reveals in Chapter 3, historians of the seventies may tire of it. According to the thinking of Professor Thelen and like-minded scholars, it is a mistake to look for the origins of a social movement in the psychological makeup of one class or another. The starting point must be issues and the times and circumstances that engendered them. But as Thelen well understands and as the subsequent readings of this volume demonstrate, one cannot separate issues from the kinds of people who took a stand on them.

One of the major issues of the Progressive era was the regulation of big business. No more than American Marxians, then found in the Socialist Party, the Socialist Labor Party, and the Industrial Workers of the World, did the Progressives have a single economic policy. Their differences came to a head in the presidential election of 1912. Theodore Roosevelt regarded bigness in business as both historically inevitable and economically beneficial. He was prepared to regulate monopoly, and called his program the New Nationalism. To Woodrow Wilson, in contrast, big business was not inevitable but artificially created, inefficient rather than beneficial, and a threat to social mobility. He promised to use the federal government to destroy monopoly, so that America could return to an older, more competitive, more individualistic economy of small enterprise. Wilson called his program the New Freedom.

Most historians of the Progressive movement favor the New Nationalism over the New Freedom. In this they echo such advanced intellectuals of the 1910s as Walter Lippmann and Herbert Croly of the *New Republic*, who argued that the need of the twentieth century was not Manchester liberalism, but organization, control, order, and governmental direction. Yet liberal historians have managed to acclaim Wilson as well as Roosevelt. The current consensus is that President Wilson implemented the New Nationalism once in office.

The Progressives hoped to control the economy through the regulatory agency or commission. That device was not their creation—it dates from a much earlier time in American history—but the Roosevelt-Wilson-La Follette generation resorted to it more than ever before. How reformist was it in theory and practice? Few historians have addressed themselves to that question, and Part Two of this book of readings offers the Federal Trade Commission as a test case. According to G. Cullom Davis, reformers set up the FTC to police big business, but conservatives later captured the agency and perverted its original purpose. To Gabriel Kolko's way of thinking, however, the FTC, like all other regulatory commissions, was designed by big business to further its own, selfish interests.

Part Three of *The Progressive Era* is about the issue of political reform. There was a wide spectrum of Progressive panaceas: the initiative, referendum, and recall; direct primaries; the direct election of Senators; woman suffrage; corrupt-practices laws: the commission and city-manager forms of municipal government; and still other measures. But Progressives were hardly unanimous in their view of political reform. Wilson and Roosevelt, for example, seriously disagreed over the merits of judicial recall.

Again, we come back to the question, which Progressives do historians think are the most representative of the Progressive movement? According to Samuel P. Hays, "the upper class" took the lead in changing the structure of municipal government. Equally important for Professor Hays' point, the foe of municipal reform was the immigrant-based machine. For his own part, John D. Buenker makes a convincing case for the crucial role of the machine in securing the adoption of the Seventeenth Amendment, which, in the name of reform, provided for the direct election of senators.

With regard to welfare, the subject of Part Four, Progressives also proposed a variety of measures. The more important of them were workmen's compensation, old-age insurance, widows' pensions, the abolition of child labor, the regulation of the employment of women, factory inspection, and tenement-house reform. Meanwhile, in the slums of industrial cities across the country, a generation of college-bred men and women–epitomized by Robert A. Woods of Boston and Jane Addams of Chicago–set up more than 400 settlement houses by 1912 to cater to the needs of poor immigrants and their children.

As with political change and the regulation of the economy, historians offer different interpretations for the impulse behind welfare reform. Was it merely an expression of rational self-interest by big businessmen? That is the position taken by James Weinstein, who, together with Kolko, points to the large corporations as the driving power behind the Progressive movement. But Robert L. Buroker, whose overview is similar to Robert H. Wiebe's search-for-order thesis, contends that the modern welfare state originated with a Progressive generation of professional men and women. Buroker allows for humanitarian considerations; Weinstein for none.

It is sometimes forgotten that the National Association for the Advancement of Colored People, the longest-lived defense organization of its kind, was founded at the height of the Progressive movement. The connection between the two was hardly coincidental, as Gilbert Osofsky reminds us in Part Five. Yet, as Nancy J. Weiss shows in her examination of segregation in the Wilson administration, Progressives were no more united on the issue of racial equality than they were on other issues.

Part Six, the concluding section, begins with the question, what was the effect of World War I on the Progressive movement? Richard Hofstadter, in an interpretation that runs back in a straight line to liberal opinion since the 1920s, argues that the war killed Progressivism. Allen F. Davis, on the other hand, cites evidence to support the thesis that the war was a spur to social justice. Yet, it is generally agreed that, after the war was over and the peace treaties were concluded, the Progressive movement no longer had the strength it previously had had. Why was that so? And in what ways did the movement express itself in the 1920s? Arthur S. Link considers both questions in his piece.

The final chapter, written by the editor of this book of readings, attempts to show that the Progressive movement was America's alternative to Marxian socialism.

If readers of this second edition of *The Progressive Era* are like those of the first, they are bound to ask, which historians are to be believed? Three centuries ago, in his *Essay Concerning Human Understanding*, John Locke proposed two questions to test the validity of an idea. Does it explain the known facts? Is it internally consistent? Philosophers of history have yet to improve on Locke. Evidence and logic remain the twin bases of historical truth.

More is involved still. Today the developing nations—which is to say the majority of the world's population—want to create urban societies of their own. If any of them succeed in doing so they will discover, as did the Americans during their "take-off point," that severe social problems accompany modernization. In trying to cope with the problems of their times, the Progressive generation had to make hard choices between this or that public policy for the economy, the political process, welfare, race, and still other aspects of American life. How well did the Progressives choose? The student can no more avoid that question than have the writers who appear in this book of readings. Doing history requires that one not only re-create the past as it probably was, but that one also place a judgment on it. In addition to knowledge and understanding, the process of decision calls for moral values.

Chapter 1 A CONTEMPORARY STATEMENT

BENJAMIN PARKE DE WITT *(1889-1965), the first historian of the Progressive movement, was only twenty-four when he submitted his manuscript to The Macmillan Company in the spring of 1914. "I do not know anything else," wrote Professor Richard T. Ely in a confidential report to De Witt's publisher, "that describes the Progressive Movement so accurately and so interestingly." A government teacher and academic administrator at New York University, De Witt was a native New Yorker and charter member of Theodore Roosevelt's Bull Moose Party, which had been founded in 1912. Yet he recognized, as is revealed by the opening pages of his book below, that the Progressive movement was broader than a single party or man. Note in particular the three objectives that De Witt defined as central to the movement.*

The term "progressive movement" has been so widely used, so much discussed, and so differently interpreted that any exposition of its meaning and principles, to be adequate, must be prefaced by careful definition. To some—comparatively few—the progressive movement stands for the attempt of one man, disappointed in his efforts to control his political party, to found another and return himself to power.* To others, who are willing to concede that the movement is not confined to a single leader, it represents the efforts of a small body of self-seeking politicians to gain position and influence by making capital of a movement that is temporarily popular. To others, the movement expresses the effort of a few sincere but misguided enthusiasts to carry out an impossible and chimerical program of social

From Benjamin Parke De Witt, *The Progressive Movement: A Non-Partisan, Comprehension Discussion of Current Tendencies in American Politics* (New York: The Macmillan Company, 1915), pp. 3-5.

*De Witt was referring to former President Theodore Roosevelt, who, in 1912, bolted the Republican party to head the newly-founded Progressive party.

reform through government and legislation. Some believe that the movement is partisan, limited to the party that bears its name; others believe that it is broader than any single party and that its supporters are found in political parties everywhere. Some believe it is new, fleeting, and evanescent, destined to disappear quickly from our political life; others hold that it is permanent, deep-seated, and fundamental, involving a modification and readjustment of our political theories and institutions.

Whatever difference of opinion may exist concerning the meaning of the progressive movement, every thinking man and woman must be convinced that the nation to-day is passing through a severe political crisis. After a period of unprecedented industrial and commercial expansion, during which time little or no attention has been given to the problems of government, the people have suddenly realized that government is not functioning properly and that radical changes are needed. Manifestations of this excitement and unrest are seen on every hand. Men write of a new democracy[1] and a new freedom.[2] In 1912 the vote of the Socialist party—the party of protest against existing conditions—almost reached the million mark; and in the same year a new political party, appealing to new ideals and new standards, polled four million votes. The Democratic party in the nation, after a stormy convention, nominated and elected as President, in 1912, a leader who insists upon high standards of public service; and the Republican party, chastened by defeat, and forced to recognize the present political tendencies, has already set about the work of party regeneration in many states. Everywhere there are evidences that the nation has passed into a new political era.

In this widespread political agitation that at first sight seems so incoherent and chaotic, there may be distinguished upon examination and analysis three tendencies. The first of these tendencies is found in the insistence by the best men in all political parties that special, minority, and corrupt influence in government—national, state, and city—be removed; the second tendency is found in the demand that the structure or machinery of government, which has hitherto been admirably adapted to control by the few, be so changed and modified that it will be more difficult for the few, and easier for the many, to control; and, finally, the third tendency is found in the rapidly growing conviction that the functions of government at present are too restricted and that they must be increased and extended to relieve social and economic distress. These three tendencies with varying emphasis are seen to-day in the platform and program of every political party; they are manifested in the political changes and reforms that are advocated and made in the nation, the states, and the cities; and, because of their universality and definiteness, they may be said to constitute the real progressive movement.

Notes

1. Woyl, *The New Democracy*.

2. Wilson, *The New Freedom*.

Part One

WHERE DID PROGRESSIVISM COME FROM?

Chapter 2 FROM ABOVE

In the article from which the following excerpt is taken, GEORGE E. MOWRY *(1909-) laid the foundations for the status-revolution theory, which claims that the Progressive impulse came from the WASP middle class. A doctoral student of John D. Hicks at the University of Wisconsin in the 1930s, Mowry was the first historian after World War II to question Hicks' interpretation that twentieth-century Progressivism had issued from earlier Populist demands of rural and crossroads Americans. Currently Kenan Professor of History at the University of North Carolina, Mowry through his many books and articles has earned a reputation as a leader in the field of early twentieth-century U. S. history.*

Just what was a California progressive before he took office in 1910 and before power and the exigencies of politics altered his beliefs? What were his springs of action, his personal aspirations, and his concepts of what constituted the good society? The rest of this paper is devoted to an attempt to answer these questions in the hope that it may shed some light on the origins of progressivism, not only in California but in the rest of the nation as well, and perhaps even direct a few faint rays on the class structuring of American politics before 1917.

Fortunately, the men who first organized the California progressive movement were both literate and historically minded. The nine solid collections of personal manuscripts they so considerately left behind them, the diaries, documents, and inumerable published articles afford the historian perhaps an unrivaled opportunity

George E. Mowry, "The California Progressive and His Rationale: A Study in Middle Class Politics," *Mississippi Valley Historical Review*, XXXVI (September 1949), 241-250. Reprinted with the permission of the Organization of American Historians and the author.

in recent American history to inquire into the origins of a grass roots movement. Moreover, this group was small. Fewer than a hundred men attended the two state-wide progressive conferences in 1907 and 1909 before victory swelled the number of the organization's would-be leaders. Of this number, the author has been able to discover biographical data on forty-seven men, which produces in total a striking picture of similarity in background, economic base, and social attitudes. Compositely, the California progressive was a young man often less than forty years old. A majority of them was born in the Middle West, principally in Indiana, Illinois, Wisconsin, and Iowa. A good minority was native to the state. Almost all carried north European names and many of them, with two notable exceptions, were of old American stock.

The long religious hand of New England rested heavily upon California progressivism as it has on so many American movements. Of the twenty-two progressives indicating a religious affiliation in their biographies, seven were Congregationalists, two were Unitarians, and four were Christian Scientists. Three of every four had a college education, and three of the group had studied in European universities. Occupationally, the California progressive held a significant niche in the American economic structure. In the sample obtained, there were seventeen attorneys, fourteen journalists, eleven independent businessmen and real estate operators, three doctors, and three bankers. At least one half of the journalists owned their own papers or worked for a family enterprise, and the lawyers, with two exceptions, were not practicing politicians. In the entire group apparently only two had any connection with a large industrial or financial corporation save for the ownership of shares. Obviously this was a group of traditional small independent free enterprisers and professional men.

While not wealthy, the average California progressive was, in the jargon of his day, "well fixed." He was more often than not a Mason, and almost invariably a member of his town's chamber of commerce. Finally, by all available evidence he usually had been, at least until 1900, a conservative Republican, satisfied with William McKinley and his Republican predecessors.

Naturally, some fundamental questions arise about these fortunate sons of the upper middle class. Inheriting a secure place in society, earning a reasonably good living and certainly not radical by temperament, what prompted their political revolt and what did they want? The answer to the first of these questions, of course, is clear. The California progressive reacted politically when he felt himself and his group being hemmed in and his place in society threatened by the monopolistic corporation on one side and organized labor and socialism on the other. Proof for this general conclusion is not hard to find. The earliest manifestation of what later became progressivism in California is apparent in two local movements starting in 1906, one aimed against the Southern Pacific political machine in Los Angeles and the other against the control of the Union Labor party in San Francisco. From that time until victory in 1910, the progressive literature was full of criticism for both politically organized capital and politically organized labor.

The adverb "politically" in the last paragraph is important, for the progressive revolt was not alone a matter of economics. It might be pointed out that progressivism arose in an extremely prosperous period in California, and that the men who really organized the movement were not employers of any significance. In addition, far from beggering these lawyers, journalists, and real estate operators, a good case can be made out that the Southern Pacific Railroad actually befriended many of them economically. Moreover, the California progressives never attacked the corporate form of business organization or the labor union as such. And although they believed that the closed shop was "anti-social, dangerous and intrinsically wrong," many of them repeatedly went to the union's defense when industry organized to break the unions and create open shops.

"Modern politics," Henry Adams wrote in his *Education*, "is a struggle not of men but of forces. The men become every year more and more creatures of force massed about central power houses." With the struggle for power between capital and labor penetrating to almost every level of California life in the period, and with the individual more and more ignored, the California progressive was increasingly sensitive to that drift and increasingly determined to stop it if possible. This was obvious in the progressive obsession with the nightmare of class consciousness and class rule. "Class government is always bad government," the progressive Los Angeles *Express* vehemently declared as it exclaimed that "unions had no more right to usurp the management of public affairs than had the public service corporations." Chester Rowell, probably the most intelligent of the California progressives, went on to gloss that statement. "Class prejudice among the business men," he wrote, "excuses bribery and sanctifies lawlessness and disorder among labor. When the spectre of class rule is raised, then all questions of truth, right, and policy disappear, and the contest is no longer over what shall be the government but wholly who shall be it." This class spirit on both sides, the editor of the Fresno *Republican* lamented, "is destroying American liberty." When it became predominant he predicted American institutions would have to be changed. "For upon that evil day reform ends and nothing but revolution is possible."

Clearly what troubled these independent progressives about both organized capital and labor was not alone a matter of economics but included questions of high politics, as well as group prestige, group morality, and group power. Involved also was the rising threat to an old American way of life which they represented and which they enthusiastically considered good.

The progressives were members of an old group in America. Whether businessmen, successful farmers. professional people, or politicians, they had engaged in extremely individualistic pursuits and had since the decline of the colonial aristocracy supplied most of the nation's intellectual, moral, and political leadership. Still confident that they possessed most of society's virtues, the California progressives were acutely aware in 1905 that many of society's rewards and badges of merit were going elsewhere. Although finely educated, they were all but excluded from politics unless they accepted either corporate or labor domination, a thing they were exceedingly loath to do. Their church, their personal morality, and their concept of law, they felt, were demeaned by the crude power struggle between capital and labor. Before the days of the Rotarians and kindred organizations they were excluded from, or did not care to participate in, either the Union League Club or the union labor hall.

On the defensive for the first time since the disappearance of the old aristocracy, this class of supreme individualists rationally enough developed a group consciousness themselves. Although generally overlooked by the historian, this consciousness had already evolved among some farming elements in the Populist period. Nothing else can be concluded from the words of the official organ of the Michigan State Farmers' Alliance. "It has been truly said," remarked that paper, "that the Peoples' Party is the logical and only nucleus for every element of the American population that stands for social stability and constitutional rights. It is the bulwark against anarchy of the upper and lower scum of society." Now in the twentieth century, flanked by organized labor on the one side and organized capital on the other, the urban California progressives took up that song. Their letters, journals, and speeches are full of the phrases, "Our crowd," "the better element," and "the good people of the state." Even their political enemies recognized their separateness as indicated by the names they conferred upon them. The phrases "Goo-goo" and "Our Set" dripped with ridicule. But they also indicated an awareness of the progressives' claim to ethical and political superiority. Finally, no clearer expression of the progressives' self-confidence in their own moral elevation and their contempt for the classes above and below them can be found than that in an editorial of their state-wide organ, the *California Weekly*. "Nearly all the problems which vex society," this illuminating item ran, "have their sources above or below the middle class man. From above come the problems of predatory wealth. . . . From below come the problems of poverty and of pigheaded and of brutish criminality." Despite the fact that it was made up of extremely individualistic elements, this was unmistakably an expression of a social group on the march.

The California progressive, then, was militantly opposed to class control and class consciousness when it emanated from either below or above him. This was his point of opposition. What was his positive creed? In the first place this "rank individualist," as he gladly styled himself, was in most cases an extremely religious man. His mind was freighted with problems of morality, his talk shot full of biblical allusions. He often thought of the political movement he had started as a part of the "Religion Forward Movement." As early as 1903 Arthur J. Pillsbury, who was later to become a leading progressive, praised Theodore Roosevelt for coming nearer "to exemplifying the New England conscience in government than any other president in recent times."

But if the religion of the California progressive was old American in its form, much of its content was a product of his recent past. Gone was the stern God of the Puritan, the abiding sense of tragedy, and the inherent evilness of man. As William

Allen White later wrote, the cult of the hour was "to believe in the essential nobility of man and the wisdom of God." With an Emersonian optimism, the California progressive believed that evil perished and good would triumph. Under the influence of Darwinism, the rising social sciences, and a seemingly benign world, the progressive had traded some of his old mystical religion for a new social faith. He was aware that evil still existed, but it was a man-made thing and upon earth. And what man created he could also destroy. For the then present sinful condition of man was the result of his conditioning. As Fremont Older's San Francisco *Bulletin* editorialized, "the basic idea behind this age of liberalism is the simple one that all men, prisoners and free, rich and poor are basically alike in spirit. The difference usually lies in what happens to them." And from that, one could conclude that when all men were given justice most of them would return justice to society. The progressive, then, not only wanted to abolish a supernatural hell; he was intent upon secularizing heaven.

There were, of course, individual variations from these generalizations. Chester Rowell, for one, while agreeing that men should not be treated as free moral agents, protested against considering them as "mere creatures of environment." "If we try to cure the trouble by curing the environment," Rowell argued, "we shall never go far enough, for however much we protect men from temptation there will be some left and men will fall to that. . . . Dealing with society the task is to amend the system. But dealing with the individual man the task is to reiterate forever, 'thou shall not steal' and tolerate no exceptions." But Rowell was more of a child of his age than even he himself realized. Despite his strictures on the sinfulness of man, one found him writing later that William H. Taft's peace treaties made international war impossible because "the moral influence on nations (for peace) would be tantamount to compulsion."

"The way to have a golden age," one progressive novelist wrote, "is to elect it by an Australian ballot." This was an extreme affirmation of democracy, but it followed logically from the progressive belief in the fundamental goodness of the individual. For according to progressive thought, behind every political question was a moral question whose answer "could safely be sought in the moral law." Since all men were moral agents, then public opinion was the final distillate of moral law. "It was a jury that can not be fixed," according to Lincoln Steffens, and indeed to some progressives, "God moving among men." Thus Charles D. Willard objected to Theodore Roosevelt's characterization of democracy as just a means to an end. To Willard democracy was a positive moral force in operation, a good in itself. "It is," he wrote, "a soul satisfying thing."

Back in the 1890's Senator John J. Ingalls of Kansas had remarked that "the purification of politics is an iridescent dream." Dream or not, that was one of the major goals of the California progressive a decade later. There was but one law for him—that of the churchgoing middle class—and he was convinced that it should be applied equally to the home, to government, and occasionally even to business. It was in this spirit that Hiram Johnson admonished his followers to forget how to make men richer and concentrate on how to make them better. This attitude helps to explain much of the progressive interest in sumptuary legislation. Individualism was a sacred thing as long as it was moral individualism; otherwise it needed to be corrected. Thus the progressive proposals for the abolition of prize fighting, "a form of social debauchery," gambling, slang, "since it is a coverup for profanity," prostitution, and the liquor traffic. And thus their demands for the censorship of literature, the drama, and social dancing.

In protest against these "holier than thou people" among his fellow progressives, Charles J. McClatchey, owner of the Sacramento *Bee*, wrote that he was his "brother's keeper only in so far as I should set him a good example." And though most progressives vehemently denied the full import of this statement when applied to morality, the majority of them was not in complete disagreement with McClatchey's views when they were applied to economics. Good Christian as he was, and on the whole benevolent, the California progressive did not quarrel with the doctrine of wardship provided it was not pushed too far. Thus he stood ready in 1910 to protect obviously handicapped individuals. And he was ready and even eager to eradicate what he called "special privilege," which to his mind was the fundamental factor in limiting opportunity for the man on the bottom to make his way economically upward. A few individuals on the left of the movement, like Congressman William Kent, felt that soon "property rights were going to tumble about the heads of the men who had built themselves pyramids of money in a desert of want and suffering." And Older raised the disturbing question of why men should be paid fortunes who had been lucky enough to be born with brains or in fortunate environments. One might as well go back to the feudal system, Older answered himself, because there was no more personal merit "in having talent than in having a noble lineage." But for the most part, the progressive majority was content with the basic concepts of the economic system under which 1910 American capitalism awarded its profits and pains.

What the progressive did object to in the year of his triumph was not 1910 capitalism as such but rather the ideological, moral, and political manifestations arising from that system. He was confident, at least in 1910, that there was not an inevitable causal relation between them. And he felt confident that he could cure these ills of society through the political method and through preaching and legislating morality.

The California progressive, then, wanted to preserve the fundamental pattern of twentieth-century industrial society at the same time he sought to blot out the rising clash of economic groups, and for that matter, the groups themselves as conscious economic and political entities. But he sought to do all this, at least before he had actually taken power, without profound economic reform. "The people," Rowell wrote sometime after the sweeping progressive victory in 1910, "elected Governor Johnson to get moral and political reform." The word "economic" was significantly absent from the statement.

From today's dark vantage point, the progressive aim of a capitalist commonwealth,

> Where none were for a class and all were for the state.
> Where the rich man helped the poor and the poor man loved the great,

may seem incredibly naive. His stress on individualism in a maturing industrial economy was perhaps basically archaic. His refusal or inability to see the connection between the economic institutions and the rising class consciousness indicated a severe case of social myopia. His hopes to avert class strife by political and moral reform alone were scarcely realistic. And paradoxical in extreme was his antipathy to the class consciousness of organized capital and labor without his being aware of his own intense group loyalties.

When the California progressives confidently took control of the state in 1910, the road ahead was uncertain indeed. What, for example, would happen to the fundamental beliefs of this group if they found their ends could not be achieved without substantial economic reform, or, if in spite of their efforts, labor through one program or another threatened their economic and political estate, or if many of them became economically and psychologically absorbed by the advancing corporate system, or again in a less prosperous age than 1910, if the clash between economic groups for a livelihood created an intense social friction? Would their moral calculus, their spirit of benevolence, their faith in men, and their reverence for democracy still persist? The answers to these questions, of course, lay beyond 1910 and belong to another story, another chapter.

But the composite California progressive in 1910 was perhaps the best his economic and social group produced. He was educated, intelligent, able. A man of unquestioned sincerity and public integrity, he was also benevolently aware of the underprivileged groups around him. Devoted to the extension of political democracy and civil rights, he stood as a worthy representative of that long historical lineage of Americans who had dreamed and worked for a better commonwealth. If such a small group is ever able to amend or to alter a little the drift of society, the California progressive's chances seemed better than an even bet.

Chapter 3 FROM BELOW

Of the new methods in history since the 1950s, none is more important than the quantitative method. As applied to political history, it consists of studying elections through the statistical breakdown of voting returns. Through that method in the following excerpts from their book, MICHAEL PAUL ROGIN *(1937-   ) and* JOHN L. SHOVER *(1927-   ) show that California Progressivism was popular with workingmen, who were predominantly Catholic and immigrant. But if Rogin and Shover are right, does it follow that Mowry was wrong about the Protestant, old-stock-middle-class background of California's Progressive leaders? Professor Rogin, currently at the University of California, Berkeley, is a political scientist; Professor Shover, who teaches at the University of Pennsylvania, is an historian of social movements.*

The interpretation of progressivism as a political movement of a disaffected middle class, frightened by the power of monopolistic corporations and fearful of organized labor, rests upon inferences drawn from public statements and, in a few instances, private thoughts, of a leadership elite. Chapter 2 has advanced the hypothesis that a distinct realignment of voting patterns took place in California midway in the period of Progressive ascendancy. Although Hiram Johnson was elected in 1910 with strongest support from areas preponderantly rural, native stock, and Protestant—the pattern of support that would be anticipated from the interpretations of Mowry and Hofstadter—a distinct change took place by 1914, and Progressive appeals henceforth were most effective in areas more urban, more working class and with greater foreign-born populations.

This hypothesis, supported in Chapter 2 by data drawn from counties and ecological areas of California, merits more specific analysis. The present chapter will explore the nature of progressivism's political support; it will not only turn from consideration of leadership to consideration of voters, but will add two additional sources of data to the evidence in the last chapter. First, we will examine the response of labor leaders and the labor press to progressivism. Second, we will attempt to determine the distribution of support for Progressive candidates and measures in California's two major metropolitan counties, San Francisco and Los Angeles.

Progressive insurgency and the factionalism it wrought in the dominant Republican party were the central issues in California politics from 1910 until 1930. California progressivism was greater than Hiram Johnson, but there can be little doubt that the forceful governor and senator was the prime representative of the movement in the state. Although Progressive leadership was fractured after 1920, Johnson still laid claim to the mantle of reform leadership, and neither his supporters nor his enemies were inclined to deny him the title. A focus primarily upon the political support for Johnson therefore provides a good index of the nature of the Progressive voting constituency. During the period considered here, 1910 to 1924, Johnson appeared as a candidate on the California ballot ten times: in the Republican primary for governor, 1910; Republican candidate for governor, 1910; Progressive vice-presidential nominee in 1912; Progressive candidate for governor, 1914; candidate in two Senatorial primaries and Republican nominee in two general elections, 1916 and 1922; delegations pledged to him were entered in two presidential primaries, 1920 and 1924. He lost the state in only one election, the presidential primary of 1924.

Labor Leaders, the Labor Press, and Hiram Johnson

If California Progressives harbored a bias against labor, it was never obvious to contemporary labor or political leaders. No labor leaders were numbered among the top advisers of Hiram Johnson, but this apparently had little effect upon their support for the governor. Paul Scharrenberg, longtime executive secretary of the California State Federation of Labor and a central figure in the San Francisco labor movement, was asked in 1954: "Do you think Johnson was prolabor generally?" He replied:

> Oh, there was no question about it. Some of Mowry's statements in here are perfectly ridiculous. Hiram Johnson was started on his career by the Teamsters' Union of San Francisco. He'd been their attorney for some time. And John P. McLaughlin, who was secretary of the Teamsters' Union and was later appointed Labor Commissioner by him, he was the boy that rounded them up. And I was one of the first converts. I was inclined to be for Bell, you know. (I was a

> Democrat then.) I swung in line and so did all the other leaders, but the rank and file in the labor districts of San Francisco, they were Democrats. And they couldn't just switch over because some new guy appeared on the horizon and said, 'Here, vote for me.' So when someone told Mowry that the leaders of labor were not for Johnson, he's got the thing upside down. The leaders of labor were for Johnson, they dragged the rank and file along. After the election and one or two sessions of the legislature, then the rank and file didn't have to be persuaded any more. They came along all right—on state issues. On national issues, that's something else again.

Scharrenberg also recalled that the labor movement in San Francisco had backed the Progressive initiative and referendum measures.

Franck Havenner, who served as Hiram Johnson's private secretary, managed his California campaign in the presidential primary of 1924 and later served as congressman from a San Francisco district, commented:

> Johnson through his policies as governor won strong support from organized labor and I think that after that the organized labor forces of San Francisco supported Johnson. . . . As Hiram Johnson gradually acquired the support of organized labor in Northern California . . . he began to lose some of his old anti-labor so-called Progressive support in Southern California.

Chester Rowell, once designated by Johnson as his heir apparent but by 1920 at bitter odds with the senator over the League of Nations, appraised the political situation in California prior to the Hoover-Johnson presidential primary of 1920. He noted that Johnson had the labor vote and that of the political Irish and Catholics. He had the support of all important labor leaders and both the Old Guard and Progressive machines in San Francisco, while Hoover commanded the support of the women, the Protestant church, the anti-Irish and anti-Catholics, and both the Old Guard and Progressive machines in southern California.

Organized labor, particularly in San Francisco, generally refrained from partisan political endorsements. Nevertheless, the sympathies of the labor press for Hiram Johnson were scarcely veiled. The *Labor Clarion*, organ of the San Francisco Central Labor Council, quoted Scharrenberg that Johnson's "uncompromising attitude for an effective Workmen's Compensation Act . . . should ever endear him to the men and women of labor." The *Clarion* refrained from comment during the campaign of 1914, but after the balloting it "rejoiced" in the reelection of Governor Johnson. The paper had discreet blessing for Johnson during his first senatorial campaign in 1916.

When the California State Federation of Labor took a political stance in the 1920s, its support for Senator Johnson was unequivocal. During the 1924 presidential primary, a flyer signed by the president and secretary of the State Federation urged all members who registered Republican to vote for Johnson. *The Southern*

California Labor Press (Los Angeles) editorialized on March 21: "The labor movement of California always has supported Mr. Johnson, on account of his record as governor." The four labor councils of Los Angeles–central labor, building trades, metal trades, and allied printing trades–unanimously endorsed Johnson's presidential candidacy. The *Sacramento Bee* noted that the labor councils had taken this stand "in every campaign in which Senator Johnson has figured."

Did the workers of California, organized and unorganized, follow the lead of union leaders and the labor press? The extent of working-class support for Johnson and progressivism can be determined best by examining voting statistics from California's two major metropolitan centers, San Francisco and Los Angeles.

Labor Politics: San Francisco and Los Angeles

The two counties provided upwards of 40 percent of the total vote cast in any California election. Both cities contained a sizable working-class population, but there the similarity ended. San Francisco was predominantly Catholic and ethnically diverse; 28 percent of its population in 1920 was foreign-born, with Irish and Italians predominating. Los Angeles was peopled by immigrants, but they were Protestant Anglo-Saxons from the small towns and farms of the South and Midwest. Only 18 percent of the county's population was foreign-born, and a quarter of these were from England and Canada. San Francisco was a closed-shop town; union membership at its peak in 1918 totaled approximately 100,000. In contrast Los Angeles was virtually an open-shop city; 40,000 belonged to unions in 1919. Labor influence loomed large in San Francisco city politics. Abe Reuf's Union Labor party, built independently of formal union support, was broken by the 1906 graft prosecutions, but P. H. McCarthy, head of the powerful Building Trades Council, managed to pick up the pieces and win election as mayor in 1909.

By 1911, however, the San Francisco Labor Council, a rival organization that had supported the graft prosecutions and opposed McCarthy, emerged as the dominant power group in San Francisco labor. More cosmopolitan than the locally centered Building Trades, the Labor Council lobbied in Sacramento, and its leaders, such as Scharrenberg, identified with the Progressive administration of Johnson. Los Angeles labor, on the other hand, locked in a futile battle with powerful antilabor interests, assumed a radical posture lacking in San Francisco. Job Harriman, a Socialist supported by labor, barely lost the race for mayor in 1911, and several Socialist assemblymen won seats in Sacramento. Although weak, Los Angeles labor was not politically impotent. Labor-endorsed candidates usually held several posts on the city council and in May, 1925, eight of eleven approved candidates were elected.

The Changing Progressive Constituency: San Francisco

San Francisco was allotted thirteen assembly districts in the reapportionment of

1911. Voting returns were tabulated by assembly district, and since there was no further reapportionment until 1929, political boundaries remained fixed through the Progressive period. To characterize the political constituency of the various San Francisco assembly districts is relatively easy. Tradition has it that the working class lived south of Market Street along the bay shore and in the Mission District, while the nabobs peered down upon them from Nob Hill, Russian Hill, and Pacific Heights in the north, and an upwardly mobile middle class resided in the trim row houses of Sunset and Richmond on the ocean side of the city. The accuracy of these impressions can be confirmed by such indexes as the vote on an antipicketing referendum in 1916 (an indication of where labor sentiment was strongest), the vote for Socialist candidates, and ethnic data from the 1920 census tabulated by assembly district.

When Hiram Johnson, prosecutor of the Reuf machine and opponent of the Southern Pacific Railroad, first sought the governorship in 1910, he was not popular in his home town. Contesting with five other candidates in the Republican primary, he ran second with 36 percent of the vote while he was carrying Los Angeles County by a clear majority of 52 percent. Johnson carried, all by plurality, only three of San Francisco's eighteen assembly districts—these three encompassed the Sunset and Richmond areas, Pacific Heights, and an apartment house district stretching north from the present Civic Center toward Nob Hill. He ran weakest in the working-class areas south of Market Street and in the Mission District. His 43 percent won him San Francisco County in a three-way race in November, but at the same time he garnered 46 percent in Los Angeles. Johnson carried ten assembly districts but won a majority only in A.D. 41 and 42, the silk-stocking Pacific Heights, and midtown apartment house areas.

The election was complicated by the presence on the ballot of a Socialist who received 8 percent of the city's vote but won more than 20 percent in five of the "south of the slot" working-class districts. Although Johnson carried five of the districts south of Market Street, the votes that won for him ranged from a low of 38 percent to a high of 44 percent. Johnson victories in 1910 owed little to San Francisco; he had won the "better" neighborhoods, but the vast majority of the working-class population had voted their preference for Democratic or Socialist candidates.

An abrupt change in the Progressive voting constituency took place in 1914. Campaigning as a Progressive party candidate in his bid for reelection and opposed by both major parties, Johnson polled 55 percent of the vote in San Francisco and 53.5 percent in Los Angeles. More important was the vote distribution. Johnson secured a majority in nine of the thirteen assembly districts including all those south of Market Street and in the Mission District. In 1910, for example, Johnson polled 38 percent of the vote in the assembly district situated in the Potrero Hill area; in 1914 in the new A.D. 22, which circumscribed much the same area, he received 67 percent of the vote. The Socialist vote there in 1910 had been 24 percent; in 1914 it was 7 percent. Johnson's poorest showing in the entire city (39.5 percent) was in A.D. 31, located in the Pacific Heights area, its boundaries only slightly modified from the district that had given him 52 percent of its vote in 1910. In addition he ran below his city average in A.D. 27 (Sunset), 28 (Richmond), 32 (Russian Hill, downtown apartment house area), 30 (Western Addition), and 33 (Italian, North Beach). Johnson won San Francisco with a base of support quite different from that which placed him in the state house four years earlier. His success resulted from strong new support in working-class districts, which more than compensated serious losses in the more exclusive residential areas.

The voting patterns of 1914 became a permanent part of the San Francisco political landscape. As Table 12 indicates, in seven contests between 1914 and 1924, Johnson's landslide victories derived most from the vote in A.D. 21 through 26 and 29, all but two of them south of Market Street or in the Mission District.

. . . [T]he correlation figures underscore the close relationship of the vote for Hiram Johnson with prolabor sentiment in San Francisco. In the election of 1916, the city's voters passed by a narrow margin Charter Amendment #8, an antipicketing ordinance modeled on that of Los Angeles and supported by business interests determined to limit union power. The vote for Johnson in the primary correlated .949 with the votes "No" on this crucial index of labor sentiment. In the general election of 1914 and in each primary in which Hiram Johnson was a candidate, the correlation of his vote with the vote "no" on the antipicketing ordinance was above .90.

The fact that Johnson absorbed the socialist vote in San Francisco indicates further the political inclinations of areas in which he gathered his most loyal supporters. His percentage in 1914 correlated .67 with the percentage for Eugene V. Debs in the 1912 election; in 1920 when Johnson was a candidate in the May presidential primary and Debs in the November election, the correlation was .88.

Johnson's working-class backers in San Francisco recognized Progressives regardless of the party label they wore. Woodrow Wilson carried the city in 1916 with 52 percent of the vote; Robert La Follette, listed on the California ballot in 1924 as a Socialist, won 46 percent of the San Francisco vote. The distribution of Wilson's 1916 vote by assembly district correlated .905 with that of Johnson in the Republican primary and .245 with his Republican senatorial vote in November. . . . The latter figure is especially significant: against the normal expectation of a close identity between a party's presidential and senatorial candidate, Johnson's vote correlated positively with that of Wilson and negatively (–.245) with that of Hughes. Given the decisive importance of the close California vote in 1916, could Charles Evans Hughes have ridden on Johnson's coattails in San Francisco, he would have become president of the United States.

The high correlation of .986 between the backing given Johnson in the 1924 presidential primary and the vote for La Follette in the general election evidences almost a complete identity of support. . . . La Fallotte's strength in San Francisco

Table 12
Johnson's Percentage Vote in San Francisco

	Governor 1914 % of Vote	*Senator (Primary) 1916 % of Vote*	*Senator 1916 % of Vote*	*President (Primary) 1920 % of Vote*	*Senator (Primary) 1922 % of Vote*	*Senator (Primary) 1922 % of Vote*	*President (Primary) 1924 % of Vote*
City Total	54.6	59.2	71.9	73.4	60.7	67.9	59.[illegible]
Working-class A.D.s							
21	60.0	70.1	68.2	80.5	70.8	64.5	67.5
22	67.7	77.3	77.5	84.2	75.6	70.2	78.8
23	66.3	75.2	72.7	87.5	78.7	70.4	79.9
24	66.5	72.9	74.3	84.1	73.5	71.8	70.6
25	62.6	64.2	74.9	84.9	73.6	75.6	75.2
26	56.2	60.0	73.8	79.7	67.0	69.0	64.3
29	59.4	63.3	70.7	80.3	71.6	71.4	70.4
Middle- and upper-class A.D.s							
27	53.7	55.9	71.1	71.8	58.7	67.6	50.7
28	51.1	53.6	70.8	68.8	50.7	68.0	43.5
30	46.5	57.5	67.7	74.8	61.7	65.7	57.4
31	39.5	42.2	71.3	52.7	38.7	60.7	31.5
32	45.4	49.1	70.0	62.0	48.0	62.6	38.6
Italian working-class A.D.							
33	47.4	57.0	74.3	63.7	52.3	67.1	48.0

was in the same districts that had overwhelmingly endorsed Johnson, opposed the antipicketing ordinance, and voted most heavily for Wilson in 1916.

Table 14
Johnson Vote and Prolabor Sentiment in San Francisco

	Governor 1914	*Senator (Primary) 1916*	*Senator 1916*	*President (Primary) 1920*	*Senator (Primary) 1922*	*President (Primary) 1924*
Charter Amendment No. 8	.921	.949	.358	.914	.947	.959

There was an important ethnic element in Hiram Johnson's vote. In general, the greater the number of foreign-born and first-generation immigrants in an assembly district, the higher the vote for Johnson (Table 16). Most striking was the high relationship between the number of foreign-born Irish and the Johnson vote. The Irish population was diffused throughout San Francisco with slightly higher concentrations in A.D. 21, 24, and 25, the former south of Market Street on the bay shore and the latter two in the Mission District. All three were Johnson political strongholds. One ethnic group, representing the largest foreign-born component in the

Table 16
Correlation: Nativity, Foreign Born, and the Progressive Vote

	Nativity 1920*	*Foreign-Born Irish*	*Foreign-Born German*
Johnson, Governor, 1914	.545	.796	.545
Johnson, Primary, 1916	.756	.692	.455
Johnson, Senator, 1916	.432	.469	.07
Wilson, 1916	.522	.751	.630
Charter Amendment #8	.703	.733	.530
Johnson, Primary, 1920	.524	.780	.686
Johnson, Primary, 1922	.687	.747	.613
Johnson, Senator, 1922	.305	.604	.414
Johnson, Primary, 1924	.644	.735	.578

*"Nativity" refers to the percent of the total population of the city or an assembly district who were *not* native whites of native white parentage.

city, was little attracted to progressivism. Assembly District 33, where 19 percent of the population were native Italians, ran consistently below the city average for Johnson and voted 60.2 percent "Yes" on the 1916 antipicketing ordinance. The Irish, foreign born, and first generation were concentrated in working-class districts; whether they voted as they did because they were members of a nationality group or because they were part of the laboring class cannot be determined accurately. However, the higher correlation figures indicate that the vote against the 1916 antipicketing ordinance would have been a better predictor of the future political behavior of a district than the percentage of Irish or nonnative white population.

San Francisco voting returns lend scant support to any hypothesis that progressivism in California was sustained by middle-class votes. Alleged bias against unions did not deter the great majority of these San Franciscans who voted "No" on the antipicketing ordinance from at the same time marking their ballot for Hiram Johnson. As governor and senator, Johnson had amazing drawing power in San Francisco and did win middle- and upper-class votes, particularly in general elections. Yet, as 1910 demonstrated, his base became weak when these constituted his principal support. A new Progressive constituency centered in working-class assembly districts emerged in 1914. It carried the city for Johnson every time he was a candidate; it won the city—and the presidency—for Woodrow Wilson in 1916; and it provided the core of La Follette's support in 1924. As the Progressives gained strong labor support, they were deserted by voters in "better" neighborhoods. Had Johnson lacked the urban lower-class support that allowed him to garner huge majorities in San Francisco to offset losses in southern California, his political career would have been terminated at an early date.

The Changing Progressive Constituency: Los Angeles

Analysis of the support for Hiram Johnson in Los Angeles County must take into account that the original enthusiasm southern California voters demonstrated for progressivism waned rapidly after 1914. In the 1910 primary, Johnson ran twenty percentage points ahead of the strongest of his four opponents and carried Los Angeles County with a 52 percent majority. In the general election, his 46 percent was ten percentage points above that of the Democratic candidate. In 1914, the governor far outdistanced the field, winning 53.5 percent of the county's vote against Republican, Democratic, Prohibition, and Socialist opponents. In the four ensuing primaries—two senatorial and two presidential—while Johnson was winning more than 60 percent of the San Francisco Republican vote in each, he carried Los Angeles County in not one. . . .

Los Angeles voting returns reveal a pattern similar to, although less distinctive, than that of San Francisco. Whether this less distinctive pattern is the result of actual voting returns or of the more generalized data from Los Angeles County employed here cannot be determined. Suburban voters in increasing numbers, particularly in Pasadena and Long Beach, like those in San Francisco's Richmond District and Pacific Heights, abandoned Hiram Johnson on election day. As his popularity in the state's largest county declined, those who remained his most steadfast supporters were residents of urban neighborhoods, which not only impressions but more concrete data, such as skepticism toward prohibition, occasional support for Socialists, and diverse ethnic composition, would identify as working class.

Conclusion

To accept the conclusion of this chapter and the preceding one, coupled with a recent and complementary study by Alexander Saxton would require a recasting of widely accepted interpretations of the Progressive movement. Neither the statements of political and labor leaders nor the voting records from California's two major metropolitan centers sustain the thesis that it was primarily a middle-class movement. The rank-and-file urban voters who consistently backed Progressive candidates lived in working-class areas. In consequence, the hypothesis that the California Progressive represented a particular strain of middle-class individualism and became militant when he felt himself hemmed in between the battening corporation and the rising labor union, seems scarcely tenable. Any antilabor tinge in the thought of leaders of California progressivism appears to have had little political significance.

A reevaluation of progressivism taking into account its urban lower-class support would necessitate a new focus upon the social reform program of Progressive governors and legislators, certainly in California and perhaps elsewhere. Between 1911 and 1915, *some* factor transformed working-class voters from apathy to vigorous support of progressivism, and by the same token, *some* factor incited the suspicions of middle- and upper-class electors, causing them to drift away.

If the testimony of labor leaders and the evidence from the labor vote are to be accepted, the working class and its leaders considered the social legislation of the Progressives a major and positive achievement. While this legislation was often qualified and tempered, the labor constituency obviously was more impressed by the gains they had made, rather than by the demands—such as an anti-injunction bill—they had lost.

In like fashion, it would appear that in 1910 when the Progressive program was largely a negative one aimed at destroying the power of the Southern Pacific machine, there were among its leaders—and perhaps voting supporters—individuals, particularly from southern California, who had little sympathy with the demands of labor. As the Johnson legislative program unfolded, these antilabor elements fell by the wayside, and by 1916 the main line of California progressivism was firmly tied to a working-class base. In this perspective, the humanitarian and labor legislation of the first Johnson administration assume major political significance.

A reinterpretation that credits the urban laboring population with a central political role in the Progressive movement will restore a sense of continuity to the study of American reform. Hence, the upsurge of working-class and immigrant power that dominated American politics during the depression, and at least a decade thereafter, would no longer appear as a sudden phenomenon that burst forth in an Al Smith revolution in 1928. In California, the political upheaval of the 1930s marked the augmenting and coming to power of the same groups that had sustained Johnson, Wilson, and La Follette, buttressed the Progressive reforms two decades earlier, and kept what remained of reform politics alive through the 1920s.

Chapter 4 NOT CLASSES, BUT ISSUES

A native Californian, DAVID P. THELEN *(1939-) teaches history at the University of Missouri and is best known for his book on the origins of Progressivism in Wisconsin. The following article contains the substance of that book. Critical of the tendency to attribute a social movement to this or that social group, Professor Thelen shows that individuals from many different groups formed a Progressive coalition to cope with the problems of the 1890s depression. In seeking the causes of Progressivism in society, to what extent is Thelen's approach like De Witt's, a half century and more ago?*

Recent historians have explained the origins of the Progressive movement in several ways. They have represented progressivism, in turn, as a continuation of the western and southern farmers' revolt, as a desperate attempt by the urban gentry to gain status from the new robber barons, as a thrust from the depths of slum life, and as a campaign by businessmen to prevent workers from securing political power. Behind such seemingly conflicting theories, however, rests a single assumption about the origins of progressivism: the class and status conflicts of the late-nineteenth century formed the driving forces that made men become reformers. Whether viewed by the historian as a farmer, worker, urban elitist, or businessman, the progressive was motivated primarily by his social position; and each scholar has painted a compel-

David P. Thelen, "Social Tensions and the Origins of Progressivism," *Journal of American History*, LVI (September 1969), 323-341. Reprinted with the permission of the Organization of American Historians and the author.

ling picture of the insecurities and tensions felt by the group that he placed in the vanguard of progressivism. Pressures and threats from other social groups drove men to espouse reform. In these class and status conflicts can be found the roots of progressivism.

How adequately does this focus on social tensions and insecurities explain the origins of progressivism? Since some of these scholars have invoked concepts from social science to support their rejection of earlier approaches, the validity and application of some of the sociological and psychological assumptions which make up the conceptual framework for the idea that social tensions impelled the progressive require analysis. Is the focus on social classes relevant to the rise of political movements like progressivism? It is useful to rely upon a narrow, untestable and unproved conception of motivation when other approaches are available? How much of a concrete situation does an abstract model explain?

First, theories borrowed from one discipline are not designed to encompass the data of another. In questioning the application of models from physiology and physics to psychology, the noted personality theorist George A. Kelly explained: "We are skeptical about the value of copying ready-made theories which were designed for other foci of convenience"; and he urged his fellow psychologists to resist the temptation of "poking about in the neighbors' back yards for methodological windfalls." Just as physiology and physics encompass only part of the psychologist's realm, so psychology, sociology, and political science are concerned with only part of the historian's realm.

Those historians who have borrowed the idea that social stratification explains the rise of political movements like progressivism illustrate the dangers inherent in borrowing theories from other fields. Most sociologists and political scientists now doubt the relevance of social stratification to the emergence of political movements. Reinhard Bendix, for example, maintained that "the study of social stratification, whether or not it is adumbrated by psychological analysis, is not the proper approach to an understanding of the role of cumulative political experience." In their pleas for more pluralistic approaches to political power, such political scientists as Nelson W. Polsby and Robert A. Dahl have found that social stratification is largely irrelevant to the exercise of political power. So severe were these criticisms of the assumption that social class determined political power that one sociologist, reviewing the literature of the field in 1964, concluded that "the problem has simply been dropped."

But an even greater problem with placing emphasis on social tensions is that it is ahistorical. Even sociologists like Seymour M. Lipset and Bendix have complained about the "increasingly ahistorical" drift of the focus of this field. After analyzing the major models of social change, another sociologist concluded that the fundamental error of these models was their failure to incorporate the dimension of time. Few scholars would deny that social tensions exist at all times and in all societies. For at least twenty years before 1900, various business groups had tried to take political power away from workers and bosses. But to focus on the social class motivation of businessmen is to obscure the basic historical problem of why progressivism emerged *when* it did. Conflicts between businessmen and workers were hardly unique to the years around 1900. The emphasis on social tensions obscures chronology. When sociologists are disturbed about this problem, historians should be wary indeed.

The assumption that progressivism derived from social tensions is at least as vulnerable to attack by phychologists. If the kinds of questions historians generally ask about the origins of political and social movements are reduced to the psychological level, then the theories of class and status motivation would seem to be premised on very debatable assumptions about individual motivation. Most historians would want to know the conditions that existed before a change occurred, why the change happened, and what were the results of that change.

The first problem—the conditions before a change occurred—reduces in psychological terms to the way an individual perceives himself, his self-image. Psychologists have approached this question in many ways, but a theory of change which assumes that social tensions were the basic cause implicitly accepts only one of these approaches. It assumes that an individual defines himself primarily in terms of his particular social role, that his behavior is motivated mainly by his class and status role perceptions. Only about one out of every three psychologists, however, would accept this premise to any real extent. Even some sociologists and anthropologists, who have traditionally seen individual behavior as primarily determined by culture, have retreated from that position and now see a more symmetrical interaction in which personality also influences culture. An overwhelming majority of psychologists have rejected role theory as an adequate explanation for the way an individual who enlists in a reform movement forms his self-image.

The second problem—why the change happened—reduces in psychological terms to the mechanism by which an individual feels impelled to join a political movement like progressivism. Here again those scholars who emphasize social tensions have implicitly chosen only one of several alternatives offered by psychologists. They assume that the threat from some other social group frustrated the would-be progressive who, in turn, reacted aggressively against that threat. Very few psychologists, however, would claim that social tensions are the main source of frustration. Furthermore, individuals are generally capable of reacting to new roles without experiencing any major frustrations. The different ways in which Theodore Roosevelt and Calvin Coolidge, for example, remade the role of the presidency to fit their own personalities suggest how flexible roles can be without deeply frustrating an individual. Furthermore, different members of the same social class will perceive social challenges in different ways; many will experience no frustration at all.

Even if historians concede that social stresses can frustrate an individual, does it follow that he will react aggressively toward the source of that frustration? The frustration-produces-aggression model is one of the most debated propositions in psychology. Extreme critics have called it "nonsensical." Others have shown that frustration more often produces anxiety, submission, dependence, or avoidance than aggression. Even presumably simpleminded creatures like rats and pigeons do not necessarily react aggressively when they are frustrated. If some psychologists have shown that aggression is only one possible result of frustration, others have shown that frustration is only one possible source of aggression. Indeed, prior to 1939 most psychologists accepted Sigmund Freud's *Beyond the Pleasure Principle*, which contended that aggression derived from the Death Wish. Others have found the source of aggression in neither frustration nor the Death Wish. The assumption that social tensions will frustrate an individual and drive him to react aggressively has been riddled by the artillery of a great many psychologists. For historians to continue to assume that men react primarily to social threats is to ignore an impressive body of psychological literature.

The third problem—what were the results of that change—reduces in psychological terms to the way an individual outwardly expresses the internal change. If an individual felt angry following threats from another social group, how would he express that anger? The idea that he will sublimate his aggressive propensities into cries for political reform is one which is endorsed by many Freudians who follow *Civilization and Its Discontents.* But even some psychoanalysts claim that Freud never adequately explained sublimation. Other personality theorists have asserted that "everyone recognizes . . . that at present we have no theory which really explains the dynamics" of sublimation. Many psychologists have seen sublimation as only one possible way of expressing aggressive proclivities. Political reform is only one of hundreds of directions an individual can channel hostile impulses. But most personality theorists are so unimpressed by the concept of sublimation that they simply ignore it in their own theories.

By assuming that social tensions produced progressivism, historians have approached the basic questions about social and political movements from a very narrow psychological viewpoint. Even more important, the psychological underpinnings of this assumption are either disproved, disputed, ignored, or "untestable" by modern psychologists.

Moreover, the whole psychological framework which includes these theories has recently come under attack. Both behaviorists and psychoanalysts had previously assumed that individuals were motivated by "a state of tenseness that leads us to seek equilibrium, rest, adjustment, satisfaction, or homeostasis. From this point of view, personality is nothing more than our habitual modes of reducing tension." Men became reformers to relieve tensions, perhaps impelled by class and status anxieties. Now, however, many psychologists contend that personality theorists too long overemphasized the irrational components in motivation. As early as 1953 Gordon Allport reported that the trend in motivational theory was away from the tension reduction approach and toward an emphasis on the rational and healthy side of individuals. By stressing the rationality of free choice, these psychologists have argued that a commitment to reform, for example, may in fact be the ultimate expression of a mature personality and reflect a man who is capable of getting outside of his self-preoccupation. Indeed, Erich Fromm has said that the revolutionary leader might well be the only "sane person in an insane world." The decision to embrace progressivism may simply represent a conscious choice between alternative programs, not an attempt to reduce tensions which grew out of a man's efforts to maintain his social position.

There is another problem in borrowing models: the more inclusive the model, the farther it is removed from the reality it is attempting to explain. The data must be squeezed and distorted to make them conform to the model. Many social scientists themselves have revolted against the top-heavy and abstract models which have prevailed in their fields. One student of social stratification, for example, concluded from a review of 333 studies that his field suffered from "the disease of over-conceptualization." Similarly, many psychologists have rejected the abstract personality constructs used to explain motivation because they are too far removed from the reality of individual people. Arguing for a focus on the "life style" of each person, Allport has attacked theories which emphasize "the abstract motivation of an impersonal and therefore non-existent mind-in-general," preferring "the concrete, viable motives of each and every mind-in-particular." In a like vein, Kelly has argued that most psychological constructs ignore an individual's "private domain, within which his behavior aligns itself within its own lawful system." These abstract constructs can only account for the individual as "an inert object wafted about in a public domain by external forces, or as a solitary datum sitting on its own continuum." Allport even charged that psychologists who build universal models to explain human motivation are seeking a "scientific will of the wisp"; the " 'irreducible unlearned motives' of men" they are seeking cannot be found because they do not exist.

This is not a critique of any particular psychological theory or approach to behavior. Rather it is a plea to be aware of the dangers in building a conceptual approach to such a problem as progressivism upon so many rickety psychological foundations. Historians should recognize that psychologists are not that different; they are at least as divided in their interpretations as we are. For historians to accept the assumptions that underlie the idea that social tensions produced progressivism would be similar to a psychologist borrowing Frederick Jackson Turner's frontier hypothesis of his research. Many of us would complain that there are other explanations for the development of American history; and a great many psychologists, in effect, are shuddering at the weak psychological underpinnings of the assumption that their social backgrounds made men become reformers.

The real test for the soundness of any approach is not theoretical, of course, but empirical. In this case the inadequacy of sociological and psychological ideas which inform the assumption that social tensions produced progressivism becomes obvious after an examination of the types of men who became progressives and conservatives. If social tensions were relevant to the rise of progressivism, then clearly the class and status experiences of progressives should have differed in some fundamental way from those of the conservatives.

How different, in fact, were the social origins of progressives and conservatives? Following George E. Mowry's publication in 1951 of *The California Progressives*, several scholars examined the external social class attributes of progressive leaders and concluded that the reformers were drawn from the young urban gentry. But because they neglected to sample a comparable group of conservatives, these studies failed to prove their contention that class and status experiences impelled the progressives. Subsequent profiles of both progressive and conservative leaders in the election of 1912 and the legislative sessions of 1911 in Washington and 1905 in Missouri showed that both groups came from nearly the same social background. Objective measures of their social origins failed to predict the programs and ideologies of political leaders.

Scholars may not accept this finding because they question whether the 1912 campaign reflected political ideologies so much as the personalities of leaders and the desire for office. The studies of legislatures in Washington and Missouri might be questioned because in a single session such extraneous pressures as the personality of a powerful governor or the use of bribes might have interfered with a legislator's expression of his natural preferences. Furthermore, neither Washington nor Missouri was ever noted as a banner progressive state. Perhaps the issues in these states were not as hotly contested—and hence did not reveal as sharp social tensions—as in the more radical states.

The following profile of Wisconsin legislators was designed to avoid some of the possible objections to the other studies. Since contemporaries and historians alike have agreed on the pivotal position of Wisconsin, it is an ideal state to test whether social tensions were important in the development of progressivism. This sample begins with the 1897 session because it was then, for the first time, that the Progressive Republicans identified in their speeches, platforms, and votes the issues which divided them from the stalwarts, and concludes with the 1903 session, when many of their programs were enacted. The index for "progressivism" was based on votes growing out of the campaigns for a more equitable distribution of the tax burden, for regulation of quasi-public corporations, and for purification of the electoral and legislative processes. These were the issues which gave the thrust and tone to Wisconsin progressivism and served as the dividing lines between the old guard and the insurgents.

During these four sessions there were 286 roll calls on these issues. A "progressive" legislator was defined as one who voted for more than 75 percent of the progressive measures; a "moderate" favored between 50 and 75 percent of the progressive measures; and a "conservative" opposed more than half of the progressive measures. Of the 360 Republican legislators included in this profile, 40 percent were progressives, 38 percent were moderates, and 22 percent were conservatives.

If social conflicts were important to the emergence of progressivism, the variable which would be most likely to reveal that fact would be the occupations of legislators. Convincing generalizations from the following chart would need to be based upon large statistical differences, since the relatively small sample is divided so many ways. Occupation clearly made little difference in a legislator's vote on progressive measures.

Table 1

	Farmer	*Merchant*	*Professional*	*Manufacturer*	*Financier*	*Worker*
	Percent	Percent	Percent	Percent	Percent	Percent
Progressives	20	27	26	13	9	5
Moderates	22	24	29	6	13	6
Conservatives	12	27	32	16	10	3

The extent of a man's education helps to locate his social position. In Wisconsin neither progressives (22 percent), moderates (24 percent), nor conservatives (27 percent) were dominated by college graduates. At a time and place where college degrees were rare, perhaps a better measure of educational aspirations would be the proportion of men who sought any kind of formal schooling—high school, business college, night school—beyond the level of the common school. Here again, however, the differences in achievement between progressives (58 percent), moderates (60 percent), and conservatives (66 percent) are insignificant.

The place of a man's birth also indicates his social background. But the nativity of Wisconsin's legislators failed to differentiate progressives from conservatives (see Table 2).

Table 2

	Midwest	*East and New England*	*Canada*	*Europe*
	Percent	Percent	Percent	Percent
Progressives	47	29	6	18
Moderates	61	24	2	13
Conservatives	49	30	5	16

If the Wisconsin sample corresponds roughly to those of other states in the occupations, education, and nativity of political leaders, it differs from them in two other respects. Students of the 1912 election found the progressives to be considerably younger than the conservatives in both age and political experience, a fact which led them to see progressivism as a revolt of the young, would-be politicians. In Wisconsin, however, progressives and conservatives both had an average age of forty-eight, and the moderates averaged forty-six. The median ages of progressives (49), moderates (45), and conservatives (47) likewise fail to suggest the existence of any generational conflict between progressives and conservatives

Nor were Wisconsin's progressives the most politically immature of the rival factions. While service in the legislature is only one measure of political experience, it does reveal the effectiveness of politicians in winning renomination from their local organizations. Although Wisconsin's conservatives had the longest tenure in the legislature, they contrasted not so much with the progressives as with the moderates. Table 3 indicates the number of previous sessions attended by legislators.

Table 3

	None	*One*	*Two or more*
	Percent	Percent	Percent
Progressives	52	28	20
Moderates	62	27	11
Conservatives	35	37	28

The social origins of Wisconsin legislators between 1897 and 1903 clearly suggest that no particular manner of man became a progressive. Such variables as occupation, education, nativity, age, and previous legislative experience fail to differentiate the average progressive from the average conservative. The theories that progressivism was motivated by status or class tensions felt by the urban gentry, the businessmen, the workers, the farmers, or the incipient politicians are challenged in Wisconsin by the fact that members of these groups were as likely to become conservatives as progressives. And the Wisconsin profile parallels other studies. To the extent that social class allegiance can be measured by such attributes as occupation, nativity, education, and age, social tensions were apparently irrelevant to the formation of progressivism since the "typical" progressive and conservative came from the same social background.

Collective statistical profiles can, however, obscure more than they reveal. The five more prominent early Wisconsin progressive leaders, the men who forged the issues which Robert M. La Follette subsequently adopted, were most noteworthy for their different social origins. The man contemporaries hailed as the "father of Wisconsin progressivism" was Albert R. Hall, a small dairy farmer in the western part of the state. Nephew of national Grange head Oliver Kelley, Hall was basically an agrarian radical who developed the reputation of a fearless enemy of the railroads and other large corporations. No less important was John A. Butler, the lengthened shadow of the powerful Milwaukee Municipal League. A sharper contrast to Hall could scarcely be found than this independently wealthy and highly educated Brahmin who seemed to spend more time in his villa than he did in his

Milwaukee law office. Milwaukee also contributed Julius E. Roehr, organized labor's leading champion in the legislature. Born in New York City—the son of German immigrants—this hardworking lawyer and dissident Republican politician would have been extremely uncomfortable with the smells of either Hall's farm or Butler's villa. James H. Stout, the most respected of the early progressives in the legislature, was born and raised in Iowa and educated at the University of Chicago. A fabulously wealthy lumber baron, Stout used his company town of Menomonie to pioneer in vocational education and in welfare benefits for his workers. The orator of these early legislative progressives was James J. McGillivray, a self-made Canadian-born architect and manufacturer who lived in Black River Falls and authored the state's antitrust acts. It would seem almost pointless to hunt for a common social "type" in these early progressives. A Brahmin man of leisure and self-made manufacturer, an agrarian radical who knew no workers and a lawyer who never lived outside a large city and was the workers' champion, young men and old men, Yankees and immigrants, these were the leaders who made common cause in Wisconsin and developed the progressive program.

The widely scattered backgrounds of the most prominent early leaders and the remarkable collective similarity between the average progressive and conservative confirm the weaknesses in the sociological and psychological framework for the assumption that progressivism was rooted in social tensions. The widespread emphasis on social tensions is unsound sociologically because it draws upon only a narrow spectrum of personality theory, and those models upon which it does draw are either unproved or unprovable. The statistical profiles from Wisconsin and elsewhere reveal empirically that the origins of progressivism cannot be found by studying the social backgrounds and tensions of progressive leaders. Remembering Kelly's injunction to avoid "poking about in the neighbors' back yards for methodological windfalls," historians must develop alternative approaches which encompass not only the realm of sociology and psychology but also that of history.

Such an alternative approach should at least restore chronology, a major casualty in the repeated emphasis on men's class and status feelings, to a more prominent position. At this point it is possible to offer a tentative explanation for the origins of progressivism when that movement is placed in the context of the chronological evolution of both industrialism and reform.

When the Progressive era is put against the backdrop of the growth of industrialism in America, the remarkable fact about that period is its relative freedom from social tensions. If conflicts between city and farm, worker and boss, younger and older generations, native-born and immigrant are more or less natural results of industrialization, then the years between the late 1890s and the early 1910s stand as a period of social peace when contrasted with either the Gilded Age or the 1920s, when those conflicts were raw and ragged. Not competition but cooperation between different social groups—ministers, businessmen, workers, farmers, social workers, doctors, and politicians—was what distinguished progressivism from such earlier reform movements as Mugwumpery, Populism, the labor movement, and civil service reform. To the extent that men and groups were motivated by tensions deriving from their class and status perceptions, they would have been unable to cooperate with men from different backgrounds. In focusing on the broadly based progressive thrust, the real question is not what drove groups apart, but what drove them together? To answer this question, progressivism must be located in the development of reform in the late-nineteenth century.

The roots of progressivism reach far back into the Gilded Age. Dozens of groups and individuals in the 1880s envisioned some change that would improve society. Reformers came forward to demand civil service reform, the eight hour day, scientific agriculture, woman suffrage, enforcement of vice laws, factory inspection, nonpartisan local elections, trust-busting, wildlife conservation, tax reform, abolition of child labor, businesslike local government, regulation of railway rates, less patronizing local charity, and hundreds of other causes which would subsequently be identified with progressivism. Younger social scientists, particularly economists, were not only beginning to lambast the formalism and conservatism in their fields and to advocate the ideas which would undergird progressivism but they were also seeking to force governments to accept their ideas. Richard T. Ely's work on the Maryland Tax Commission in the mid-1880s, for example, pioneered in the application of the new economics to government and generated many of the programs which future reformers and politicians would soon adopt.

But this fertility of reform in the Gilded Age did not conceal the basic fact that individuals and groups remained fragmented. There was no common program which could rally all groups, and the general prosperity tended to reassure people that industrialism might cure its own ills. As late as 1892 one editor, reflecting this optimistic frame of mind, could state that "the rich are growing richer, some of them, and the poor are growing richer, all of them." Men and groups seeking major changes, whether elitists or Populists, were generally stereotyped as cranks who were blind to the vast blessings and bright future of industrialism. Circumscribed by such problems and attitudes reformers were understandably fragmented in the Gilded Age.

The catastrophic depression of 1893-1897 radically altered this pattern of reform. It vividly dramatized the failures of industrialism. The widening chasm between the rich and the poor, which a few observers had earlier called a natural result of industrialism, could no longer be ignored. As several tattered bands of men known as Coxey's Army tramped from town to town in 1894, they drew attention to the plight of the millions of unemployed and vividly portrayed the striking contrasts between the way of life of the poor and the "conspicuous consumption" of the rich. Furthermore, as Thorstein Veblen observed, they showed that large numbers of Americans no longer cherished the old gospel of self-help, the very basis for mobility in a democratic society. As desperation mounted, businessmen and politicians tried the traditional ways of reversing the business cycle, but by

1895 they realized that the time-honored formulas of the tariff and the currency simply could not dispel the dark pall that hung over the land. Worse still, President Grover Cleveland seemed utterly incapable of comprehending, let alone relieving, the national crisis.

The collapse of prosperity and the failure of national partisan politicians to alleviate the crisis by the traditional methods generated an atmosphere of restless and profound questioning which few could escape. "On every corner stands a man whose fortune in these dull times has made him an ugly critic of everything and everybody," wrote one editor. A state university president warned his graduates in 1894 that "you will see everywhere in the country symptoms of social and political discontent. You will observe that these disquietudes do not result from the questions that arise in the ordinary course of political discussion . . . but that they spring out of questions that are connected with the very foundations of society and have to do with some of the most elemental principles of human liberty and modern civilization." Was the American dream of economic democracy and mobility impossible in an industrial society? Would the poor overthrow an unresponsive political and economic system? Such questions urgently demanded answers, and it was no longer either wise or safe to summarily dismiss as a crank anyone who had an answer. "The time is at hand," cried one editor, "when some of the great problems which the Nineteenth century civilization has encountered are crying for a solution. . . . Never before in the history of the world were people so willing to accept true teaching on any of these subjects and give to them a just and practical trial." A man's social origins were now less important than his proposals, and many men began to cooperate with people from different backgrounds to devise and implement solutions.

This depression-inspired search for answers sprouted hundreds of discussion groups at which men met, regardless of background, to propose remedies. These groups gave men the habit of ignoring previously firm class lines in the face of the national crisis. When Victor Berger urged the Milwaukee Liberal Club to adopt socialism as the answer, for example, his audience included wealthy bankers, merchants, and lawyers. In the same city, at the Church and Labor Social Union, banker John Johnston urged a "new society" where "class privileges will be abolished because all will belong to the human family," and the discussion was joined by Populists and Socialists as well as clergymen and conservative editors. In this context, too, all types of people sought the wisdom of the men who had made a career of studying the social and economic breakdown. No one was surprised when unions, Granges, women's clubs, and other groups wanted University of Wisconsin economists like Ely to address them. Maybe they had an answer. The social unrest accompanying the depression weakened class and status allegiances.

The direct political effects of the depression also broke down the previous rigidity and fragmentation of reform. The depression created a clear sense of priorities among the many causes which Gilded Age reformers had advocated. It generated broadly based new issues which all classes could unite behind. One such program was the urgent necessity for tax reform. When the depression struck, individuals and corporations were forced to devise ways of economizing as property values, sales, and revenues declined precipitously. Caught between higher taxes to cover the rising costs of local government and their own diminishing revenues, many wealthy individuals and corporations began to hide their personal assets from the assessors, to lobby tax relief through local governments, and even to refuse to pay any taxes. The Progressive program was forged and received widespread popular support as a response to these economies. Citizens who lacked the economic or political resources to dodge their taxes mounted such a crusade against these tax dodgers that former President Benjamin Harrison warned the wealthiest leaders that unless they stopped concealing their true wealth from the tax assessors they could expect a revolution led by enraged taxpayers. The programs for tax reform—including inheritance, income, and ad valorem corporation taxes—varied from place to place, but the important fact was that most citizens had developed specific programs for tax reform and had now agreed that certain individuals and corporations had evaded a primary responsibility of citizenship.

A second major area which proved capable of uniting men of different backgrounds was "corporate arrogance." Facing declining revenues, many corporations adopted economies which ranged from raising fares and rates to lobbying all manner of relief measures through city and state governments. Even more important, perhaps, they could not afford necessary improvements which elementary considerations of safety and health had led local governments to demand that they adopt. Corporate arrogance was no longer a doctrinaire cry of reformers. Now it was an unprotected railway crossing where children were killed as they came home from school or the refusal of an impoverished water company to make improvements needed to provide the healthful water which could stop the epidemics of typhoid fever. Such incidents made the corporation look like a killer. These specific threats united all classes: anyone's child might be careless at a railroad crossing, and typhoid fever was no respecter of social origins.

From such new, direct, and immediate threats progressivism developed its thrust. The more corporations used their political influence to resist making the small improvements, the more communities developed increasingly radical economic programs like municipal ownership or consumer-owned utilities and fought to overthrow the machines that gave immunity to the corporations. Political reforms like the initiative, direct primary, and home rule became increasingly important in the early stages of progressivism because, as William Allen White said, men had first to get the gun before they could hit anything with it. But it was the failure of the political system to respond to the new and immediate threats of the depression that convinced people that more desperate programs were needed.

Perhaps there are, after all, times and places where issues cut across class lines. These are the times and places where men identify less with their occupational roles as producers and more with their roles as consumers—of death-dealing water, unsafe railway crossings, polluted air, high streetcar rates, corrupt politicians—which serve to unite than cross social barriers. There are also universal emotions—anger and fear—which possess all men regardless of their backgrounds. The importance of the depression of the 1890s was that it aroused those universal emotions, posed dramatic and desperate enough threats to lead men of all types to agree that tax dodging and corporate arrogance had to be ended and thereby served to unite many previously fragmented reformers and to enlist the support of the majority that had earlier been either silent or enthusiastic only about partisan issues like the tariff or symbols like Abraham Lincoln. The conversion of the National Municipal League showed how issues were becoming more important than backgrounds. Originally composed of elitists who favored such Mugwumpish concerns as civil service reform, the League by 1898 had become so desperate with the domination over political machines by utility companies that it devoted its energies to municipal ownership and to political devices which promised "more trust in the people, more democracy" than its earlier elitism had permitted. The attitude of moral indignation, such an obvious feature of the early stages of progressivism, was not rooted in social tensions but in the universal emotion of anger.

Whether this emphasis on the results of the depression—unrest, new threats and new issues, and cooperation among social groups—has widespread relevance or validity remains to be seen, but it does help to explain the roots of progressivism in Wisconsin. The most important factor in producing the intensity of Wisconsin progressivism was the cooperation between previously discrete and fragmented social groups both in forging popular issues and getting reforms adopted. And the most important factor in defining the popular issues was the arrogance of certain corporations. In Milwaukee the traction and electricity monopoly between 1894 and 1896 alone, for reasons ranging from extreme overcapitalization to confidence in its political powers, raised both its lighting and streetcar fares, refused to arbitrate with its striking employees, enjoined the city from enforcing ordinances lowering its fares, and used its political power—the company's chief manager was the state's leading Republican boss—to cut its tax bill in half, kill an ordinance which would have prevented it from polluting the air, and thwart generally popular attempts at regulation. Each time the monopoly refused to obey an order, lobbied special favors from the city or state, or prostituted the Republican party to the company, the progressive coalition grew. By the end of the depression, the coalition drew together both ends of the economic spectrum—the Merchants and Manufacturers Association and the Chamber of Commerce as well as several labor unions and the Federated Trades Council. Politically it included the country Republican Club, the Democratic Jefferson Club, and the Socialists and Populists. The Mugwumpish and upper-class Municipal League was joined by German social clubs like the Turnvereine. So defiant was the company—so desperate were the people—that the traction managers became the state's most hated men by 1899; and humorist-politician George Peck observed that Wisconsin's parents "frighten children when they are bad, by telling them that if they don't look out," the traction magnates "will get them." Four hundred miles away, in Superior, the story was remarkably similar. Angered by the repeated refusals of that city's water company to provide the city with healthful enough water to prevent the typhoid fever epidemics that killed dozens of people each year, and blaming the company's political power within both parties for the failure of regulation, labor unions and Populists co-operated with business and professional men and with dissident politicians to try to secure pure water and to overthrow the politicians owned by the company. In Superior, political debate had indeed narrowed, as an editor observed, to a fight of "the people against corporate insolence." The water company, like the traction monopoly at Milwaukee, stood isolated and alone, the enemy of men from all backgrounds. In Wisconsin, at least, the community's groups continued to perform their special functions; and, by the end of the depression, they were all agreed that corporate arrogance had to be abolished. Their desperation made them willing to speak, lobby, and work together.

If, as the Wisconsin experience suggests, cooperation was the underpinning of progressivism, historians should focus on reformers not as victims of social tensions, but as reformers. At any given time and place, hundreds of men and groups are seeking supporters for their plans to change society and government. The basic problem for the reformer is to win mass support for his program. In Wisconsin a reformer's effectiveness depended on how well he manipulated acts of corporate and individual arrogance that infuriated everyone in order to demonstrate the plausibility of his program. Desperate events had made tax dodging, corporate defiance and control of politics the main political issues and had allowed this program to swallow the older reformers at the same time that they created a much broader constituency for reform. The question then becomes: Why did some succeed while others failed? North Dakota never developed a full-blown progressive movement because that state's progressives never demonstrated the plausibility of their programs. Wisconsin's early progressives did succeed in drawing together such diverse groups as unions, businessmen, Populists, and dissident politicians because they adapted their program and rhetoric to the menacing events which angered everyone. Reformers operate in their hometowns and not in some contrived social background which could as easily apply to New York or Keokuk, and it is in their hometowns that they should be studied. Historians should determine why they succeeded or failed to rally the support of their communities to their programs, for the most significant criterion for any reformer is, in the end, his effectiveness.

When the progressive characteristically spoke of reform as a fight of "the people" or the "public interest" against the "selfish interests," he was speaking quite literally of his political coalition because the important fact about progressivism, at least in Wisconsin, was the degree of cooperation between previously discrete social groups now united under the banner of the "public interest." When the progressive politician denounced the arrogance of quasi-public corporations and tax-dodgers, he knew that experiences and events had made his attacks popular with voters from all backgrounds. Both conceptually and empirically it would seem safer and more productive to view reformers first as reformers and only secondarily as men who were trying to relieve class and status anxieties. The basic riddle in progressivism is not what drove groups apart, but what made them seek common cause.

Part Two

THE REGULATION OF THE ECONOMY

Chapter 5 PROGRESSIVE INTENTIONS OVERTURNED

The history of regulatory agencies has not received the attention it deserves. In the following article, which won the Mississippi Valley Historical Association's Pelzer Award for 1962, G. CULLOM DAVIS *(1935-) broke new ground in tracing the first fifteen years of the Federal Trade Commission's history. Conceived as a reformist agency, according to Davis, the FTC later fell under conservative control. The reader, in anticipation of Gabriel Kolko's interpretation that comes next, should note that behind Davis' thesis lies the assumption that the world is full of surprises. Now teaching at Sangamon State University, Professor Davis is involved in an oral history project of his native Illinois.*

During the presidential campaign of 1920, Republican candidate Warren G. Harding sought the support of the American electorate in inaugurating an era of "less government in business and more business in government." In the years that followed, this campaign pledge was fulfilled to such an extraordinary degree that historians of the 1920s have constructed as one of the central pillars of "normalcy" the pro-business orientation of the federal government. A related phenomenon was the mounting hostility with which progressive reformers viewed this rapprochement between government and the business community.

At the focal point of government-business relations was the Federal Trade Commission. Still relatively untested when the decade began, the Commission under-

G. Cullom Davis, "The Transformation of the Federal Trade Commission, 1914-1929," *Mississippi Valley Historical Review*, XLIX (December 1962), 437-455. Reprinted with the permission of the Organization of American Historians and the author.

went a severe trial when confronted with the sweeping transition from progressivism to "normalcy." After a few years of stubborn resistance, it sharply if belatedly altered its activities in 1925 to conform more closely to prevailing views in Congress and the White House. As a consequence, the attitudes of those two opposing groups—progressives and businessmen—which had been, respectively, its warmest defenders and its sharpest critics before 1925 were suddenly reversed. A close study of its behavior and stature during the years from 1914 to 1929 should produce insights into the nature of the Commission and into the temper of American politics in the 1920's.

The passage of the Federal Trade Commission Act in September, 1914, had been considered by many observers of the political scene as the final solution of a long-standing controversy over methods of regulating business. The dispute, which had puzzled and divided reformers since the turn of the century, had centered on the question of whether business could be regulated more effectively by stringent legislation to reinforce the Sherman Anti-Trust Act, or by an administrative commission vested with far-reaching powers. Exponents of the latter view had argued that the ideal instrument of regulation was a small, independent commission, composed of carefully selected experts and isolated from the corrupting and fluctuating influences of everyday politics. Originating chiefly within the ranks of progressive reformers, the controversy had quickly spread to the two major political parties and had served as a prominent issue in the heated presidential campaign of 1912. Now, in 1914, the issue had seemingly been settled by the creation of the Federal Trade Commission. That agency, vested with unprecedented powers to investigate, publicize, and prohibit all "unfair methods of competition," represented a crowning triumph for advocates of the commission concept of regulation. Its five members, appointed by the President, would presumably administer an impartial and consistent policy in accordance with the progressive ideals of strict regulation and vigorous antitrust activity.

General agreement on the importance of the Federal Trade Commission Act did not, however, mean general approval of its provisions. The public was sharply divided on the wisdom and potential benefits of the law. Among progressives the reaction was generally enthusiastic. The bill had been passed by a comfortable majority, with the outcome in the Senate determined largely by the co-operation of the reform-minded senators of both parties. Theodore Roosevelt, still reigning as the patriarch of progressivism, asserted that its enactment meant that the Democrats had adopted "a little of the Progressive Platform," while President Wilson, who had exerted strong pressure for its passage, was proud to claim it as a major accomplishment of his "New Freedom" program. The attitude of the Republican progressives was summed up tersely in the following statement by Senator Albert B. Cummins of Iowa: "I am not half-hearted in my support of this measure. I believe in it thoroughly. I look forward to its enforcement with a high degree of confidence." Similar expressions of approval also came from some of the leading reform journals of the period. The *New Republic*, for example, in one of its early issues, commended the establishment of a regulatory commission and hopefully predicted that it would produce "historic political and constitutional reform"; and in his weekly journal, *La Follette's Magazine*, Senator Robert M. La Follette contributed an editorial praising the law and anticipating "much relief to the public and to honest business."

In contrast to the united support offered it by progressives, the Federal Trade Commission received a divided reaction from the business world. As the *Outlook* observed, many businessmen hoped that the law would produce "genuine co-operation" between business and government, but there were others who viewed the new agency "with foreboding." The former group, whose attitude might have been described as cautious optimism, included the powerful United States Chamber of Commerce. Through its official publication, *The Nation's Business*, the Chamber observed that the Commission's value would have to be judged on the basis of its future course of action. So long as it acted as a "constructive and timely aid to business," rather than as an enemy, it would enjoy the businessman's support. But it would lose that support, the Chamber warned, if it undertook "investigations of no constructive significance" or if it acted as "a court of inquisition."

Less optimistic business interests viewed the Commission with apprehension and hositility. They feared that it would become an all-powerful agency, combining the functions of all three branches of government and endeavoring to dissolve free enterprise into small, unprofitable units. Illustrative of this position was the attitude of Senator Frank B. Brandegee of Connecticut, who had stubbornly opposed the Trade Commission bill, and who warned that the Commission would be "a burden upon the varied business interests of the land" and, even worse, the first fatal step toward a "socialistic program of government." Although this extreme point of view was relatively rare among businessmen in 1915, it was an accurate forecast of the conservative attitude that was to evolve in the next ten years.

In its first decade of activity, the Federal Trade Commission proved a disappointment to many of its original supporters. Progressives generally placed the blame for this failure outside the Commission itself. They correctly judged that its poor record was due to a combination of three damaging factors: a series of adverse court decisions, the active opposition of many congressmen, and an uncooperative attitude on the part of many businessmen. The commissioners themselves, or at least a majority of them, worked hard to fulfill the original purpose of the Federal Trade Commission Act. Consequently, in spite of its disappointing record, the Commission continued up to 1925 to enjoy the support of progressives.

It would probably be accurate to say that before 1925 a majority of the commissioners desired to execute a strict regulatory policy in accordance with the progressive ideals of economic reform. Most of President Wilson's appointees shared this progressive view, and because commissioners were appointed for seven-year terms the progressive majority remained intact for a few years following Wilson's departure from office. Consequently, it was not until 1925 that the remaining Wilson appointees faced a majority selected by Warren G. Harding and Calvin Coolidge. Up to a point, then, the Commission was able to operate independently and to maintain a consistent policy in spite of the changing complexion and policies of the White House.

The work of the Federal Trade Commission was just beginning when the United States entered the First World War. During the conflict its regulatory activities were necessarily curtailed in the interest of the war effort, and the Commission functioned chiefly as a fact-finding bureau for the War Industries Board and other temporary agencies. Thus, the duties which it was created to perform did not really begin until after 1918, but as soon as conditions permitted it initiated a program of vigorous investigation. Its first target was the meat-packing industry, where it undertook an extensive investigation of the five largest firms. In a lengthy report, issued late in 1919, it pointed out that the major meat packers were engaged in profiteering activities that constituted unlawful restraints of trade. This revelation, and the broad punitive recommendations which accompanied it, provoked a sharp congressional controversy which resulted in the first major setback for the Commission. Led by Senator James E. Watson of Indiana, a leading right-wing Republican, conservatives in Congress condemned the investigatory methods and findings of the Commission. The outcry had a damaging effect, both direct and indirect, upon the stature and effectiveness of the Commission. The clamor served to stall proceedings in the case to such an extent that formal action was never taken against the defendants, and the Commission was rebuked in the Republican platform of 1920 for "unfair persecution of honest business." And in 1921 Congress added its own reproach in the Packers and Stockyards Act, which transferred jurisdiction over meat packers to the Department of Agriculture.

Not only in Congress but also in the courts, the Federal Trade Commission encountered crippling obstacles. The most serious blow, delivered in a series of judicial decisions, was denial of the Commission's right to define the specific meaning of "unfair methods of competition." Instead, this power was assumed by the courts, which generally defined it in such narrow terms that many Commission rulings were reversed. The courts also insisted on the right to review not only the Commission's procedure in cases, but its findings of fact as well. In other words, factual evidence gathered by the Commission was not accepted *prima facie*, but became subject to review and hence to possible dismissal by the courts. According to Nelson B. Gaskill, who served as one of the more active and conscientious members of the Commission from 1920 to 1925, these adverse rulings "completely devitalized" the Commission and "reduced it to terms of a futile gesture."

In its contacts with businessmen, the Federal Trade Commission met with increasing defiance and animosity. Its investigators were denied access to company records or were permitted to examine only selected materials. In some cases its rulings were actually ignored or defied, the most notable instance being in the case against the Aluminum Company of America. Following an intensive investigation, the Commission in 1924 ordered the company to halt certain illegal practices. Reports that this ruling had not been obeyed led to a second investigation, but by that time the Commission membership had changed, and the case was eventually dropped. Thus hampered by the unfriendliness of Congress, the courts, and the business community, members of the Commission experienced the futility and frustration of striving to carry out a vigorous regulatory policy in an environment which was decidedly hostile to such action.

The commissioners' disappointment over their record contrasted sharply, however, with the unswerving and heartening loyalty expressed by leading progressives. Up to 1925 progressives looked with confidence to the Federal Trade Commission as their most effective weapon in the war against monopoly and unfair business practices. The very failures of the Commission served to reinforce the arguments in favor of its existence, for so long as the commissioners themselves remained dedicated to the principles of progressivism, the Commission appeared to be the only potentially effective regulator of business. The fact that its work had been sabotaged by the exponents of a pro-business viewpoint merely emphasized the virtues of a strong, independent commission. This continuing loyalty of progressives to the Commission was accurately expressed in *La Follette's Magazine*: "The Federal Trade Commission was intended by Congress to do exactly the things it has done, as an independent body, non-partisan in its personnel and unhampered by interference from other branches of the government."

That progressives continued to rely upon the Federal Trade Commission up to 1925 is also indicated by the fact that they frequently sought aid and information from it. Many of its investigations of business activities were initiated at the request of liberal reformers in Congress. A noteworthy example was the investigation of the utilities industry. In 1924 a number of leading progressives, including Senators George W. Norris and Thomas J. Walsh and Governor Gifford Pinchot of Pennsylvania, expressed their alarm at the expanding network of interconnected utility corporations, which they called the "power trust." Certain large companies were suspected of monopolistic control over many other utilities representing an aggregate capital investment of hundreds of millions of dollars. Progressives urged that the federal government take action, and they unhesitatingly selected the Federal Trade Commission as the proper agency to direct an investigation. Senator Norris' resolution embodying these demands was finally passed in February, 1925. Thus, until the early months of 1925 progressives were willing and even eager to intrust important investigative and regulatory tasks to the Commission.

Probably the most frequent and consistent favorable publicity for the work of the Commission during the early years of its activity appeared in *La Follette's Magazine*. Senator La Follette utilized the journal to publicize attempts in Congress to "hamstring the Federal Trade Commission" by cutting its appropriation, and he was also quick to praise the Commission's accomplishments, which he considered numerous and important. After his death in 1925, this policy was continued, and in 1926 an editorial reviewing the Commission's achievements prior to 1925 made the statement that "the Federal Trade Commission during the past ten years has not only restrained the greed of the steel trust, but it has investigated the packers, the harvester trust, grain exchanges, lumber trusts, aluminum trust, fertilizer trust, and other great organizations." In short, the editorial concluded, "the Commission was the friend of labor, of the farmers, of cooperative organizations, and of the small business men."

Another progressive, Senator William H. King of Utah, also summarizing the accomplishments of the Commission before 1925, argued that it "performed service of the very highest character, and did much to protect honest business from unfair practices." This view was echoed by Josephus Daniels, who had served as secretary of the navy under President Wilson. Daniels observed that the Commission had "done much good and proved . . . a deterrent to unfair practices in business," in spite of the heavy opposition which it had encountered. Progressives were of course disappointed that the Commission had not completely fulfilled its original aims, but they nevertheless continued to support it on the grounds that its shortcomings were the result of a hostile environment rather than of any inherent defects. This unbroken loyalty bolstered the Commission against the increasing attacks being made upon it by representatives of business.

During the same ten-year period the attitude of businessmen toward the Commission had shifted from their initially divided and uncertain reaction of 1915 to a steadily increasing united opposition to its work. Their criticism ranged from mild displeasure and vexation at the Commission's investigations to sharp attacks upon its very foundations. Viewed collectively, the businessmen's attacks called for either a radical transformation or the outright abolition of the Commission.

Those voices which expressed displeasure in subdued language included prominent individuals and publications in the business world. The *Nation's Business*, which had hopefully adopted a "wait and see" policy in 1915, revealed a growing exasperation in the years that followed by publishing articles criticizing the Commission's activities. One of these essays, contributed by a New York banker, attacked the alleged tendency of regulatory commissions to become "prosecuting functionaries" and concluded that the very principles of investigation and regulation, which of course formed the basis for the Commission's existence, "instead of simplifying a complex situation . . . tended to make it more complicated and obscure." This view was reiterated in other articles in the same journal. Writing in 1925, former Secretary of Commerce William C. Redfield warned that "after ten years of endurance, the business world is rebelling against the unjust methods of the Federal Trade Commission." He added that the Commission had wrongly assumed the functions of "accuser, judge, and jury," thereby becoming "a disappointment and a scourge to the business world." Another article in the same issue charged that instead of helping business as it was originally intended to do, the Commission had placed "every possible obstacle in its way and . . . condemned and maligned businessmen for practices of which they were innocent." Another business publication, the *Wall Street Journal*, bluntly depicted the Federal Trade Commission as "a crusading, muck-raking body."

A more extreme form of attack by businessmen was forcefully expressed by William E. Humphrey, the man who was to play the key role in the Commission's transformation in 1925. Humphrey was a former congressman from the state of Washington, an active Republican party regular, and one of President Coolidge's campaign managers in the 1924 election. His close connection with northwestern lumber interests, which had suffered the unfavorable publicity of a Federal Trade Commission investigation, made him a particularly bitter foe of its work. He charged that the pre-1925 Commission was "an instrument of oppression and disturbance and injury instead of a help to business," and asserted that "No other governmental agency ever had a practice so tyrannical and so repugnant to every sense of justice." Although Humphrey's views were probably more extreme than the typical businessman's attitude, they nevertheless revealed the extent to which many business spokesmen had become hostile to the Commission by 1925.

Thus if the Federal Trade Commission had not lived up to its initial promise prior to 1925, the blame for this failure clearly lay in circumstances beyond that agency's control. This conclusion is indicated not only by the record of the Commission itself, but also by the conflict between the views of progressives and businessmen toward it. An organization which continued to enjoy the support of progressive reformers, and which at the same time incurred the mounting hositility of business interests, was plainly still directed toward the progressive ideals which had given it birth. The Commission's survival thus constituted by 1925 one of the last remaining bulwarks of progressivism against the rising tide of reaction and conservatism in the federal government. Its continued existence, however, was precarious. With a total membership of five men, the Commission was destined eventually to come under the control of a conservative majority. Opponents of the Commission, who had attacked it frontally in Congress and in the courts, had also succeeded in quietly placing two staunch conservatives on its board by 1925. In that year they were able, as one progressive journal angrily observed, to "destroy it from the inside" by appointing a third and pivotal conservative to its membership. That development, with its important repercussions, quickly elevated the Commission to new heights of controversy and criticism.

The year 1925 stands out, therefore, as a critical turning point in the early history of the Federal Trade Commission. As a result of the vital change in its membership and leadership from a progressive to a conservative majority in that year, it experienced a far-reaching transformation of its fundamental purpose and practices. And in consequence of this transformation, it became the subject of serious concern, re-evaluation, and controversy among government officials and professional students of politics. This controversy revealed a remarkable reversal in the roles of the Commission's former allies and enemies as progressives and businessmen exchanged their positions with regard to the Commission itself. Businessmen overnight became loyal defenders of the Commission, while progressives united in attacking it and even in demanding its abolition. On one point, however, every one agreed after 1925: the Federal Trade Commission had now broken with its progressive origins and ideals and had completely if belatedly reorientated its activities to conform to the prevailing pattern of "normalcy."

To place responsibility for these changes upon a single person is to invite disbelief and a charge of oversimplification. With minor qualifications, however, the general conclusion is inescapable that the appointment of William E. Humphrey as a member of the Federal Trade Commission in February, 1925, set off a chain reaction which eventually included all of the developments summarized above. Under these circumstances, a careful study of the man and his appointment is warranted.

It has been noted that Humphrey was one of the Commission's more formidable opponents before 1925. During his career as a congressman he was known as a sincere and staunch exponent of the business viewpoint. This reputation was further substantiated after 1917, when he became a lawyer and vigorous lobbyist for northwestern lumber interests. There was nothing secretive about Humphrey's work; he was proud of his business associations. An article in *The Nation* in 1925 paid him the supreme compliment when it pointed out that "big business has no warmer friend or defender," and Senator Norris, who had served with Humphrey in the House, characterized him as "a fearless advocate of big business" and "one of the greatest reactionaries." The most revealing evidence of this conservative viewpoint, however, was provided by Humphrey himself. He once declared, for example, that many years of experience in Washington had given him "a profound distrust of the reformer." Such language was scarcely calculated to endear its author to the progressives.

Up to the time of Humphrey's appointment, the Federal Trade Commission was controlled by a progressive-minded majority. Early in 1924, four Wilson appointees remained to direct the activities of the five-man Commission. These were Huston Thompson, who had served as assistant attorney general under Wilson; Victor Murdock, who prior to his 1917 appointment was a progressive congressman from Kansas; Nelson B. Gaskill, who later wrote a book lamenting the disappearance of the progressively oriented Commission; and John F. Nugent, who resigned from the Senate in 1921 to become a commissioner. Gradually, however, the Harding and Coolidge appointees gained in number. Vernon W. Van Fleet, a friend of Indiana's Senator Watson and a former lobbyist for the National Association of Manufacturers, was appointed in 1922. Victor Murdock was replaced in 1924 by Charles W. Hunt, whom *La Follette's Magazine* briefly characterized as a "reactionary Republican of Iowa." Thus with the appointment of Humphrey to succeed Nelson Gaskill in February, 1925, majority control over the Federal Trade Commission passed into the hands of the more recent appointees.

Progressives sharply but unsuccessfully opposed Humphrey's appointment. Its effect was "to set the country back more than twenty-five years," according to Senator Norris, who pictured the Commission as now standing "three to two in favor of the big-business idea." *La Follette's Magazine* asserted that the Commission consisted of "three reactionaries and two Progressives," and *The Nation* charged the Coolidge administration with the "deliberate breaking down of governmental safeguards against the evils of big business." In spite of these attacks, however, and of the obvious implications of Coolidge's selection, Humphrey's appointment was easily confirmed in the Senate by a vote of 45 to 10.

This controversial change in the personnel of the Federal Trade Commission was but the prelude to a still more significant transformation of its rules of policy and procedure. The Commission adopted the first three of a new set of rules of procedure in March, 1925. In the first of these it specified that henceforth its investigations were to be confined strictly to those cases which included definite allegations of unfair practices detrimental to the public interest. This restricting rule was designed to end the congressional practice of authorizing the Commission to undertake sweeping economic studies of a general nature. A second change was the announcement that in the future the Commission would strive to settle most of its cases by "stipulation," or informal agreement, rather than through the costlier and more time-consuming process of formal action by either the Commission or some other government agency. Settlement by stipulation was considered desirable because it would give defendants the benefits of reduced legal expenses, less public exposure of their misdeeds, and a friendlier relationship with the government.

A third new rule gave defendants the opportunity to present their arguments informally and confidentially in a preliminary hearing before a board of review. The record of those hearings was not to be printed or given any publicity, so that defendants could speak freely without fear of being held responsible at some later date for their informal testimony. In insisting upon the adoption of this rule, Commissioner Humphrey charged that in the past the Commission had been employed all too often as "a publicity bureau to spread socialistic propaganda." A fourth rule change, adopted a few weeks later, providing that stipulation agreements were to be made confidentially without any public announcement of the settlements, further emphasized a determination to curtail the Commission's ability to publicize its actions. Thus stipulation now became all the more attractive to defendants, because it offered them a means of avoiding altogether any unfavorable or damaging publicity.

The guiding influence behind this transformation was the newly appointed commissioner, William E. Humphrey, who had immediately assumed vigorous leadership of the conservative majority. His virtual domination of the commission served, as one writer has observed, "to inaugurate a 'new era' in its activities." Humphrey himself freely and proudly acknowledged his responsibility for the new era. "I certainly did make a revolutionary change in the method and policies of the commission," he was quoted as saying in 1928. "If it was going east before, it is going west now." Humphrey's influence was also decisive in other important developments within the Federal Trade Commission. He was chiefly responsible, for example, for the decision against reopening the earlier case against the Aluminum Company of America, thus thwarting the demands of progressives who charged that the original Commission order had been disobeyed by the company. He also succeeded in enlarging the Commission's board of review—which conducted the informal preliminary hearings—frankly admitting that his purpose was to "stack" the board with a compliant majority. "What of it?" he asked brazenly in answer to criticism. "Do you think I would have a body of men working here under me that did not share my ideas about these matters? Not on your life. I would not hesitate a minute to cut their heads off if they disagreed with me. What in hell do you think I am here for?"

Humphrey's pro-business attitudes also led him to encourage more extensive use of a procedure through which the Commission had permitted industry-wide meetings, or "trade practice conferences," to formulate their own rules of behavior. If these rules fell within the Commission's jurisdiction, they could be approved by that agency and given the force of law. Despite their appealing informality and sense of co-operative effort, such conferences had been infrequent prior to 1926. In that year, however, Humphrey brought about the creation within the Commission of a new department, the trade practice conference division, whose purpose was to encourage industrial self-regulation. The new procedure, it was pointed out, "permits an industry to make its own rules of business conduct . . . in cooperation with the commission." The plan was effective, for after 1926 the average number of trade practice conferences jumped from less than three to about sixteen per year. The general effect was to introduce an atmosphere of co-operation and common effort into relations between business and the Commission and to promote a tendency toward less governmental interference on the one hand and more corporate independence on the other.

Viewed together, these procedural changes constituted a sharp departure from earlier Commission policy and from the progressive ideal of strict regulation. Essentially, the new policy was friendlier, more trusting, and more co-operative toward business. In the first place, the Commission had now expressed a strong preference for settling cases by informal, confidential agreement rather than by formal Commission order. Second, it had taken steps to curtail its powers of publicity and investigation, thereby shielding defendants from public embarrassment and criticism. Finally, it now exhibited such confidence in the ability and willingness of business to regulate itself that its own function in the regulatory process was being performed more as partner than as overseer. The members themselves summarized the new viewpoint in 1927, when they declared that "helping business to help itself wherever and whenever it can be done . . . is the principle of this new policy." In that same year they asserted that "the legitimate interests of business are in perfect harmony with the true interests of the public." In other words, after 1925 the majority of the Commission no longer viewed business as an actual or even potential enemy to be investigated suspiciously and regulated stringently, but rather as a friend and partner to be assisted and encouraged in pursuit of common aims.

Within a period of one year, therefore, the Federal Trade Commission had undergone a radical transformation of its fundamental purpose and policy, and it was only natural that the two groups most directly concerned should mirror this change in their attitudes toward the Commission. Progressives and businessmen continued as before to view the Commission from opposite positions, but their respective attitudes were completely reversed. Instead of criticizing and attempting to weaken the Commission, businessmen after 1925 began to defend its activities. Conversely, progressives ceased supporting what had once been a vital part of their reform program and began to attack the Commission and even to demand its abolition.

The attitude of the business community toward the new policy of the Commission was perhaps most revealingly expressed by Humphrey himself. He observed in 1927 that "the businessmen who have come in contact with the Commission during the last year realize this change in attitude, and I know that they fully endorse it." In 1926 the Commission itself testified to this response of businessmen when it noted "an increasing degree of cooperation on the part of business." Humphrey dismissed the critics as "the vocal and beatific fringe, the pink edges that border both of the old parties." "No longer," he noted with satisfaction, would the Commission serve "as a means of gratifying demagogues."

Other voices from the business world expressed these same sentiments. A prominent New York banker wrote in the *Nation's Business* that the Commission was finally coming to the correct conclusion that "the only way to regulate business effectively is to let it regulate itself," and the United States Chamber of Commerce expressed its formal approval of the Commission's course of action. In its annual meetings of 1925 and 1926 the Chamber passed resolutions endorsing the new rules of those two years. One resolution happily predicted that the changes would make the Commission "increasingly constructive, effective, and helpful to American business." The *Magazine of Wall Street*, a trade periodical of banking and finance, lauded the new rules as "an encouraging development" in the campaign to end the Commission's "legalized persecution of business." Thanks to the work of Humphrey, it added, the Commission had been converted from a "hectoring, tyrannical and . . . tireless snooper" into "an instrument of protection," thus heralding a "new trend toward making government the fair and understanding arbiter of business."

Progressives, shocked by the rapid and disastrous transformation of the Federal Trade Commission, were vociferous critics of the new policy. The progressive reaction, both spontaneous and sharp, appeared in the remarks and activities of politicians and in leading news publications. One of the first to complain was Commissioner Huston Thompson, whose experience enables him to anticipate the probable outcome of Humphrey's rules changes. Thompson attacked those changes which curtailed the Commission's publicity power as "wholly dangerous and subversive to the public welfare," paving the way for "a new system of government by secrecy." Thompson was joined by John F. Nugent, the other progressive remaining on the Commission, and in vain the two men warned that the revised rules would convert the Commission into a "star-chamber." Progressives in Congress were equally critical. Senator Thomas J. Walsh charged that Commissioner Humphrey's changes were intended "to limit, if not utterly destroy, the usefulness of the commission." William E. Borah of Idaho claimed that the Commission could no longer fulfill its original purpose, and Senator Norris, who had accurately predicted the probable effect of Humphrey's appointment, also joined in the attack.

Among progressive publications, the sharpest reaction came from *La Follette's Magazine*. In what proved to be his final editorial contribution, the ailing Senator La Follette wrote a bitter epitaph for the Federal Trade Commission. "The last of the Commissions at Washington to be taken over by the forces it was intended to regulate," he said, "the Federal Trade Commission has been packed with its worst enemies, its rules have been perverted, the law under which it was created has been emasculated, and its usefulness has been destroyed." The finishing blow, according to La Follette, had been dealt by the three conservative commissioners, and he concluded that pro-business control of the Commission had done much more to subject the public to business exploitation "than was accomplished by [Secretary of Interior Albert B.] Fall when he turned the naval reserves over to the oil monopoly." Similar criticism appeared in other progressive magazines. George Soule, co-editor of the *New Republic*, warned that the new rules refusing to publicize certain types of cases might enable "business malefactors" who enjoyed influence with the Commission to "get away with murder." An editorial in *The Nation* complained that the Commission had lost its real power, and that its probable future course of action would be "to do only what business desires."

Following their initial reaction of surprise and bitter criticism, progressives became even more convinced of the uselessness and actual disservice of the Federal Trade Commission as it was now constituted. Fearful that the Commission might begin to do more harm than good, they attempted in Congress either to restrict its activities or to abolish it altogether. The possibility that a regulatory commission could serve the interests it was designed to control was not new to the progressives of the 1920's. As early as 1892 Richard Olney, who later became President Cleveland's attorney general, had observed that the Interstate Commerce Commission could be "of great use to . . . railroads" by serving as "a sort of protection against hasty and crude legislation hostile to railroad interests." This possibility appeared to have been dramatically verified by the recent policy changes of the Federal Trade Commission. Progressives therefore publicized the process in their mounting attacks upon the Commission.

Within a year following the first rules changes a serious movement, championed by leading reformers and progressive publications, was under way to abolish the

Federal Trade Commission. One of the first to take up the proposal was Representative Tom Connally of Texas, who remarked that the Commission was "suffering from pernicious anemia" and charged that it had become "a city of refuge to which the guilty may flee, a sanctuary for those who violate and defy the laws of the United States." The original sponsor of the bill to abolish the Commission was Senator William H. King of Utah. In explaining the need for such action King asserted that the Commission had become "not only a useless appendage, but . . . a real menace." King's bill was fated to die in committee, but in the course of the debate other progressives spoke in its behalf. One of these was Senator Norris, who denounced the Commission as "the refuge for monopoly, unfair competition, and unfair business methods." Norris was joined by his Nebraska colleague in the Senate, Robert B. Howell, who described the Commission as "the sanctuary of utility corporations," and Senators Borah of Idaho and Carter Glass of Virginia also supported the proposal for dissolution.

Frustrated in their efforts to abolish the Commission, progressives next attempted to relieve it of any duties which could be more satisfactorily handled by some other government agency. They believed that even if it should remain under the control of pro-business commissioners, its evil influence might still be minimized, and it was this argument that prompted Senators Walsh and Norris to urge in 1928 a new investigation of the utilities industry, to be conducted by a Senate committee rather than by the Federal Trade Commission.

Progressives were especially dissatisfied with the results of an investigation which had recently been made by the Commission at their insistence, and whose findings, published in 1927, had reported no evidence either of illegal activities in the utilities industry or of the existence of the alleged "power trust." In February, 1928, therefore, Walsh introduced a resolution calling for a new investigation by a special committee of five senators. He insisted that the task should not be given to the Commission because, he said, any investigation by that agency would "not be . . . of any value." During a three-day debate on this resolution Walsh was supported by Norris and Senator William J. Harris of Georgia. An alternative motion, designating the Commission as the investigating agency, was attacked by the progressives as a sinister maneuver engineered by big business. Senator Harris, who had served on the Federal Trade Commission from 1915 to 1918, warned that the defeat of Walsh's motion "would be a great victory for the Water Power Trust." Such progressive publications as *La Follette's Magazine* and the *New Republic* also supported Walsh's demand for a Senate investigation, but once again the efforts of a handful of progressives against an essentially conservative majority in Congress were doomed to failure. The Walsh motion was defeated, and the alternative resolution passed easily.

Thus, within a startling brief period of time, the Federal Trade Commission experienced a radical transformation of its functions as well as its friends and foes. As a result of the important policy changes promoted by Commissioner Humphrey, businessmen abruptly halted their campaign against the Commission and became its loyal supporters. Progressives, on the other hand, reacted bitterly against the change and now attacked the Commission with the same scorn that they had directed against the other conservative institutions of the period. It was ironic that this agency, which had been one of the most important and auspicious products of the progressive program, should have been transformed after 1925 into a pro-business institution which threatened not only to weaken but even to subvert the entire regulatory process. Under these circumstances, it is not surprising that the progressive estrangement from the Federal Trade Commission was bitter, almost vengeful. Disillusioned and disaffected, liberals experienced the frustrations of a thoroughly hostile political environment from 1925 until changing economic conditions made possible their resurgence after 1929.

Chapter 6 DESIGNED BY AND FOR BIG BUSINESS

From the preceding chapter, it is clear that the Progressives did not build proper safeguards to regulate the regulators. In the following selection, GABRIEL KOLKO *(1932-) addresses himself to another, although related problem–namely, who, in the first place, designed the regulatory state? His answer is, big business. Born in New Jersey and currently teaching at York University, Canada, Professor Kolko has written at length about the shortcomings of American liberalism in both domestic and foreign affairs. In contrast to G. Cullom Davis, who describes himself as "an old-fashioned Progressive," Kolko's overview is similar to that of many a Marxian during the Progressive era. Which of the two historians is to be believed about the FTC?*

During most of 1913 Woodrow Wilson and his aides were preoccupied with banking reform and tariff legislation. But the pressure for more extensive federal regulation of corporations and business was great, and the New Freedom also obligated the Administration to take action in this area. To precisely what was Wilson committed? The New Freedom was, in the final analysis, intended to serve as a campaign document, and the doctrine was full of inconsistencies. "I am for big business, and I am against the trusts," Wilson declared, but he could not define the major differences between the two and he never gave the matter serious thought. He proclaimed that "The development of business upon a great scale . . . is inevitable," and also expressed satisfaction that businessmen were beginning to reform themselves.

The guidelines utilized by Wilson were amorphous. What was certain, however, was the demand of leading businessmen for federal regulation designed to meet their problems. Since the failure of Perkins, Gary and the National Civic Federation forces to enact the Hepburn Bill in 1908, important segments of big business had sought to overcome the condition of uncertainty that existed in innumerable industries. Federal incorporation had been prominently mentioned as a possible solution for well over a decade, but Congress was never willing to act on the principle. The idea of a trade commission similar to the I.C.C. was actively promoted by George W. Perkins and many others from early 1911 on, and both the Progressive and Republican Parties endorsed the proposal in 1912. Gary and Carnegie were even suggesting government price-fixing! Armed with the National Civic Federation's business opinion poll of late 1911, big businessmen stridently called for federal regulation of the economy.

It was obvious that without strong Executive support there could be significant legislative advances toward a political capitalism only as a result of irate public opinion manipulated to satisfy business ends. Save in railroad legislation, much of the real progress toward political capitalism from the beginning of the century until 1913 had been an incidental byproduct of scandals and amorphous reform enthusiasm among the wider public. In 1913 Wilson had little guidance save from fundamentally conservative individuals, of whom Colonel House was the foremost, who directed Wilson's unclear but moderate impulses toward conservative ends. Bryan, despite his emotional radicalism, was also a shrewd politician, and it was difficult to reduce his arsenal of phrases and clichés to specific proposals for concrete changes. Moreover, Wilson could barely tolerate Bryan's style and manners, and relied on him only when it was absolutely necessary. During 1913, despite a few dramatic antitrust cases by the fundamentally conservative but literal-minded Attorney General, James C. McReynolds, Wilson was responsive to the pressures and desires of big business. There was more progress in the fulfilment of big business interests through the Federal Reserve Act alone than there had been in well over five years.

Wilson's ideological conservatism has been appreciated by historians. The extent of that conservatism can only be fully understood, however, when we pass from Wilson as an intellectual to Wilson as an administrator. The New Freedom, after all, was not merely a doctrine—in any serious sense it was hardly that. The New Freedom was, more than anything else, government regulation of banking, industry, and railroads. Wilson during his eight years as a trust-buster initiated substantially fewer cases than Harding and Coolidge during their two terms. Wilson's other reforms were, for the most part, of no great significance to a wider public.

Wilson and Business

Wilson did not enter office under any sort of cloud that might have made big business apprehensive. "... we shall get more experience with respect to economic and industrial policies," Senator Joseph B. Foraker predicted immediately after the election, and even Taft found it possible to approve Wilson's new Cabinet, an approbation that was eventually to blossom to admiration for Wilson in general. J. P. Morgan, on his deathbed, was full of optimism for the new administration, and he offered his services to the President through George Harvey.

Senator Francis G. Newlands, the old Democratic advocate of federal incorporation, by 1912 was ready to try instead to obtain a commission, and Wilson's victory made him chairman of the crucial Senate Committee on Interstate Commerce. Despite the increasing possibilities for action in 1913, very little was done. Pressure for action existed, of course, but it was mild in a prosperity year. Roosevelt kept up his demand for an interstate trade commission, but George Wickersham denied the need for any serious changes in the Sherman Act. Letters continued to pour into the Department of Justice, as they had in previous years, asking for opinions on the legality of various actions. And, as Arthur Eddy told a Department of Justice official, "I am interested in seeing passed broad and comprehensive legislation, legislation which will really reach the evils the industrial world suffers, at least as effectively as the Interstate Commerce Law reaches some of the evils of transportation."

It was logical that the Department of Justice concern itself with the problem of the relationship of the government to business. It was even more logical, however, that the Bureau of Corporations try to reconsider the problem in light of the commitments of the New Freedom. Joseph E. Davies, the new head of the bureau, pondered about the matter and in July, 1913, sent Secretary of Commerce William C. Redfield a memo on the topic; Redfield approved it and immediately sent it along to Wilson. Perhaps the Davies memo was really a rationale for larger appropriations for the bureau—he asked for a tripling of its budget—but it is at least of significance as an example of an attempted definition of the role of the executive in the New Freedom. Big business had implications to the general political structure insofar as it had the power to create a state within a state, and it had the power to affect labor, Davies admitted. Both of these problems were beyond the interest of the bureau. What was of concern, Davies suggested, was the effect of big business on the costs of production and prices. In addition to its specific industry investigations, it was time for the bureau to discover "what principles or laws generally underlie industry and its relation to society and to the state. . . ." Questions to be explored were the relationship of size to efficiency and prices, and "whether the regulation of practically monopolistic units or the restoration of competitive units is the true and correct solution." This task, Davies modestly proposed, was to be completed in a five months period. As if this were not enough, state corporation laws and trade agreements would also be studied in great detail. If state laws could be made uniform it "would eliminate one of the principal arguments for centralization of power in the National Government for the regulation of corporations. . . ." Moreover, a really serious study of trade agreements could determine which ones ought to be exempted from the Sherman Act. The Davies memo indicated the doubt and confusion that existed among so many crucial leaders around Wilson, and left the door wide open to those who knew what they wanted. Davies' ambitious answers were never produced.

By October, 1913, however, it was increasingly obvious that Wilson's current legislative preoccupations were going to attain fulfilment and that "antitrust" legislation would be a serious issue in 1914. In late October, Ralph W. Easley, the director of the National Civic Federation, wrote McReynolds about antitrust legislation. Referring to the unhappy experience with the Hepburn Bill under Roosevelt, Easley indicated that he had another draft bill available that had been produced by Seth Low, James R. Garfield, C. A. Severance, Samuel Untermyer, John B. Clark, and J. W. Jenks. An audience was requested and immediately granted. The federation's plan provided for a seven-man Interstate Trade Commission chosen by the President and with powers of investigation and subpoena, and the ability to refer its complaints to the courts and fine companies $5,000 for each violation. The commission could license corporations, and would require annual reports. Its jurisdiction would apply to companies with sales of $10 million and up. The proposal received an important circulation and a copy was sent to Wilson, while Davies also discussed the matter with Easley in detail.

By the end of 1913 Wilson was feeling very mellow toward business. It had been most cooperative–indeed its aid had been crucial–in the campaign to obtain banking reform. On December 19 he wrote McReynolds that "I gain the impression more and more from week to week that the businessmen of the country are sincerely desirous of conforming with the law, and it is very gratifying indeed to be able to deal with them in complete frankness and to be able to show them that all that we desire is an opportunity to cooperate with them." During the same month, conscious of the long preceding effort to obtain a federal commission, the House Committee on the Judiciary, chaired by Henry D. Clayton of Alabama, opened hearings on the entire problem of trust legislation. And from late 1913 on the leaders of the business community began shifting their attention to the need for greater federal regulation of the industrial economy.

The President was fully aware of the fact that the business community resented the insecurity of the Sherman Act and wished to attain a measure of predictability and confidence that had been lacking under Taft. He was certainly familiar with the call for a "Federal Trade Commission" in the Republican platform of 1912, and the obsessive concern of the Progressive Party with the issue. Was it not Wilson, in the closing days of the campaign of 1912, who warned that "If the government is to tell big businessmen how to run their business, then don't you see that big businessmen have to get closer to the government even than they are now?" But the campaign was over, and by January, 1914, the pressure for a federal commission was very great indeed. Virtually everyone, from Rep. Dick T. Morgan of Oklahoma to members of top Wall Street circles, wanted some form of commission—for their own reasons. Only Senator William E. Borah and a few others condemned the movement toward commissions and boards, the movement which would take decisions "entirely away from the electorate," and expose these boards to "the influence and the power that affect other men. . . ."

On January 20 Wilson appeared before a joint session of Congress and made it clear that future trust legislation would be just as responsible as banking legislation had been.

> What we are purposing to do . . . is happily, not to hamper or interfere with business as enlightened businessmen prefer to do it, or in any sense to put it under the ban. The antagonism between business and government is over. . . .The Government and businessmen are ready to meet each other half way in a common effort to square business methods with both public opinion and the law. The best informed men of the business world condemn the methods and processes and consequences of monopoly as we condemn them; and the instinctive judgement of the vast majority of businessmen everywhere goes with them.

There would have to be a prohibition of interlocking directorates, Wilson told Congress. But the main burden of his Message was to strike a most responsive chord.

> The business of the country awaits also, has long awaited and has suffered because it could not obtain, further and more explicit legislative definition of the policy and meaning of the existing anti-trust law. Nothing hampers business like uncertainty. . . . And the businessmen of the country desire something more than that the menace of legal process in these matters be made explicit and intelligible. They desire the advice, the definite guidance and information which can be supplied by an administrative body, an interstate trade commission.

Businessmen were delighted with the conservatism and reasonableness of the President's address, and messages of congratulation poured in from all over the country, from small and big businessmen alike. "It has had a very reassuring effect on the business community here in New York . . . ," a member of Speyer & Co. wrote Wilson. "By your temperate, sober, earnest way in handling these important matters," a member of the Union League Club of New York assured Wilson, "you have in our opinion (the opinion of life-long Republicans) proved yourself a *safe* man to be at the head of the country!" Seth Low, however, wrote Wilson that he would have considerable difficulty defining a trust. The President, admitting he was aware of the problem, assured him "You may be sure we shall not attempt the impossible and will not even try to define a trust, but confine ourselves to very specific provisions."

The Campaign for Legislation

Although numerous bills for trust legislation and a federal commission had been introduced throughout 1913, the first politically serious bills were not introduced in Congress until January 22, 1914, when Rep. Clayton and Senator Newlands presented a rather timid bill, similar to Newlands' earlier bills, providing for a five-man commission to supersede the Bureau of Corporations. The proposal allowed the commission to subpoena all necessary materials and to recommend action to the Attorney General, who had the power to arrange voluntary reorganization. The bill as it stood failed to appeal to the Attorney General's office, but it became the basis of discussion for subsequent legislation. To complicate the matter, Clayton also introduced four tentative bills amending the Sherman Act. The first forbade attempted efforts at monopolization via price discrimination, but contained so many clauses it became meaningless. The second extended "restraint of trade" to include agreements between companies, a position long maintained by the Supreme Court. The third bill forbade interlocking directors among banks, railroads, and competitive industries, and the fourth was intended to eliminate interlocking stockholdings.

In the meantime, the advocates of special proposals and concrete steps were given ample opportunity to exert pressures wherever possible, and to voice their criticisms of the tentative bills. The concept of a commission was never seriously opposed by any important segment interested in the topic, and Wilson was quite properly confident "that the businessmen themselves desire nothing so much as a trade commission." At the hearings held by the House Committee on the Judiciary, and by the Senate Committee on Interstate Commerce during February-June, 1914, the three major business concerns for future legislation were specifically with interlocking directorates, fair trade laws, and the status of trade unions under the antitrust act.

Big business and bankers opposed a possible prohibition on interlocking directorships in industry and banking. There was, in fact, little reason for their anxiety, since one or two interlocks on a board are insufficient for control if the outside directors do not represent some significant power, in which case the leverage the power provides exists even without interlocking directorships. In brief, short of a total transformation of existing economic relations, the prohibition of interlocking directorships is not too important. Nevertheless, many big businessmen found the suggestion obnoxious, and the American Bankers Association, the Railway Executives' Advisory Committee, and numerous individuals opposed any prohibitions. Even Louis Brandeis suggested that a blanket ban on interlocks was not desirable. At the same time that big business attacked the possibility of prohibiting interlocking directorates, representatives of small business associations of merchants, druggists, and grocers, as well as large manufacturers, called for the legalization and even the enforcement of fair trade price-fixing, a cause that Brandeis supported and that was to be revived periodically. Virtually all businessmen, big or small, endorsed the general principle of a trade commission.

While the various tentative bills were under discussion, two business organizations were to become especially important among the many petitioning their Congressmen and appearing before Congressional hearings, and were to shape the final legislation. The Chicago Association of Commerce strongly desired a trade commission, and under the leadership of Thomas Creigh, attorney for the Cudahy Packing Company, it took a prominent part in the agitation for a trade commission that could eliminate business uncertainty by giving business advice on the legality of proposed actions. This goal became the heart of the Chicago Association's program, although it also favored a commission with the power to issue desist orders before handing a complaint over to the Attorney General. The National Chamber of Commerce also strongly endorsed the need for a commission, but only a minority of the members of the Chamber, led by Charles R. Van Hise, president of the University of Wisconsin, accepted the Chicago position for a commission to advise business on the legality of prospective actions. Although a few major city and state groups, such as the Philadelphia Bourse and the New York State Chamber of Commerce, opposed the basic premises of the tentative bills, there is no doubt that the National Chamber of Commerce or the Chicago Association of Commerce reflected the overwhelming opinion of virtually all levels and types of business. And Congress knew business would support any action in this direction, since Senator Newlands had submitted three bills to businessmen in December, 1913, and favorable opinion in support of the basic principle flowed in.

Until March 16, when the Trade Commission Bill was finally separated from the proposed amendments to the Sherman Act and unity imposed over the bevy of competing measures sponsored by the same men, no conclusive and final business position was possible. Moreover, the exact provisions of a future Administration bill were unknown. Various business organizations knew what they wanted, but they were not sure of what they had. La Follette regarded the existing bills as "flabby and without teeth," and Henry Lee Higginson opposed the assortment as they stood. The Interstate Trade Commission Bill of March 16 was so weak that there was little question that it would be amended. Introduced by Rep. James H. Covington of Maryland, the new bill provided for a five-man trade commission that could investigate a corporation to see if it was complying with the antitrust law, gather information, and advise the Attorney General concerning dissolutions and prosecutions. The bill, on the whole, was just as weak as it had been in its earlier confused form. And on April 14 Rep. Clayton merged the basic contents of his various tentative bills into one coherent draft, the Clayton Antitrust Bill.

The revision of the Sherman Act was entirely unsatisfactory to labor unions, who objected to the equivocal wording that "Nothing contained in the anti-trust laws shall be construed to forbid the existence and operation of labor organizations." Unionists wished an outright declaration that the antitrust laws did not apply to unions at all, and efforts by several members of the House Committee on the Judiciary to obtain such a clause failed. Changes in the wording of the Clayton Bill applying to unions were made, but as historians have commonly agreed, the Clayton Bill did not free unions from prosecution under the antitrust laws. Despite intensive pressure by organized labor, Wilson regarded all efforts to have labor excluded from the law as class legislation, and the final bill, notwithstanding the embarrassed attempt of Gompers to find some concession in it to justify six years of support for the Democrats, was also hailed by antilabor elements.

The initial Trade Commission Bill was most unsatisfying to those business elements that had long been interested in such legislation. On the other hand, disunity among businessmen as to what type of legislation was desirable became increasingly apparent during the spring of 1914, although the sentiment for some form of legislation was nearly universal. Both the N.A.M. and the Chamber of Commerce split evenly on the desirability of a strong trade commission with the power to pass on proposed business actions. The N.A.M. convention, meeting in May, decided to take no stand whatsoever, and failed to approve a committee resolution condemning legislation. The Chamber of Commerce, on the other hand, began shifting its position, and it was apparent that Charles R. Van Hise, hitherto only a minority voice on the Chamber's committee on trust legislation, spoke for a significant proportion of the business community. In mid-April the Chamber sent a referendum to its members on the extent and form of trade commission legislation, asking them to vote on the trust committee's recommendations. On the creation of the commission and its power to investigate, the members endorsed their committee's positive recommendations by overwhelming majorities. The committee's refusal to endorse commission powers to pass on the legality of proposed actions, however, was reversed by a vote of 307 to 306. Even before the Chamber's committee received the results of the referendum, however, it moved to endorse the Clayton Bill in general, urging that legislation be "expressed in terms of principles only," but also favoring the prohibition of interlocking directors and stock ownership lessening competition. More significant was the committee's focus on the Stevens Bill, a hitherto obscure measure presented by Rep. Raymond B. Stevens of New Hampshire that assumed that it would be the function of a Federal Trade Commission to decide if a business' actions violated the more general provisions of the antitrust laws.

The Stevens Bill was no coincidence. The Chamber's trust committee included among its members George Rublee, an attorney who had been in the Progressive Party and generally shared its trust orientation. The Chamber's committee held its first meetings in February, 1914, and Rublee was directly interested in the legislative history of the various bills from that point on. Rublee knew Stevens and the Congressman agreed to allow him to draft a bill that was introduced on April 13. The Stevens Bill provided for a commission with powers to issue cease and desist orders, subject to court review, where unfair methods of competition were being utilized. The Stevens Bill, and the general concept of a strong trade commission, had few supporters in Congress, and its attraction was mainly to men like Rublee, Creigh, and Van Hise. On June 5, as an illustration of its unformulated casual attitude, the House passed the Covington Bill by a voice vote, defeating a motion to recommit by 151 to 19. No one was overly excited by the weakness of the measure, save those circles that had long advocated a trade commission as a means of giving business stability and predictability.

At the beginning of June, Rublee, Stevens, Brandeis, and Charles McCarthy went to see Wilson about the obscurity of the Clayton Bill, pointing to the need for a stronger trade commission to give it substance. The group's comments managed to swing Wilson from his not-too-firm position , and he indicated his willingness to see the heart of the Stevens Bill incorporated into the Federal Trade Commission Bill as Section 5. Senator Newlands, always anxious to please and certainly no radical, responsed to Wilson's new position by modifying his Senate equivalent of the Covington Bill to include the heart of the Stevens Bill. Despite some debate in the Senate on the meaning of unfair competition and the extent of judicial review, virtually everyone agreed the amended Newlands Bill was an important advance, and on August 5 it passed by 53 to 16.

The Clayton Bill, while the trade commission was being debated, passed the House on June 5 by a vote of 277 to 54, somewhat altered to allow the F.T.C. and I.C.C. to have greater responsibility for its enforcement and to eliminate imprisonment and fines for certain violations. It was obvious that legislation was almost universally desired, and the leaders of the small business organizations were especially pleased with the steps that had been taken by July, even though a reconciliation of the House and Senate Trade Commission Bills was still months off. Wilson, for his part, moved to reassure business, if assurance was needed, that the New Freedom could be trusted. He had, by mid-1914, attained considerable insight into the economy, and he was now able to evaluate the future needs of the nation in the light of recent progress. Speaking to the Virginia Editorial Association on June 25 "as a friend of business and a servant of the country," Wilson appraised the larger problem faced by a democratic society in an age of big business and industrialism. Perhaps it was once thought that America was ill and in need of progressive economic cures, but "as the diagnosis has progressed it has become more and more evident that no capital operation is necessary; that at the most a minor operation was necessary to remove admitted distempers and evils." The tariff and currency bills had been two minor operations, and the economy was now undergoing another operation in the form of trust legislation. But when this was completed "business can get and will get what it can get in no other way—rest, recuperation, and successful adjustment."

Thomas Creigh of the Chicago Association of Commerce felt disappointed with the Trade Commission Bill and and the even vaguer Clayton Bill, and in mid-July he and a group of his Chicago associates visited Wilson to discuss the entire legislative situation. They left Washington "feeling much encouraged," thinking the "objectionable parts" of the Clayton Bill would be dropped "and the Trade Commission Bills strengthened, especially, in Section 5, so that it would more fully embrace our ideas." The Chicago group, with its belief in a strong commission that could pass on the legality of business proposals, was doubly reassured when Davies privately indicated to it that many of its suggested changes would be made.

Davies consolation was significant, for it was the head of the Bureau of Corporations, more than any other individual within the Administration, that helped formulate the Trade Commission Bill. Besides Wilson, he gave direction to the plastic Senator Newlands, the chief figure in the Senate. This was as it should have been, since the commission was to supersede the bureau. Davies, for his part, relied heavily on the advice of interested business lawyers such as Rublee, Creigh, and Gilbert H. Montague, the author of the Merchants' Association of New York's commission plan and a friend of the Chicago Association of Commerce's proposals. Montague, along with Creigh, sent Davies memoranda, letters, and proposals designed to strengthen the power of a commission, and even to protect any future commission from broad judicial review. Davies appreciated the assistance, and he used it in keeping Wilson behind a strong commission position while the debates on judicial review in congress attracted attention during the summer. Business lawyers told him that they did not want long litigation, Davies assured Wilson, and that they preferred narrow judicial review. Although we cannot expect everything in the first bill, Davies assured Creigh, the efforts of the Chicago Association of Commerce "have procured so much a better bill than I thought would be possible at this time. . . ."

The Federal Trade Commission Bills of both the House and the Senate remained in conference until early September, when they were reconciled in favor of the Senate. The Senate passed the report 43 to 5, and the Act was signed by Wilson September 26. There was a moderate broadening of judicial review in the compromise bill, the debate over which historians have overexaggerated in importance; the final vote in the Senate is an accurate gauge of the seriousness of the disagreement. The Clayton Bill also passed through both branches with large majorities. The Senate approved it in early September by a vote of 46 to 16, over strong condemnation of its ineffectiveness by Western Senators. The conference report was passed by the House in early October by a vote of 244 to 54, and Wilson signed the law on October 16.

The End of the New Freedom

The Federal Trade Commission Act specified that a commission of five was to be appointed by the President with the approval of the Senate, with not more than three members from any party. "Unfair methods of competition" were declared "unlawful," and the commission was authorized to prevent them from being used.

Upon calling a hearing, the commission could issue "cease and desist" orders which could be enforced by Circuit Courts. The commission might also compel the production of information and utilize the power of subpoena, with penalties for refusal to cooperate. The commission could gather and issue information of a more general sort, and advise the Attorney General on correcting illegal corporate actions. All in all, the Act was vague and unclear, failed to exclude businessmen from membership on the commission, and left a great area for free interpretation of the law.

By comparison to the Clayton Act, however, the Federal Trade Commission Act was a model of precision. It was the intention of Congress to allow the commission and courts to settle most of the vagueness in the Clayton Act, and no greater clarity in the antitrust law was established. Price discrimination was forbidden, but with ample "due allowances." The Act also condemned tieing contracts to prevent purchasers from buying from a company's competitors if they lessened competition . It forbade purchases of stock that reduced competition and prohibited interlocking directorates among banks with more than $5 million resources, between railroad directors or officers and construction or maintenance companies with which they did a substantial business, and directors of competitive industries. The new Act was most detailed in its specification of mechanical procedures for cease and desist orders and appeal procedures. On the whole, it reflected the deep ambivalence of Congress on the topic of business concentration. There were no means, needless to say, by which concentration could be reversed. Precedent was still the major criterion for action, and precedents were to be defined by judicial and administrative bodies dominated by men who, in the last analysis, had little more than their ideological commitments to guide them.

Although bankers disliked the interlock prohibitions, big business as a whole was very pleased, to put it mildly, with the new state of affairs. The provisions of the new laws attacking unfair competitors and price discrimination meant that the government would now make it possible for many trade associations to stabilize, for the first time, prices within their industries, and to make effective oligopoly a new phase of the economy. In part the new mood of confidence was a result of the President's repeated assurances that he favored a conservative approach to business —a public statement on the need for greater railroad profits on September 10 was only one of many examples—and a realization that a Federal Trade Commission was to serve as a stabilizing factor in the economy and a protector against public attacks. The unions were no better off, despite Gompers' effusive support of the Clayton Act, and the last stone in the foundation of a comprehensive political capitalism involving the banks, railroads, and industry had been laid.

The new measures were quickly endorsed by the long-time advocates of federal regulation, with the exception of George W. Perkins, who was deeply motivated by political considerations. ". . . these laws largely coincide with the principles we have urged," the president of the Chicago Association of Commerce telegraphed Wilson. "The Democratic National Administration deserves unmistakable approval," Francis Lynde Stetson announced in mid-October. Arthur J. Eddy, the architect of the trade association movement, also agreed that the new laws were progressive and constructive.

What is truly significant about the passage of the two bills, however, is that it marked the conscious completion of the legislative objectives of the New Freedom just at the very time that the most important goals of business advocates of political capitalism were attained. In late 1914 Wilson drew the line on reform, and reiterated innumerable times his belief that federal regulation had gone far enough. In late October Wilson began explicitly formulating his retreat from legislative action. "The situation is just this," he wrote a friend: "the reconstructive legislation which for the last two decades the opinion of the country has demanded . . . has now been enacted. That program is practically completed." Further changes would have to await the end of the European war and the experience of using the "instrumentalities already created." By mid-November Wilson was ready to make a public statement of policy in a letter to McAdoo that was immediately sent to the press.

> Ten or twelve years ago the country was torn and excited by an agitation which shook the very foundations of her political life, brought her business ideals into question, condemned her social standards, denied the honesty of her men of affairs, the integrity of her economic processes, the morality and good faith of many of the things which her law sustained.

Businessmen and politicians had been exposed to abuse, but any of the evils that may have existed were now corrected, and all of the older ideals and foundations were now being reasserted. "The spirit of co-operation which your letter breathes is an example to all of us," Frank Trumbull, head of the Railway Executives Association, immediately wrote Wilson. Stimulated by similar professions and the congratulations of Davies and urgings of Tumulty, Wilson bid his final farewell to the New Freedom in his Annual Message to Congress on December 8. Appearing before a joint session, Wilson's stand was unequivocal:

> Our program of legislation with regard to the regulation of business is now virtually complete. It has been put forth, as we intended, as a whole, and leaves no conjecture as to what is to follow. The road at last lies clear and firm before business. It is a road which it can travel without fear or embarrassment.

What the President ignored, of course, was that the road had never been charted by him; and that the New Freedom, in its concrete legislative aspects, was little more than the major demands of politically oriented big businessmen. They had defined the issues, and it was they who managed to provide the direction for change. If they did not always manage to shape every detail of each reform measure, it was only because, in a political democracy, legislative situations have their own unpredictable, uncontrollable qualities. But in its larger outlines it was they who gave progressivism its essential character. By the end of 1914 they had triumphed, and to the extent that the new laws were vague and subject to administrative definitions by boards and commissions, they were to totally dominate the extensive reign of political capitalism that had been created in the United States by 1915.

Part Three POLITICAL REFORM

Chapter 7 THE UPPER CLASS TAKES THE LEAD

The article below, by SAMUEL P. HAYS *(1921-), is a standard piece in anthologies of American history. After taking issue with various theories of interpretation–among them the status-revolution theory–Hays asserts that the key to municipal reform is "the upper class." Even if he is correct in that interpretation, does it follow that all political reform derived from that social base? A member of the University of Pittsburgh faculty since 1960, Professor Hays is well known for two books, one on the conservation movement, and the other an overview of the Progressive era.*

Available evidence indicates that the source of support for reform in municipal government did not come from the lower or middle classes, but from the upper class. The leading business groups in each city and professional men closely allied with them initiated and dominated municipal movements. . . .

The character of municipal reform is demonstrated more precisely by a brief examination of the movements in Des Moines and Pittsburgh. The Des Moines Commercial Club inaugurated and carefully controlled the drive for the commission form of government. In January, 1906, the Club held a so-called "mass meeting" of business and professional men to secure an enabling act from the state legislature. P. C. Kenyon, president of the Club, selected a Committee of 300, composed prin-

Samuel P. Hays, "The Politics of Reform in Municipal Government in the Progressive Era," *Pacific Northwest Quarterly*, LV (October 1964), 159-169. Reprinted with the permission of the *Pacific Northwest Quarterly* and the author.

cipally of business and professional men, to draw up a specific proposal. After the legislature approved their plan, the same committee managed the campaign which persuaded the electorate to accept the commission form of government by a narrow margin in June, 1907.

In this election the lower-income wards of the city opposed the change, the upper-income wards supported it strongly, and the middle-income wards were more evenly divided. In order to control the new government, the Committee of 300, now expanded to 530, sought to determine the nomination and election of the five new commissioners, and to this end they selected an avowedly businessman's slate. Their plans backfired when the voters swept into office a slate of anticommission candidates who now controlled the new commission government.

Proponents of the commission form of government in Des Moines spoke frequently in the name of the "people." But their more explicit statements emphasized their intent that the new plan be a "business system" of government, run by businessmen. The slate of candidates for commissioner endorsed by advocates of the plan was known as the "businessman's ticket." J. W. Hill, president of the committees of 300 and 530, bluntly declared: "The professional politician must be ousted and in his place capable business men chosen to conduct the affairs of the city." I. M. Earle, general counsel of the Bankers Life Association and a prominent figure in the movement, put the point more precisely: "When the plan was adopted it was the intention to get businessmen to run it."

Although reformers used the ideology of popular government, they in no sense meant that all segments of society should be involved equally in municipal decision-making. They meant that their concept of the city's welfare would be best achieved if the business community controlled city government. As one businessman told a labor audience, the businessman's slate represented labor "better than you do yourself."

The composition of the municipal reform movement in Pittsburgh demonstrates its upper-class and professional as well as its business sources. Here the two principal reform organizations were the Civic Club and the Voters' League. The 745 members of these two organizations came primarily from the upper class. Sixty-five per cent appeared in upper-class directories which contained the names of only 2 per cent of the city's families. Furthermore, many who were not listed in these directories lived in upper-class areas. These reformers, it should be stressed, comprised not an old but a new upper class. Few came from earlier industrial and mercantile families. Most of them had risen to social position from wealth created after 1870 and in the iron, steel, electrical equipment, and other industries and they lived in the newer rather than the older fashionable areas.

Almost half (48 per cent) of the reformers were professional men: doctors, lawyers, ministers, directors of libraries and museums, engineers, architects, private and public school teachers and college professors. Some of these belonged to the upper class as well, especially the lawyers, ministers, and private school teachers. But for the most part their interest in reform stemmed from the inherent dynamics of their professions rather than from their class connections. They came from the more advanced segments of their organizations, from those in the forefront of the acquisition and application of knowledge. They were not the older professional men, seeking to preserve the past against change; they were in the vanguard of professional life, actively seeking to apply expertise more widely to public affairs.

Pittsburgh reformers included a large segment of businessmen; 52 per cent were bankers and corporation officials or their wives. Among them were the presidents of fourteen large banks and officials of Westinghouse, Pittsburgh Plate Glass, U.S. Steel and its component parts (such as Carnegie Steel, American Bridge, and National Tube), Jones and Laughlin, lesser steel companies (such as Crucible, Pittsburgh, Superior, Lockhart, and H. K. Porter), the H. J. Heinz Company, and the Pittsburgh Coal Company, as well as officials of the Pennsylvania Railroad and the Pittsburgh and Lake Erie. These men were not small businessmen; they directed the most powerful banking and industrial organizations of the city. They represented not the old business community, but industries which had developed and grown primarily within the past fifty years and which had come to dominate the city's economic life.

These business, professional, and upper-class groups who dominated municipal reform movements were all involved in the rationalization and systematization of modern life; they wished a form of government which would be more consistent with the objectives inherent in those developments. The most important single feature of their perspective was the rapid expansion of the geographical scope of affairs which they wished to influence and manipulate, a scope which was no longer limited and narrow, no longer within the confines of pedestrian communities, but was now broad and city-wide, covering the whole range of activities of the metropolitan area.

The migration of the upper class from central to outlying areas created a geographical distance between its residential communities and its economic institutions. To protect the latter required involvement both in local ward affairs, and in the larger city government as well. Moreover, upper-class cultural institutions, such as museums, libraries, and symphony orchestras, required an active interest in the larger municipal context from which these institutions drew much of their clientele.

Professional groups, broadening the scope of affairs which they sought to study, measure, or manipulate, also sought to influence the public health, the educational system, or the physical arrangements of the entire city. Their concerns were limitless, not bounded by geography, but as expansive as the professional imagination. Finally, the new industrial community greatly broadened its perspective in governmental affairs because of its new recognition of the way in which factors throughout the city affected business growth. The increasing size and scope of industry, the greater stake in more varied and geographically dispersed facets of city life, the effect of floods on many business concerns, the need to promote traffic flows to and from work for both blue-collar and managerial employees—all contributed to this larger interest. The geographically larger private perspectives of upper-class, professional, and business groups gave rise to a geographically larger public perspective.

These reformers were dissatisfied with existing systems of municipal government. They did not oppose corruption per se—although there was plenty of that. They objected to the structure of government which enabled local and particularistic interests to dominate. Prior to the reforms of the Progressive Era, city government consisted primarily of confederations of local wards, each of which was represented on the city's legislative body. Each ward frequently had its own elementary schools and ward-elected school boards which administered them.

These particularistic interests were the focus of a decentralized political life. City councilmen were local leaders. They spoke for their local areas, the economic interests of their inhabitants, their residential concerns, their educational, recreational, and religious interests—i.e., for those aspects of community life which mattered most to those they represented. They rolled logs in the city council to provide streets, sewers, and other public works for their local areas. They defended the community's cultural practices, its distinctive languages or national customs, its liberal attitude toward liquor, and its saloons and dance halls which served as centers of community life. One observer described this process of representation in Seattle:

> The residents of the hill-tops and the suburbs may not fully appreciate the faithfulness of certain downtown ward councilmen to the interests of their constituents. . . . The people of a state would rise in arms against a senator or representative in Congress who deliberately misrepresented their wishes and imperilled their interests, though he might plead a higher regard for national good. Yet people in other parts of the city seem to forget that under the old system the ward elected councilmen with the idea of procuring service of special benefit to that ward.

In short, pre-reform officials spoke for their constituencies, inevitably their own wards which had elected them, rather than for other sections or groups of the city.

The ward system of government especially gave representation in city affairs to lower- and middle-class groups. Most elected ward officials were from these groups, and they, in turn, constituted the major opposition to reforms in municipal government. In Pittsburgh, for example, immediately prior to the changes in both the city council and the school board in 1911 in which city-wide representation replaced ward representation, only 24 per cent of the 387 members of those bodies represented the same managerial, professional, and banker occupations which dominated the membership of the Civic Club and the Voters' League. The great majority (67 per cent) were small businessmen—grocers, saloonkeepers, livery-stable proprietors, owners of small hotels, druggists—white-collar workers such as clerks and bookkeepers, and skilled and unskilled workmen.

This decentralized system of urban growth and the institutions which arose from it reformers now opposed. Social, professional, and economic life had developed not only in the local wards in a small community context, but also on a larger scale had become highly integrated and organized, giving rise to a superstructure of social organization which lay far above that of ward life and which was sharply divorced from it in both personal contacts and perspective.

By the late 19th century, those involved in these larger institutions found that the decentralized system of political life limited their larger objectives. The movement for reform in municipal government, therefore, constituted an attempt by upper-class, advanced professional, and large business groups to take formal political power from the previously dominant lower- and middle-class elements so that they might advance their own conceptions of desirable public policy. These two groups came from entirely different urban worlds, and the political system fashioned by one was no longer acceptable to the other.

Lower- and middle-class groups not only dominated the pre-reform governments, but vigorously opposed reform. It is significant that none of the occupational groups among them, for example, small businessmen or white-collar workers, skilled or unskilled artisans, had important representation in reform organizations thus far examined. . . .

In Des Moines working-class representatives who in previous years might have been counted members, were conspicuously absent from the "businessmen's slate." Workingmen acceptable to reformers could not be found. A working man's slate of candidates, therefore, appeared to challenge the reform slate. Organized labor, and especially the mineworkers, took the lead; one of their number, Wesley Ash, a deputy sheriff and union member, made "an astonishing run in the primary, coming in second among a field of more than twenty candidates. In fact, the strength of anticommission candidates in the primary so alarmed reformers that they frantically sought to appease labor.

The day before the final election they modified their platform to pledge both an eight-hour day and an "American standard of wages." They attempted to persuade the voters that their slate consisted of men who represented labor because they had "begun at the bottom of the ladder and made a good climb toward success by their own unaided efforts." But their tactics failed. In the election on March 30, 1908, voters swept into office the entire "opposition" slate. The business and professional community had succeeded in changing the form of government, but not in securing its control. A cartoon in the leading reform newspaper illustrated their disappointment; John Q. Public sat dejectedly and muttered, "Aw, What's the Use?"

The most visible opposition to reform and the most readily available target of reform attack was the so-called "machine," for through the "machine" many different ward communities as well as lower- and middle-income groups joined effectively to influence the central city government. Their private occupational and social life did not naturally involve these groups in larger city-wide activities in the same way as the upper class was involved; hence they lacked access to privately organized economic and social power on which they could construct political power. The "machine" filled this organizational gap.

Yet it should never be forgotten that the social and economic institutions in the wards themselves provided the "machine's" sustaining support and gave it larger significance. When reformers attacked the "machine" as the most visible institutional element of the ward system, they attacked the entire ward form of political organization and the political power of lower- and middle-income groups which lay behind it.

Reformers often gave the impression that they opposed merely the corrupt politician and his "machine." But in a more fundamental way they looked upon the deficiencies of pre-reform political leaders in terms not of their personal shortcomings, but of the limitations inherent in their occupational, institutional, and class positions. In 1911 the Voters' League of Pittsburgh wrote in its pamphlet analyzing the qualifications of candidates that "a man's occupation ought to give a strong indication of his qualifications for membership on a school board." Certain occupations inherently disqualified a man from serving:

> Employment as ordinary laborer and in the lowest class of mill work would naturally lead to the conclusion that such men did not have sufficient education or business training to act as school directors. . . . Objection might also be made to small shopkeepers, clerks, workmen at many trades, who by lack of educational advantages and business training, could not, no matter how honest, be expected to administer properly the affairs of an educational system, requiring special knowledge, and where millions are spent each year.

These, of course, were precisely the groups which did dominate Pittsburgh government prior to reform. The League deplored the fact that school boards contained only a small number of "men prominent throughout the city in business life . . . in professional occupations . . . holding positions as managers, secretaries, auditors, superintendents and foremen" and exhorted these classes to participate more actively as candidates for office.

Reformers, therefore, wished not simply to replace bad men with good; they proposed to change the occupational and class origins of decision-makers. Toward this end they sought innovations in the formal machinery of government which would concentrate political power by sharply centralizing the process of decision-making rather than distribute it through more popular participation in public affairs. According to the liberal view of the Progressive Era, the major political innovations of reform involved the equalization of political power through the primary, the direct election of public officials, and the initiative, referendum, and recall. These measures played a large role in the political ideology of the time and were frequently incorporated into new municipal charters. But they provided at best only an occasional and often incidental process of decision-making. Far more important in continuous, sustained, day-to-day processes of government were those innovations which centralized decision-making in the hands of fewer and fewer people.

The systematization of municipal government took place on both the executive and the legislative levels. The strong-mayor and city-manager types became the most widely used examples of the former. In the first decade of the 20th century, the commission plan had considerable appeal, but its distribution of administrative responsibility among five people gave rise to a demand for a form with more centralized executive power; consequently, the city-manager or the commission-manager variant often replaced it.

A far more pervasive and significant change, however, lay in the centralization of the system of representation, the shift from ward to city-wide election of councils and school boards. Governing bodies so selected, reformers argued, would give less attention to local and particularistic matters and more to affairs of city-wide scope. This shift, an invariable feature of both commission and city-manager plans, was often adopted by itself. In Pittsburgh, for example, the new charter of 1911 provided as the major innovation that a council of twenty-seven, each member elected from a separate ward, be replaced by a council of nine, each elected by the city as a whole.

Cities displayed wide variations in this innovation. Some regrouped wards into larger units but kept the principle of areas of representation smaller than the entire city. Some combined a majority of councilmen elected by wards with additional ones elected at large. All such innovations, however, constituted steps toward the centralization of the system of representation.

Liberal historians have not appreciated the extent to which municipal reform in the Progressive Era involved debate over the system of representation. The ward form of representation was universally condemned on the grounds that it gave too much influence to the separate units and not enough attention to the larger problems of the city. Harry A. Toulmin, whose book, *The City Manager*, was published by the National Municipal League, stated the case:

> The spirit of sectionalism had dominated the political life of every city. Ward pitted against ward, alderman against alderman, and legislation only effected by "log-rolling" extravagant measures into operation, mulcting the city, but gratifying the greed of constituents, has too long stung the conscience of decent citi-

> zenship. This constant treaty-making of factionalism has been no less than a curse. The city manager plan proposes the commendable thing of abolishing wards. The plan is not unique in this for it has been common to many forms of commission government. . .

Such a system should be supplanted, the argument usually went, with city-wide representation in which elected officials could consider the city "as a unit." "The new officers are elected," wrote Toulmin, "each to represent all the people. Their duties are so defined that they must administer the corporate business in its entirety, not as a hodge-podge of associated localities."

Behind the debate over the method of representation, however, lay a debate over who should be represented, over whose views of public policy should prevail. Many reform leaders often explicitly, if not implicitly, expressed fear that lower- and middle-income groups had too much influence in decision-making. One Galveston leader, for example, complained about the movement for initiative, referendum, and recall:

> We have in our city a very large number of negroes employed on the docks; we also have a very large number of unskilled white laborers; this city also has more barrooms, according to its population, than any other city in Texas. Under these circumstances it would be extremely difficult to maintain a satisfactory city government where all ordinances must be submitted back to the voters of the city for their ratification and approval.

At the National Municipal League convention of 1907, Rear Admiral F. E. Chadwick (USN Ret.), a leader in the Newport, Rhode Island, movement for municipal reform, spoke to this question even more directly:

> Our present system has excluded in large degree the representation of those who have the city's well-being most at heart. It has brought, in municipalities . . . a government established by the least educated, the least interested class of citizens.
>
> It stands to reason that a man paying $5,000 taxes in a town is more interested in the well-being and development of his town than the man who pays no taxes. . . . It equally stands to reason that the man of the $5,000 tax should be assured a representation in the committee which lays the tax and spends the money which he contributes. . . . Shall we be truly democratic and give the property owner a fair show or shall we develop a tyranny of ignorance which shall crush him.

Municipal reformers thus debated frequently the question of who should be represented as well as the question of what method of representation should be employed.

That these two questions were imtimately connected was revealed in other reform proposals for representation, proposals which were rarely taken seriously. One suggestion was that a class system of representation be substituted for ward representation. For example, in 1908 one of the prominent candidates for commissioner in Des Moines proposed that the city council be composed of representatives of five classes: educational and ministerial organizations, manufacturers and jobbers, public utility corporations, retail merchants including liquor men, and the Des Moines Trades and Labor Assembly. Such a system would have greatly reduced the influence in the council of both middle- and lower-class groups. The proposal revealed the basic problem confronting business and professional leaders: how to reduce the influence in government of the majority of voters among middle- and lower-income groups.

A growing imbalance between population and representation sharpened the desire of reformers to change from ward to city-wide elections. Despite shifts in population within most cities, neither ward district lines nor the apportionment of city council and school board seats changed frequently. Consequently, older areas of the city, with wards that were small in geographical size and held declining populations (usually lower and middle class in composition), continued to be overrepresented, and newer upper-class areas, where population was growing, became increasingly underrepresented. This intensified the reformers' conviction that the structure of government must be changed to give them the voice they needed to make their views on public policy prevail.

It is not insignificant that in some cities (by no means a majority) municipal reform came about outside of the urban electoral process. The original commission government in Galveston was appointed rather than elected. "The failure of previous attempts to secure an efficient city government through the local electorate made the business men of Galveston willing to put the conduct of the city's affairs in the hands of a commission, dominated by state-appointed officials." Only in 1903 did the courts force Galveston to elect the members of the commission, an innovation which one writer described as "an abandonment of the commission idea," and which led to the decline of the influence of the business community in the commission government.

In 1911 Pittsburgh voters were not permitted to approve either the new city charter or the new school board plan, both of which provided for city-wide representation; they were a result of state legislative enactment. The governor appointed the first members of the new city council, but thereafter they were elected. The judges of the court of common pleas, however, and not the voters, selected members of the new school board.

The composition of the new city council and new school board in Pittsburgh, both of which were inaugurated in 1911, revealed the degree to which the shift from ward to city-wide representation produced a change in group representation. Members of the upper class, the advanced professional men, and the large business groups dominated both. Of the fifteen members of the Pittsburgh Board of Education appointed in 1911 and the nine members of the new city council, none were small businessmen or white-collar workers. Each body contained only one person who could remotely be classified as a blue-collar worker; each of these men filled a position specifically but unofficially designed as reserved for a "representative of labor," and each was an official of the Amalgamated Association of Iron, Steel, and Tin Workers. Six of the nine members of the new city council were prominent businessmen, and all six were listed in upper-class directories. Two others were doctors closely associated with the upper class in both professional and social life. The fifteen members of the Board of Education included ten businessmen with city-wide interests, one doctor associated with the upper-class, and three women previously active in upper-class public welfare. . . .

The success of the drive for centralization of administration and representation varied with the size of the city. In the smaller cities, business, professional, and elite groups could easily exercise a dominant influence. Their close ties readily enabled them to shape informal political power which they could transform into formal political power. After the mid-1890's the widespread organization of chambers of commerce provided a base for political action to reform municipal government, resulting in a host of small-city commission and city-manager innovations. In the larger, more heterogeneous cities, whose subcommunities were more dispersed, such community-wide action was extremely difficult. Few commission or city-manager proposals materialized here. Mayors became stronger, and steps were taken toward centralization of representation, but the ward system or some modified version usually persisted. Reformers in large cities often had to rest content with their Municipal Research Bureaus through which they could exert political influence from outside the municipal government.

A central element in the analysis of municipal reform in the Progressive Era is governmental corruption. Should it be understood in moral or political terms? Was it a product of evil men or of particular socio-political circumstances? Reform historians have adopted the former view. Selfish and evil men arose to take advantage of a political arrangement whereby unsystematic government offered many opportunities for personal gain at public expense. The system thrived until the "better elements," "men of intelligence and civic responsibility," or "right-thinking people" ousted the culprits and fashioned a political force which produced decisions in the "public interest." In this scheme of things, corruption in public affairs grew out of individual personal failings and a deficient governmental structure which could not hold those predispositions in check, rather than from the peculiar nature of social forces. The contestants involved were morally defined: evil men who must be driven from power, and good men who must be activated politically to secure control of municipal affairs.

Public corruption, however, involves political even more than moral considerations. It arises more out of the particular distribution of political power than of personal morality. For corruption is a device to exercise control and influence outside the legal channels of decision-making when those channels are not readily responsive. Most generally, corruption stems from an inconsistency between control of the instruments of formal governmental power and the exercise of informal influence in the community. If powerful groups are denied access to formal power in legitimate ways, they seek access through procedures which the community considers illegitimate. Corrupt government, therefore, does not reflect the genius of evil men, but rather the lack of acceptable means for those who exercise power in the private community to wield the same influence in governmental affairs. It can be understood in the Progressive Era not simply by the preponderance of evil men over good, but by the peculiar nature of the distribution of political power.

The political corruption of the "Era of Reform" arose from the inaccessibility of municipal government to those who were rising in power and influence. Municipal government in the United States developed in the 19th century within a context of universal manhood suffrage which decentralized political control. Because all men, whatever their economic, social, or cultural conditions, could vote, leaders who reflected a wide variety of community interests and who represented the views of people of every circumstance arose to guide and direct municipal affairs. Since the majority of urban voters were workingmen or immigrants, the views of those groups carried great and often decisive weight in governmental affairs. Thus, as Herbert Gutman has shown, during strikes in the 1870's city officials were usually friendly to workingmen and refused to use police power to protect strikebreakers.

Ward representation on city councils was an integral part of grass-roots influence, for it enabled diverse urban communities, invariably identified with particular geographical areas of the city, to express their views more clearly through councilmen peculiarly receptive to their concerns. There was a direct, reciprocal flow of power between wards and the center of city affairs in which voters felt a relatively close connection with public matters and city leaders gave special attention to their needs.

Within this political system the community's business leaders grew in influence and power as industrialism advanced, only to find that their economic position did not readily admit them to the formal machinery of government. Thus, during the strikes, they had to rely on either their own private police, Pinkertons, or the state militia to enforce their use of strikebreakers. They frequently found that city officials did not accept their views of what was best for the city and what direction municipal policies should take. They had developed a common outlook, closely related to their economic activities, that the city's economic expansion should become the prime concern of municipal government, and yet they found that this view had to compete with even more influential views of public policy. They found that political tendencies which arose from universal manhood suffrage and ward representation were not always friendly to their political conceptions and goals and had produced a political system over which they had little control, despite the fact that their economic ventures were the core of the city's prosperity and the hope for future urban growth.

Under such circumstances, businessmen sought other methods of influencing municipal affairs. They did not restrict themselves to the channels of popular election and representation, but frequently applied direct influence–if not verbal persuasion, then bribery and corruption. Thereby arose the graft which Lincoln Steffens recounted in his *Shame of the Cities*. Utilities were only the largest of those business groups and individuals who requested special favors, and the franchises they sought were only the most sensational of the prizes which included such items as favorable tax assessments and rates, the vacating of streets wanted for factory expansion, or permission to operate amid antiliquor and other laws regulating personal behavior. The relationships between business and formal government became a maze of accommodations, a set of political arrangements which grew up because effective power had few legitimate means of accomplishing its ends.

Steffens and subsequent liberal historians, however, misread the significance of these arrangements, emphasizing their personal rather than their more fundamental institutional elements. To them corruption involved personal arrangements between powerful business leaders and powerful "machine" politicians. Just as they did not fully appreciate the significance of the search for political influence by the rising business community as a whole, so they did not see fully the role of the "ward politician." They stressed the argument that the political leader manipulated voters to his own personal ends, that he used constituents rather than reflected their views.

A different approach is now taking root, namely, that the urban political organization was an integral part of community life, expressing its needs and its goals. As Oscar Handlin has said, for example, the "machine" not only fulfilled specific wants, but provided one of the few avenues to success and public recognition available to the immigrant. The political leader's arrangements with businessmen, therefore, were not simply personal agreements between conniving individuals; they were far-reaching accommodations between powerful sets of institutions in industrial America.

These accommodations, however, proved to be burdensome and unsatisfactory to the business community and to the upper third of socio-economic groups in general. They were expensive; they were wasteful; they were uncertain. Toward the end of the 19th century, therefore, business and professional men sought more direct control over municipal government in order to exercise political influence more effectively. They realized their goals in the early 20th century in the new commission and city-manager forms of government and in the shift from ward to city-wide representation.

These innovations did not always accomplish the objectives that the business community desired because other forces could and often did adjust to the change in governmental structure and re-establish their influence. But businessmen hoped that reform would enable them to increase their political power, and most frequently it did. In most cases the innovations which were introduced between 1901, when Galveston adopted a commission form of government, and the Great Depression, and especially the city-manager form which reached a height of popularity in the mid-1920's, served as vehicles whereby business and professional leaders moved directly into the inner circles of government, brought into one political system their own power and the formal machinery of government, and dominated municipal affairs for two decades.

Municipal reform in the early 20th century involves a paradox: the ideology of an extension of political control and the practice of its concentration. While reformers maintained that their movement rested on a wave of popular demands, called their gatherings of business and professional leaders "mass meetings," described their reforms as "part of a world-wide trend toward popular government," and proclaimed an ideology of a popular upheaval against a selfish few, they were in practice shaping the structure of municipal government so that political power would no longer be broadly distributed, but would in fact be more centralized in the hands of a relatively small segment of the population. The paradox became even sharper when new city charters included provisions for the initiative, referendum, and recall. How does the historian cope with this paradox? Does it represent deliberate deception or simply political strategy? Or does it reflect a phenomenon which should be understood rather than explained away?

The expansion of popular involvement in decision-making was frequently a political tactic, not a political system to be established permanently, but a device to secure immediate political victory. The prohibitionist advocacy of the referendum, one of the most extensive sources of support for such a measure, came from the belief that the referendum would provide the opportunity to outlaw liquor more rapidly. The Anti-Saloon League, therefore, urged local option. But the League was not consistent. Towns which were wet, when faced with a county-wide local option decision to outlaw liquor, demanded town or township local option to reinstate it. The League objected to this as not the proper application of the referendum idea.

Again, "Progressive" reformers often espoused the direct primary when fighting for nominations for their candidates within the party, but once in control they often became cool to it because it might result in their own defeat. By the same token, many municipal reformers attached the initiative, referendum, and recall to municipal charters often as a device to appease voters who opposed the centralization of representation and executive authority. But, by requiring a high percentage of voters to sign petitions–often 25 to 30 per cent–these innovations could be and were rendered relatively harmless.

More fundamentally, however, the distinction between ideology and practice in municipal reform arose from the different roles which each played. The ideology of democratization of decision-making was negative rather than positive; it served as an instrument of attack against the existing political system rather than as a guide to alternative action. Those who wished to destroy the "machine" and to eliminate party competition in local government widely utilized the theory that these political instruments thwarted public impulses, and thereby shaped the tone of their attack.

But there is little evidence that the ideology represented a faith in a purely democratic system of decision-making or that reformers actually wished, in practice, to substitute direct democracy as a continuing system of sustained decision-making in place of the old. It was used to destroy the political institutions of the lower and middle classes and the political power which those institutions gave rise to, rather than to provide a clear-cut guide for alternative action.

The guide to alternative action lay in the model of the business enterprise. In describing new conditions which they wished to create, reformers drew on the analogy of the "efficient business enterprise," criticizing current practices with the argument that "no business could conduct its affairs that way and remain in business," and calling upon business practices as the guides to improvement. . . .

The model of the efficient business enterprise, then, rather than the New England town meeting, provided the positive inspiration for the municipal reformer. In giving concrete shape to this model in the strong-mayor, commission and city-manager plans, reformers engaged in the elaboration of the processes of rationalization and systematization inherent in modern science and technology. For in many areas of society, industrialization brought a gradual shift upward in the location of decision-making and the geographical extension of the scope of the area affected by decisions. . . .

The drama of reform lay in the competition for supremacy between two systems of decision-making. One system, based upon ward representation and growing out of the practices and ideas of representative government, involved wide latitude for the expression of grass-roots impulses and their involvement in the political process. The other grew out of the rationalization of life which came with science and technology, in which decisions arose from expert analysis and flowed from fewer and smaller centers outward to the rest of society. Those who espoused the former looked with fear upon the loss of influence which the latter involved, and those who espoused the latter looked only with distain upon the wastefulness and inefficiency of the former. . . .

. . . The current task of the historian of the Progressive Era is to quit taking the reformers' own description of political practice at its face value and to utilize a wide variety of new types of evidence to reconstruct political practice in its own terms. This is not to argue that ideology is either important or unimportant. It is merely to state that ideological evidence is not appropriate to the discovery of the nature of political practice.

Only by maintaining this clear distinction can the historian successfully investigate the structure of political life in the Progressive Era. And only then can he begin to cope with the most fundamental problem of all: the relationship between political ideology and political practice. For each of these facets of political life must be understood in its own terms, through its own historical record. Each involves a distinct set of historical phenomena. The relationship between them for the Progressive Era is not now clear; it has not been investigated. But it cannot be explored until the conceptual distinction is made clear and evidence tapped which is pertinent to each. Because the nature of political practice has so long been distorted by the use of ideological evidence, the most pressing task is for its investigation through new types of evidence appropriate to it. The reconstruction of the movement for municipal reform can constitute a major step forward toward that goal.

Chapter 8 THE ROLE OF THE URBAN MACHINE

According to the preceding chapter, the chief opposition to changing the structure of government came from machine-dominated, foreign-born neighborhoods. But is that the whole story? Like many another historian who came of academic age in the 1960s, Professor JOHN D. BUENKER *(1937-), of the University of Wisconsin, Parkside, has been doing important research on the support that the immigrant masses gave to the Progressive movement. Below he makes his point in tracing the adoption of the Seventeenth Amendment. Is his interpretation irreconcilable with that of Professor Hays? Note that they deal with different aspects of the movement for political reform.*

With the possible exception of the giant corporation, no institution was so severely castigated by the middle-class progressive as the urban political machine. Viewing such civic virtues as honesty, efficiency, and economy in government as workable solutions for the complex problems of urban, industrial America, these genteel reformers often looked with horror upon the activities of the urban political machine and its constituents, who seemed preoccupied with such mundane realities as food, clothing, jobs, and votes. Historians have usually assumed that the urban political organizations were unabashed opponents of any political change which might challenge their authority.

Yet the proof of this assertion must be sought in detailed analysis of the ma-

John D. Buenker, "The Urban Political Machine and the Seventeenth Amendment," *Journal of American History*, LVI (September 1969), 305-322. Reprinted with the permission of the Organization of American Historian and the author.

chine politician's attitude toward specific reform proposals. A clear-cut test case is the enactment of the Seventeenth Amendment to the Constitution—a measure which, theoretically, struck at the big city organization's control of patronage by removing the selection of United States senators from the state legislatures, where it could be readily manipulated, and placing it in the hands of the voters where, presumably, it could not. Here, certainly, was one of the cardinal achievements of the Progressive Era, one which transformed the upper chamber from a bastion of private privilege into the more liberal of the two houses of Congress; yet, almost without exception, it was one which had the overwhelming support of the urban machines' minions in the major industrial states.

To understand this, it is necessary to identify the kinds of lawmakers who are under consideration. The urban political machine developed in the nineteenth century as a response to the industrialization, urbanization, and immigration which transformed the nature of American society and created a multitude of largely new stock wage earners who were often unable to cope with the circumstances of their new existence. By providing jobs, protection from the law, and various welfare activities, the political boss came to command large blocs of minority-group votes. Alliances between a number of ward politicians ultimately produced an organization which was able to dominate the politics of the entire city and even to exert influence at the state and national level. Generally, this amalgamation resulted in one machine and one boss, as in New York City; but sometimes it fragmented into two or three machines under different bosses, as in Chicago or Boston. The fealty of the immigrant voter was partly secured by the judicious dispensation of economic and political favors, but it also depended upon a rough sense of identification with the organization and its constituents. A study of twenty city bosses disclosed that five of them were immigrants and ten others second-generation Americans and that "there seems to be some relationship between the racial stock of municipal bosses and the dominant racial group of foreign origin in their cities." This ethnic confluence was even more apparent in the backgrounds of the urban lawmakers who considered ratification of the Seventeenth Amendment in 1913. For example, among the thirty-five Chicago Democrats who participated, there were no fourth-generation Americans; all of them were of Irish, German, Polish, Norwegian, Danish, Italian, Bohemian, Canadian, or Russian Jewish ancestry.

New stock origins alone did not automatically make a lawmaker a spokesman for the urban machine any more than an old stock background made him an independent. The correlation was high enough, however, and the chief spokesmen for the political machine generally turned out to be members of ethnic minorities—a circumstance which often caused the native, middle-class reformer to suspect the existence of a monolith. Mindful of this tendency, Richard Hofstadter has "singled out, as a phenomenon of the Progressive era, the antipathy between the ethos of the boss-machine-immigrant complex and that of the reformer-individualist-Anglo-Saxon complex . . . " identified the latter group with progressivism, and styled the former as part of the "potent mass that limited the range and achievements of Progressivism." More specifically, Hofstadter has cited the popular election of senators as one of those reforms sponsored by "Progressives" to end the power of the urban political machine—an interpretation which clearly does not square with the circumstances of the Seventeenth Amendment's ratification in the major industrial states.

Since many of the political machines were Democratic, the easy triumph of the measure in the industrial states can be attributed primarily to the party's sweeping victories in the 1912 elections. Of the eleven major industrial states, eight elected Democratic governors in 1912. In six states, both houses of the legislatures were Democratic, while in three others, the party captured one chamber and narrowly missed control of the other. Only in Pennsylvania and California was Republican rule intact, and even there it was severely shaken by Progressive incursions. Clearly, then, the attitude of the machine-oriented Democrats was crucial to the fate of the amendment.

Actually, machine support for the measure was demonstrated even when the proposal was discussed in Congress, although the nature of the matter was somewhat confused. The complicating factor was a side argument concerning the right of Congress to regulate elections for United States senators, which intruded when Senator George Sutherland, a standpat Republican from Utah, introduced an amendment to that effect. Southern congressmen, who generally favored the idea of direct, popular election of senators, were fearful that granting such control to the federal government, would open the door to enfranchisement of the Negro; and they regarded it as "a price greater than the South is willing to pay." As a consequence, they voted against the Sutherland amendment and, when it passed, either abstained or voted against the basic measure. Their attitude disturbed the northern Democrats who also favored the direct election of senators but who did not wish to alienate their southern colleagues. In the final vote, however, the majority of the northerners supported the proposed amendment, and most of the rest abstained.

The real opponents of direct election were the standpat Republicans, and they employed the divide-and-conquer technique to prevent its passage. They voted for the Sutherland amendment in order to insure southern distaste for the basic measure and later joined southern Democrats in voting against submission. In the Senate, the final test on the proposal saw the opposition emerge as a coalition of southern Democrats and Republican conservatives such as Henry Cabot Lodge, Frank Brandegee, William Lorimer, Boies Penrose, Reed Smoot, and Elihu Root. In the House, where the conservative Republicans were less influential, the proposed article passed over the objections of the southern Democrats.

Very few machine Democrats were members of the Senate, but they all voted for adoption—including James Martine of New Jersey, James O'Gorman of New York, and Atlee Pomerene of Ohio. The situation was slightly more complex in the House, where Democratic urban machine politicians were more numerous, but the great majority of the Democrats also voted in favor of the proposal. There were some notable exceptions, such as James Cox of Ohio, William Sulzer of New York, James Michael Curley of Massachusetts, George O'Shaunessey of Rhode Island, and Adolph Sabath of Illinois, all of whom abstained; and it seems highly likely, given the extraneous issue of states rights, that their hesitancy was not due to any distaste for the idea of the direct election of senators, but rather to a desire to placate the peculiar sensibilities of the southern members of their party. The Republican machine politicians, who were free from this disability, like Martin Madden of Chicago and Julius Kahn of San Francisco, supported the resolution. Moreover, one of the more stirring speeches in favor of the principle of direct election, given before the issue of federal control of elections intruded, was made by Sulzer—a readily recognizable minion of Tammany Hall—who was soon to be his party's successful candidate for governor, a post which enabled him to recommend the ratification of the amendment.

The most convincing evidence of urban machine approval of the Seventeenth Amendment is provided by an analysis of the support which it won in the various legislatures of the industrial states. There, the measure received the almost unanimous endorsement of the representatives of the urban machines. They not only acquiesced in the triumph of the proposal but they also actually seized the initiative in sponsoring it. This was clearly the case in New York. The resolution to ratify in the senate was introduced by Robert F. Wagner of New York City, a German immigrant, associate of Tammany Hall, and the Democratic majority leader. All thirty-two Democratic members of the senate voted in favor of ratification, and the twenty-two representatives of metropolitan New York City formed the bulk of that total. Of these, all but four were Irish, German, or Jewish. In addition, Buffalo's three Democratic senators added their support. The four dissenting votes were cast by upstate Republicans of old stock lineage—Elon Brown of Watertown, Henry Sage of Menands, Herbert Coots of Saranac Lake, and John Stivers of Middletown. Sage had previously denounced the measure as a "step toward pure democracy," and Brown had stigmatized it as an "act of stultification" and an admission that the legislature was unworthy.

Neither Democratic favor nor Republican distaste was as evident in the assembly, but the general outlines remained the same. The resolution to ratify was once again introduced by a Tammany Democrat, Aaron J. Levy. In the main, the party's delegation from the metropolitan area concurred with his stand—thirty-two of New York County's thirty-five Democrats and seventeen of Kings County's twenty-three voted yes. The number of abstentions, especially in Kings County, was significant and probably indicates the desire of individual Democrats to express their personal displeasure at the amendment without risking outright opposition to the party's policy. Buffalo's nine Democrats were unanimous in their approval. In the final analysis, Democrats cast 70 percent of the votes in favor of ratification, and New York contributed about 70 percent of them. Four "nay" votes were once again cast by upstate Republicans–Simon Adler of Rochester, John Jones of Carthage, John Malone of Albany, and Ransom Richardson of Fillmore. Six other Republicans abstained–including the party's candidate for speaker of the assembly, Harold J. Hinman of Albany. Still, thirty-two of the lower chamber's forty-two Republicans favored the resolution, a result which demonstrates its general popularity and contrasts sharply with the performance in the senate where over half of the party spokesmen had either opposed or abstained.

A clash between the urban-based Democrats and the more traditionally oriented Republicans over the Seventeenth Amendment was also evident in Rhode Island, where the Republicans succeeded in blocking passage mostly because of the apportionment system. General Charles R. Brayton had built an almost invincible organization upon a system of representation which allowed each town only one senator regardless of population and thus discriminated against Providence and its environs. It was estimated that twenty towns with a total population of 41,000, about 7 percent of the state's total, could actually control the upper house, a circumstance which guaranteed the selection of business-oriented Republican United States senators. Most of the population of the gerrymandered urban areas around Providence were wage earners and members of ethnic minorities–Irish, German, Italian, French Canadian, and various East European nationalities. By 1912, large numbers of these urban, new stock workers were voting Democratic and sending like-descended representatives to the state capital. Twenty-three of the party's thirty-eight representatives in 1913 were of new stock origin. Only eight of the sixty-four Republicans and Progressives in the lower house were of new stock origin, although more than 70 percent of the state's population was foreign born or second generation.

From the outset, Democrats urged ratification upon the Republicans. The resolution to ratify was introduced by James J. Dunn, an Irish Catholic Democrat of East Providence. The Republican majority promptly referred it to a committee on special legislation which consisted of five Republicans, two Democrats, and one Progressive. Predictably, the committee recommended rejection of the measure.

A spirited debate followed. Republican spokesmen argued that the existing system was devised by the Founding Fathers and that it had worked especially well in Rhode Island. The heartiest denunciations of this view were voiced by Patrick Dillon of Cumberland, who insisted that the system allowed the election of corporation men like Nelson Aldrich. Dillon was vigorously seconded by Thomas O'Niel and Albert West, both Providence Democrats. In the end, the house rejected the committee report 39-54; and it ratified the amendment.

Thirty-seven of the thirty-eight Democrats made up the largest segment of the negative votes, and only James Cummiskey of Warwick voted for the majority report. The remainder of the thirty-eight votes recorded for the motion to reject, and hence against the direct election of senators, were cast by Republicans. Almost two thirds of the Republicans opposed ratification. The bulk of Republican votes in favor were those of minority-group legislators from Providence and its environs. On balance, the contest was clearly one between the urban-based Democrats, aided by a few Progressives and Republicans from similar constituencies, and the rural and small-town based Republican organization.

In the senate, where the apportionment system virtually disfranchised urban voters, the Seventeenth Amendment was not even able to get on the floor. The resolution was smothered in a committee where the Republicans had a six-to-one majority, approximately the same ratio which obtained in the chamber as a whole. Rhode Island became one of only three states to reject the proposed amendment, and the result was clearly a triumph of the Brayton combine over the urban Democrats.

This conflict was even more intense in neighboring Connecticut. Again the apportionment system, this time in the lower house, operated against the urban areas by requiring that no town could have less than one not more than two representatives, regardless of its population. This discriminated against the state's new stock wage earners who comprised the bulk of the population of New Haven, Hartford, Bridgeport, and the other industrial cities, and who generally sent lawmakers of similar antecedents and Democratic leanings to the legislature. This enabled the Republicans under the leadership of J. Henry Rorabach to retain much of their strength in the lower house in spite of the general Democratic victory in 1912.

The division in the lower house over ratification was one of the most clear-cut. The resolution was introduced by James Lynch, an Irish-born lawyer and Democrat from Waterbury. The final vote was 151-77—a coalition of Democrats and Progressive Republicans defeated the regular Republicans. All 119 Democrats present voted yes, but the Republicans showed only thirty-two in favor and seventy-seven against. In Hartford County only ten of the thirty-two Republicans favored ratification; in New Haven County, only three of eighteen; in New London County, one of six; in Fairfield, six of fourteen; in Windham, five of seventeen; in Litchfield, ten of twenty-two; in Middlesex, seven of ten; and in Tolland County, seven of ten. Nearly all of the Republicans were old stock legislators from rural areas who were protecting their position from the challenge of the Democrats.

In the senate, where the Democrats had a three-to-two majority, the measure easily passed, but it was once again the urban lawmakers who took the lead. Ratification was proposed by Democratic Senator John Hurley of Waterbury, an Irish immigrant, and seconded by another Irish Democrat, Arch McNeil of Bridgeport. The amendment was adopted by voice vote. The results in the lower house, the identity of the sponsors, and the Democratic control of the senate clearly indicate that ratification was a victory for the state's urban Democrats.

In Massachusetts the same general lines of division obtained. The Republican party in Massachusetts had been dominant for several decades and had only recently been challenged by the resurgent Democrats. The Democratic party was largely controlled by Irish-Americans and had its greatest strength in the general area of Boston. Although some of the more recent immigrant groups such as the Italians, Poles, and French Canadians who inhabited the mill towns sometimes tended to vote Republican, the Irish, according to the foremost students of Massachusetts politics, claimed to be representative of all the minority groups in the state. Moreover, the Republican delegations to the legislature were preponderantly old stock and rural, and the Democratic delegations were overwhelmingly new stock and urban. Republican control of the legislature usually resulted in the selection of Yankee-descended, corporation-conscious Republicans like Lodge and Winthrop Murray Crane, and the Democrats saw a remedy for this situation in direct, popular election.

Actually, the Democrats began their campaign for this reform even before Congress officially proposed the amendment. In a resolution prepared by Secretary of State Frank Donahue, the Democrats called upon Congress to summon a constitutional convention in order to amend the Constitution to allow for the direct election of senators. The Republicans, endorsing a motion by Yankee George Barnes of suburban Norfolk County, proposed to amend the Donahue resolution so that it merely petitioned Congress to effect the reform in any way it saw fit. Although many Republicans undoubtedly favored direct election and were leery of the calling of a general constitutional convention which might open the door to other amendments, it is clear that many party regulars were actually opposed to the idea and that Barnes introduced his amendment as a face-saving gesture in the light of the popular sentiment for the change. When Democrat John Mack of North Adams asked Barnes point-blank if he favored the direct election of senators, the Republican admitted that he had "grave doubts" about its wisdom, was skeptical that it would produce men of the same calibre as the existing system, and would support the reform only because it "reflects the sentiment of the people."

The vote on the Barnes amendment was the nearest thing to an outright test of the policy of the two parties, and the Democrats clearly established themselves as the staunchest supporters of direct election. All thirteen Democrats, mostly Irish-Americans from the Boston vicinity, voted against the Barnes amendment and demonstrated their desire for the strongest possible position on the question. They were joined by four of the so-called "labor legislators"—Republicans with labor backgrounds and working-class constituencies. The remaining Republicans, regulars like Barnes and Calvin Coolidge, voted for the Barnes amendment, and it passed. The Democrats and their labor legislator allies, believing that "half a loaf is better than none," voted for the amended resolution which passed 35-3. Two Republican regulars apparently refused to agree to even the more modest resolution, while Democrat Francis Quigley presumably held out for the original proposal.

The same question was raised in the lower house, but the Democrats carried the day by virtue of superior numbers. The resolution calling for a convention was introduced by John Meany of Blackstone, the Democratic leader, who argued that the people had already proven their capacity to govern. Some Republicans, like

Roger Wolcott of Milton and Robert Washburn of Worcester, stated their objections to popular government, but most of the party joined the Democrats. They even refused to alter the language to read "requests" instead of "demands." The resolution passed resoundingly–162-37. All thirty-seven negative votes were cast by Republicans. With the exception of a few members who were absent, the Irish-American delegates from Suffolk, Middlesex, and Worcester Counties were unanimous in their approval–even the prototype of the Boston machine politico, Martin Lomasney.

Clearly, the urban Democrats had demonstrated a far greater preference for direct election than had their Yankee Republican opponents before the Seventeenth Amendment was proposed by Congress. Since the Republicans admitted the overwhelming sympathy of the people of Massachusetts for the reform, the legislature ratified the amendment within ten days after it had been submitted. The measure passed the lower house by a voice vote. The only inkling of opposition in the senate was provided by nine abstentions–three Democrats who apparently felt the amendment too modest and six Republicans who could not bring themselves to vote for any measure advocating direct election. The contest over the direct election of senators in Massachusetts is a concrete illustration of Richard Abram's contention that the "truly 'insurgent' groups" in the state were "the large Irish-American segment of the population, who purported to represent the newer Americans generally," aided by a few labor unionists.

Democratic machine support for the direct election of senators was also evidenced in Illinois, and the lack of any serious opposition from the Republicans resulted in an easy triumph for ratification. The urgency of the reform was all the more pressing in Illinois because of two incidents which had marred the selection of the state's senators. In 1909, the election of Republican Lorimer had been effected by bribery which allegedly involved some fifty-seven lawmakers and made the Illinois legislature a symbol for all those who desired the change to direct election. In the same 1913 session at which ratification of the amendment was being considered, the task of selecting Lorimer's successor and another full-term senator consumed almost four months of the legislature's time and interfered with other business.

At the outset, support for ratification appeared bipartisan. The ratification resolutions in both houses were introduced by downstate Republicans, and firm endorsement was given by Democratic Governor Edward F. Dunne of Chicago, an Irish Catholic and a member of the so-called Hearst-Harrison faction of the party. Dunne, in his own history of Illinois, refers to the amendment as one of his most important recommendations to the legislature and to its ratification as "the greatest victory for popular government in fifty years." Despite this apparent agreement, however, senate Republicans did make one unsuccessful attempt at blocking consideration of the amendment by trying to table a motion by Democratic Senator John Denvir–an Irish Catholic labor leader–to refer the measure to the Committee on Constitutional Amendments. The maneuver failed on an almost completely partisan vote, and the measure was referred to a committee where the Democrats had a narrow majority. After a favorable report, it was approved by the senate 50-0. No Illinois state senator was willing to declare against ratification in the light of the state's past history, although some Republicans were reluctant to allow the amendment to come to a vote.

The vote in the lower house was an equally decisive 146-1; only downstate Democrat Lee O'Niel Browne of La Salle opposed. The affirmative votes represented both factions of the Democratic party. The followers of the Chicago boss Roger Sullivan—R. E. "Bob" Wilson, John J. McLaughlin, and "Bennie" Mitchell—agreed with Michael Igoe and James Ryan of the Harrison-Dunne group. The support of the Chicago Democratic machine for the Seventeenth Amendment was at least as great as that of any other political faction in Illinois.

In two other major industrial states, Ohio and New Jersey, ratification was easily effected after a major Democratic electoral victory which temporarily strengthened the position of the urban political machine complex. In Ohio, traditionally a Republican state, the 1912 election had resulted in a Democratic sweep. Cox, a protégé of Toledo Democratic boss Edward Hanley, was elected governor; William Greenlund, a Danish-American from Cleveland and a former state senator, was chosen lieutenant governor; and two Irish Catholics, John Brennan and Timothy Hogan, were selected treasurer and attorney-general respectively. More significantly for the future of the Seventeenth Amendment, both houses of the legislature were solidly controlled by the Democrats, and even such usually Republican strongholds as Cincinnati produced Democratic lawnmakers.

Ratification in the senate came on a motion introduced by Maurice Bernstein of Cleveland. The other four Cleveland senators supported the motion, and they were joined by two of Cincinnati's three Democratic delegates; one was absent. The amendment was also approved by President Pro Tempore of the Senate William Green of Coshocton, well-known leader of the state's mine workers and future head of the American Federation of Labor, and by such acknowledged machine Democrats as Daniel F. Mooney of St. Marys and Michael Cahill of Eaton. The lone negative vote out of the thirty-one cast was that of Michael A. Broadstone of Xenia, whose biographer describes him as "an uncompromising republican."

Easy ratification, 114-0, also followed in the lower house, after the introduction of the amendment by Democrat Robert Black of Cincinnati. Floor leader Lawrence Brennan and future Senator Stephen Young were among twelve of the thirteen-man Cleveland delegation which voted yes. Except for Young and Don P. Mills, the remainder of the delegates were products of the city's Irish, German, Bohemian, and Polish minorities. Speaker Charles Swain joined seven of the ten Cincinnati Democrats to vote yes, and so did the Democratic representatives of other urban areas such as Toledo, Dayton, and Columbus.

In New Jersey the Democratic trend had begun with election of Woodrow

Wilson as governor in 1910. After the 1912 contest, the party controlled the assembly 51-8. In the senate, the margin was much narrower, 12-9, because of an apportionment law which gave each county one senator regardless of population. In the lower house especially, most of the party's strength was composed of new stock, Jersey City, and Newark lawmakers who were normally considered to be the servants of the machines bossed by Robert "Little Bob" Davis and James "Big Jim" Smith. The Democrats also dominated the two next largest delegations, those of Passaic and Union Counties. The sponsorship of the amendment in the assembly was undertaken by Charles O'Connor Hennessy, an Irish-born lawyer from Haworth in Bergen County. In the final vote, 42-0, thirty-six Democrats and six Republicans were recorded in favor. Twelve of the thirteen Essex County (Newark) Democrats and nine of the Hudson County (Jersey City) delegation voted yes. Four of Passaic's five delegates, two of Bergen's three, and all three of Union County's assemblymen were recorded in favor of ratification. The floor leader, Charles Egan of Hudson, voted yes, but most of the abstainers were Democrats from Rural areas. The machine Democrats in New Jersey's lower legislative house provided the largest bloc of votes for the direct election of senators.

Machine influence was less noticeable in the New Jersey senate, where the measure passed 18-1. The lone dissenter was Democrat Richard Fitzherbert of Dover. The Democratic senators from Bergen, Union, Passaic, and Hudson Counties and an Essex County Republican lawmaker voted yes. One member of each party abstained. Thus, in New Jersey, as in Ohio, a Democratic legislature dominated by politicians who were normally considered spokesmen for the state's urban political machines effected passage of a reform widely regarded as a blow at one of the organization's prerogatives.

The representatives of other urban Democratic organizations in somewhat less populous states also endorsed the Seventeenth Amendment. In Delaware, for example, sponsorship of the measure was undertaken by two Democrats from Wilmington, Senator John Gormley and Representative Timothy Mooney. In the lower house, where the Democrats were in control after the 1912 election, ratification occurred by an easy vote, 30-0; and Timothy Mooney and Speaker Chauncey Holcomb of Wilmington were the leading proponents. In the senate, where the Republicans held a nine-to-seven edge, the amendment was rejected by an almost perfectly partisan division, 6-10. Delaware joined Rhode Island and Utah as the only states where Republican control of the senate was the deciding factor in the rejection of the Seventeenth Amendment.

In Missouri, too, the sizeable Democratic delegations from St. Louis and Kansas City generally supported ratification. In the lower house, where the measure passed 128-1, all fourteen Democrats from the St. Louis area were recorded in favor; and all but two of them were of Irish or German extraction. Five of Kansas City's six Democrats also voted yes, and the sixth was absent due to illness. In the senate, however, nearly all the Democrats from those two cities were absent on the day the vote was taken, a development which might have portended disapproval on their part. Nevertheless, the fact that they chose to abstain rather than openly oppose, coupled with the nearly unanimous backing which the measure received from their colleagues in the house, would seem to indicate widespread approbation of the Seventeenth Amendment on the part of the machine and its constituents.

A somewhat different pattern was evident in Wisconsin, although the support of Milwaukee's Democrats was equally clear. All twelve of them voted for ratification in the lower house, as did both the city's Republicans and Social Democrats. Nearly all of these men were of new stock extraction, regardless of party label. The city's lone Democratic senator, George Weissleder, was not recorded in the vote on the Seventeenth Amendment, but since three of four Republicans and the single Social Democrat did vote in favor of ratification, the measure was obviously popular among all political factions in Milwaukee.

It seems safe to assert that the Seventeenth Amendment received an overwhelming degree of support from the representatives of urban Democratic political machines. The same assertion can be made about the Republican political machines in Pennsylvania and California, but only with certain clarifications. In both Philadelphia and Pittsburgh, the Republican party had succeeded in preventing, or at least slowing, the drift of new stock voters into the Democratic party. By collusion and other methods, they had reduced the Democratic party to the status of a subsidiary organization, which often accepted favors and took orders from the dominant Republican group headed in 1912 by Senator Penrose. The Democrats occasionally sent lawmakers from Philadelphia or Pittsburgh to Harrisburg during this period, but the Republicans retained control. However, this virtual monopoly led to factionalism within the Republican ranks and, ultimately, to a power struggle between Penrose and Philadelphia boss Edwin Vare.

This factionalism was evident in the struggle over the Seventeenth Amendment because Edwin "Duke" Vare's lieutenants apparently supported ratification more enthusiastically than did Penrose's followers. This was particularly obvious in the senate, where, despite a unanimous vote, there were some significant abstentions. Only five of Philadelphia's nine senators voted for the measure, and two of these, Richard Farley and James Nulty, were Democrats and Irish Catholic labor leaders. The three Republicans who favored ratification were in Vare's faction. The four Penrose people in the senate, however, including the senator's personal representative, James "Strawberry Jim" McNichol, abstained. All but one of the six-man Republican delegation from Pittsburgh also concurred. Thus, despite its apparent dislike for the measure, even the powerful Penrose machine was reluctant to oppose it openly.

This split in the Pennsylvania Republican ranks was less evident in the lower house, where thirty-seven of the thirty-nine Philadelphia lawmakers voted for ratification. There were two dissenters—Edward Fahey and Harry Bass, the only Negro member. The other negative vote was cast by Richard Baldwin of suburban Delaware County. Four of Pittsburgh's twenty-four-man delegation abstained, but the support of the measure among urban machine Republicans in both major cities was nevertheless clearly established.

San Francisco's Republican machine also favored ratification. In the lower house the entire Republican delegation from the Bay City area voted in favor of the amendment. Three of the four San Francisco Democrats, all Irish-Americans with labor backgrounds, voted yes. In the senate, however, two of the five city Republicans abstained, and there was no overt attempt by the machine to block ratification.

The fate of the Seventeenth Amendment in the major industrial states amply demonstrates that the urban political machine was one of the most consistent and influential supporters of this reform. In some states the machine was simply one of several political factions favoring ratification. In others—New York, New Jersey, Connecticut, and Massachusetts—machine support was unquestionably the major force behind the success of the measure. In Rhode Island and Delaware, the urban-based Democrats sponsored the amendment in the face of overwhelming Republican opposition, and it went down to defeat. No urban machine or its representatives openly opposed ratification.

The enthusiasm of the urban political machines for the Seventeenth Amendment raises a serious question about the overall attitude of these organizations toward reform in the Progressive era. It may be that ratification of the Seventeenth Amendment was a solitary exception, or that the machines had to acquiesce in the inevitable because of the clamor of public opinion, but the overwhelming nature of their support makes such an interpretation highly unlikely. It seems far more credible that the issue is a concrete illustration of the contention, first set forward by J. Joseph Huthmacher, that the machine politician's attitude toward political reform was not uniformly reactionary, but selectively pragmatic. Indeed, Huthmacher cites the ratification of the Seventeenth Amendment by the New York General Assembly as an example of his thesis. The apportionment system in the legislatures of most of the major industrial states was so weighted in favor of the non-metropolitan areas that it all but guaranteed the selection of senators who were rural, old stock, business-oriented, and Republican. This was certainly true in New England, and the difference in most of the other more populous states was only one of degree. The change to a system of direct, popular election would greatly enhance the chances of candidates who were urban, new stock, and more attuned to the needs of the industrial wage earner. This was explicit in Congressman Sulzer's contention that the apportionment system made it impossible to secure selection of a Democratic senator in New York unless that party won by a margin of at least 100,000 votes. It was clearly expressed by state representative Dillon of Rhode Island, when he asserted repeatedly that Aldrich could never be victorious in a popular election. It was strongly implied in Republican denunciations of the measure in Massachusetts, Rhode Island, and New York. It was patently obvious when

Penrose, who controlled virtually all of Pennsylvania, opposed ratification and Vare, who dominated only Philadelphia, supported it. It was also clearly indicated by the fact that the Democrats immediately began to produce urban, new stock candidates under the new system of election. The first Massachusetts Democrat to try for the Senate after the ratification of the Seventeenth Amendment was John F. Fitzgerald, and the next was David I. Walsh. In Illinois, Roger Sullivan, in Indiana, boss Thomas Taggart, and in Ohio, Timothy Hogan all entered senatorial contests. Only a few were successful, but the potential for producing future Kennedys, Wagners, and Ribicoffs was clearly established.

Although there were political advantages for the machine in direct election, many machine spokesmen also believed that more significant issues were involved. The selection of United States senators by malapportioned legislatures clearly violated the idea of American democracy and representative government. The fact that this system so uniformly discriminated against the chances of candidates with urban, industrial, immigrant backgrounds seemed to be a denial of the equality of opportunity which American life was supposed to provide. Little wonder that it was the people who were most affected by these inequities who developed the keenest sense of appreciation of the principles involved. It was, after all, the suffragettes who felt most strongly about the full participation of women in American life; and, despite the substantial contributions of white liberals, it has been Negro leaders who have demonstrated the greatest anguish about racial inequality. Moreover, as Hofstadter has observed, it was at least partly concern for their own waning power and prestige which awakened the members of the "reformer-individualist-Anglo-Saxon complex" to the full meaning of such ideals as patriotism and democracy. In any event, the spokesmen for the urban machines voiced their concern about the democratic process as eloquently as did the good-government reformer. Governor Dunne of Illinois asserted that true democracy could only be realized when all important state and national officials were elected by popular vote. Congressman Sulzer of New York maintained that the people "can and ought to be trusted." Assemblyman Dillon of Rhode Island demanded that the people and not the corporations select United States senators, and Democratic majority leader Meany of Massachusetts insisted that the people had already demonstrated their capacity to act wisely in the selection of other public officials. The urban machine politician supported the Seventeenth Amendment out of a healthy mixture of idealism and self-interest, and it is difficult to separate the one from the other.

Until recently, much of the activity of historians of the Progressive era has centered around the delineation of a movement called "Progressivism" and a group of people deemed "progressives." It has generally been assumed that the solid legislative achievements of those years flowed somehow from that movement and that group of people. Few would deny that the Seventeenth Amendment was one of the cardinal achievements of the era, yet its success was owed in large measure to the support of an entirely different segment of society—one generally considered antagonistic to the aims of the Progressive movement. It would seem appropriate, therefore, for historians to concentrate their attention less on the concept of a movement and more on the method by which the important legislation was enacted. To do this, they must also heed Huthmacher's advice and "modify the 'middle class' emphasis which has come to dominate the field and devote more attention to exploring hitherto neglected elements of the American social structure."

Part Four WELFARE

Chapter 9 IT'S GOOD FOR BUSINESS

JAMES WEINSTEIN *(1926-   ), former editor of* Studies on the Left *discusses here the movement for workmen's compensation. There can be no question but that it received support from businessmen, as Weinstein demonstrates. Two questions remain, though. First, was that the sole support it received? Second, was workmen's compensation representative of the whole welfare movement during the Progressive era?*

Social reform and the regulation of business enterprise and banking first became widely accepted as a legitimate function of the federal and state governments during the Progressive Era. In large part this was the result of an understanding by many of the more sophisticated financiers and corporation leaders that such reform would strengthen the system; that if the new trusts were to stabilize their dominant position in American society, the demands of other groups must be met at least in part. This did not mean that the initial demands for particular reforms were made by business leaders; most movements for reform were initiated by those suffering under intolerable conditions. But it did often mean that success, in the sense of legislation enacted, followed upon the adoption of particular reform programs by big business leaders. Gabriel Kolko has demonstrated that this was so in respect to

James Weinstein, "Big Business and the Origins of Workmen's Compensation," *Labor History*, VIII (Spring 1967), 156-174. Reprinted by permission of *Labor History*.

the pure food and drug legislation and the Federal Trade Commission Act. This article will examine the process whereby big business came to sponsor workmen's compensation legislation, as well as its striking legislative success in so doing.

The socially uncontrolled entrepreneurial initiative that led to America's leap into world predominance as an industrial power in the last third of the nineteenth century was accompanied by a ruthless spirit of competition that left little room for concern about the welfare or working conditions of those at the bottom. Accidents and injury abounded in American industry at the turn of the century, and few seemed to care, except the victims themselves and a small circle of "do-good" reformers. When, in 1905, Werner Sombart set out to show that American capitalism was the greediest on earth, he used as evidence the relative accident rates on the railways of the United States and Austria. In 1903 American railroads injured 11,066 workers, compared to the Austrian figure of 172, according to Sombart. Both by kilometer of road and by millions of passengers carried, American railroads killed and injured many times their European counterparts. Many popular writers exposed working conditions in the railroad, steel and packing industries during these years. They revealed that the monthly average of 328 American railroad workers killed during the years 1888-1908 made up only ten percent of an estimated 35,000 killed and 536,000 injured workers in American industry each year. As the muckraker William Hard reported in "Making Steel and Killing Men," in 1906 the South Chicago plant of the United States Steel Company alone killed 46 men and wounded an estimated 598.

Not only were American working conditions worse and accidents more frequent than in European industry, but provisions for the injured worker were virtually non-existent in the United States, while they were extensive in Europe. Until the end of the first decade of the new century, in fact, the law in almost every state had been handed down from decisions made in pre-industrial England and the United States. A worker killed or injured at work had recourse to damages only through the courts; even after expensive and drawn-out litigation, his or his heirs' chances of recovery were slight. The defenses available to the employer were such that only an estimated 15 percent of the injured employees ever recovered damages, even though 70 percent of industrial accidents were estimated to be the result of the nature of the work or of employer negligence.

There were three common law defenses available to an employer: the fellow-servant doctrine, the assumption of risk, and contributory negligence. Under the fellow-servant doctrine an injured employee was held responsible for the negligence of other employees, on the theory that he should acquaint himself with the bad habits of his co-workers and exercise a salutary influence upon them. In one case an employee on the night shift at the United States Steel plant in South Chicago plugged an open hearth carelessly. A few minutes later, when the day shift man had relieved him, the plug blew out and several tons of molten steel engulfed the day man. The night man was eighteen-years old. He had worked at his job only one week. The two men had met only once. Yet the court held that the day man had no claim against the company because he and his fellow servant "had ample opportunity to exercise upon each other an influence promotive of care and prudence in the matter of performing their work.

In another case, made famous by Theodore Roosevelt in 1913, a young woman, Sarah Knisley, had her arm torn off by the unprotected gears of a grinding machine on which she was working. The state law provided that the gears should be covered; Miss Knisley had complained to her employer that they were not, and expressed fear about working at the machine in its present condition. But the employer warned her to do her job or quit, and she complied out of need of the job. The court held that in so doing she had assumed the risk of the dangerous condition and could not recover damages. Had she not known or complained of the illegal condition she would have had a cause of action; her knowledge made her liable.

In Arizona, a railroad engineer had been forced to work thirty hours straight when his replacement failed to appear. As a result, he fell asleep on the job and was involved in an accident. The law limited straight working hours on railroads to sixteen, and the engineer agreed to continue work only under the threat of discharge. Nevertheless, the court held him negligent. He had the free choice of cooperating in a violation of the law or of terminating his employment. His decision to cooperate was held to be contributory negligence.

As early as 1898, in response to a workman's compensation act passed in Great Britain the year before, the Social Reform Club of New York introduced a bill calling for automatic compensation for injury in some types of industrial accidents. But labor did not generally support the idea of compensation at this time. In New York, the Workingmen's Federation argued instead for modification of the traditional common law defenses so that employers would be liable for those injuries where the worker was not negligent. This position was also taken by the several railway brotherhoods in 1899. Agitation along this line by labor produced employer liability laws of some kind in twenty-six states by 1907. Most of these modified the fellow servant doctrine; a few limited the assumption of risk and contributory negligence doctrines as well.

Labor's opposition to compensation legislation was based in part upon its belief that a weakening of the employer's defenses would produce many court victories and much higher payments than automatic compensation could provide. Equally important, almost all unionists, socialist or conservative, opposed government regulation of working conditions on the theory, often only implicit, that government was controlled by business, either directly or indirectly through conservative politicians and judges whose thinking on labor questions was identical to that of leading businessmen. Samuel Gompers, for example, opposed minimum wage and maximum hours legislation for men, and only grudgingly accepted the idea for women; the conception that employers were "the trustees of the property of the world, and hence that they are to be the guardians of the welfare of the employees" made him uneasy. He preferred a voluntary organization of wage workers prepared to advance labor's interests independently. Even minimum wages for women were opposed by craft unionists at times. Such opposition was based on the fear that state action would weaken labor's prerogatives and "carry with it disintegration of the vital forces of labor." Though, in the face of such state programs, unions might persist in name "and even grow in membership," the union would be "deprived of its essentials of independence, self-direction and elastic adaptation to the needs of a forceful mass mechanism." Workmen's compensation raised another objection: state satisfaction of the guild-like provision of pensions and other welfare benefits would reduce the craftsmen's loyalty to the union.

In contrast to labor's opposition to compensation, some of the largest of the new trusts had come to favor such plans. George W. Perkins, a Morgan partner and a director of the International Harvester and United States Steel corporations, explained the principle that underlay big business support of compensation and other welfare plans to the National Civic Federation in 1909. "Co-operation in business," he said, "is taking and should take the place of ruthless competition." If "this new order of things is better for capital and better for the consumer, then in order to succeed permanently it must demonstrate that it is better for the laborer." Profit sharing, pensions, sick and accident insurance, Perkins emphasized, "must mean co-operation between capital and labor." Perkins then described the International Harvester welfare program. It included a stock purchase plan and a company benefit plan under which the worker paid 2 percent of his wages in return for two years' pay for accidental death, one year's pay for death by sickness, and half pay for sickness or disability through injury. Seventy-five percent of the workers were said to have joined, and the company had contributed $50,000. No waiver of the right to sue the company was demanded. In addition, a pension plan provided a minimum of $18.00 per week, and a maximum of $100.00 per week.

The Harvester Company, Perkins explained, "did not do this out of pure philanthropy," but was motivated by a "purely business spirit." The idea was "that the plans would so knit [the company's] vast organization together, so stimulate individual initiative," so "strengthen and develop the *esprit de corps*" that it would enable the company to increase its earning.

The United States Steel Corporation announced a similar plan for voluntary workmen's compensation in 1910. Modeled on the workmen's compensation laws in Germany and other European countries, the plan provided 35 percent of weekly wages for injured single workers, 50 percent for married workers, and an extra 5 percent for each child over five years of age. Elbert H. Gary carefully explained that these were actually relief payments, not compensation, since an estimated 75 percent of the cases would involve no legal liability on the part of the company. The paternalistic nature of the plan was emphasized in the announcement that the progressive step was not the result "of any demand or suggestion of the employees." One commentator on the United States Steel plan observed that its merit, from the manager's standpoint, was that it helped keep "intact a non-union working force." Raynal C. Bolling, assistant general solicitor of the Corporation, in speaking of the Steel plan and workmen's compensation laws, went further; he hoped that "the progress of workmen's compensation should be a rebuke and a rebuttal" to those who "assert that the workingmen get nothing except by contest and struggle." In short, company workmen's compensation plans were designed to reduce the need for independent political action by labor, as well as the appeal of unionism in the large corporation.

There were limitations to private welfare and compensation plans, however. Workers often resented the paternalism inherent in them, and only the largest corporations had the resources necessary to their successful operation. Smaller manufacturers agreed in principle with the objectives of such plans, but as the chairman of the Committee on Employer's Liability of the National Association of Manufacturers (N.A.M.) pointed out, small industrialists could not afford voluntary systems such as the United States Steel Corporation had instituted. Ninety-five percent of the 25,000 employers to whom the N.A.M. sent questionnaires in 1910 favored automatic compensation for industrial accidents; few had the resources to institute such programs privately. The Association therefore endorsed the idea of workmen's compensation legislation.

By the time the N.A.M. reached this conclusion, labor had been induced to change its mind on compensation. In part, this was the result of agitation, starting in 1907, by the American Association for Labor Legislation (A.A.L.L.), a middle-class reform organization financed by such men as John D. Rockefeller, Elbert H. Gary, and V. Everitt Macy. But trade unionists had little use for the A.A.L.L. Much more important in winning the support of labor and the attention of state politicians was the role of the National Civic Federation, which after 1908 threw its whole weight into the fight for compensation legislation.

Organized in 1900 by Ralph M. Easley, the National Civic Federation claimed to represent business, labor and the public. Its early purposes centered around a program of conciliation and mediation between the unions and the large corporations. From the beginning the Civic Federation was led by big businessmen themselves. Marcus A. Hanna was its first president; others among its early members were Samuel Insull, the Chicago banker Franklin McVeagh, Charles Francis Adams, Andrew Carnegie, George B. Cortelyou of Consolidated Gas and several J. P. Morgan partners. By 1903 almost one-third of the 367 corporations with a capitalization of more than $10,000,000 were represented in the National Civic Federation, as were sixteen of the sixty-seven largest railroads in the United States. Labor was also represented by its top leaders. Samuel Gompers was the original First Vice President of the Federation, a position he retained until his death in 1925. John Mitchell of the United Mine Workers was an active member and full-time head of the Trade Agreements Department from 1908 to 1911. The heads of the major railroad brotherhoods and many A.F.L. international unions were also on the executive committee. The members of the executive committee representing the public included at one time or another Grover Cleveland, William H. Taft, Charles J. Bonaparte (Roosevelt's Attorney General), Nicholas Murray Butler, Charles W. Eliot, Benjamin Ide Wheeler (President of the University of California), and many other prominent figures in politics and the professions.

The Civic Federation's leading members were, of course, not narrowly anti-union. They were more concerned with molding the character and direction of the labor movement and hoped to help the conservative unionists as much as to hinder the spread of the movement. In the minds of many financial and corporation leaders, there existed a constant tension between these two goals. Some members of the civic Federation saw the necessity of conservative unionism as an abstract principle, but opposed unions in their shops; outstanding among them were Cyrus McCormick, George W. Perkins, Elbert H. Gray, Henry W. Phipps, and Henry P. Davidson of the International Harvester and United States Steel companies. Although these men were among the most generous contributors to the Federation and participated in its activities, their companies became increasingly anti-union between 1903 and 1910; the Steel corporation, in fact, remained a bastion of anti-unionism until the early days of the New Deal.

Other employers were less ambivalent. William C. Brown, senior vice president of the New York Central Railroad, wrote in 1908 that "organized labor has done a tremendous work for labor," and, at the same time, "by raising the standard of intelligence," it had "been beneficial to all interests." Certainly, Brown concluded, "this is true so far as it relates to organized railroad labor." Similarly, Mark Hanna had early recognized the value of unions and the need for trust between capital and labor. As Samuel Gompers remarked upon Hanna's death in 1904, he had been one of the "pioneers among employers to not only recognize but to come to agreements with labor in its organized capacity."

Whatever the attitude of different businessmen in the Civic Federation toward recognition of unions within their own enterprises, all were agreed on the need to uphold conservative unionism as against the Socialists or the Industrial Workers of the World, and all feared labor's entrance into politics as an organized force. "Class politics" was anathema to the business leaders of the Federation, yet the A.F.L. had moved steadily toward independent politics from 1906 to 1908. Impelled by the losses suffered as a result of the National Association of Manufacturers' open-shop drive, by the increasing effectiveness of N.A.M. anti-labor lobbying in Congress, and by a series of anti-labor injunctions in the courts, the A.F.L. drew up a Bill of Grievances to present to Congress in 1906 and then campaigned against the most anti-labor congressmen in the fall election. More important, inspired by the success of the Union Party in San Francisco, local and state organizations were instructed to nominate straight labor candidates where regular nominees ignored labor's demands. Six union men were, as a result, elected to Congress in 1906. Then, in early 1908 the Executive Council of the A.F.L. met with farm organization leaders to discuss a farmer-labor alliance, and the A.F.L. strongly supported Bryan in the presidential elections, after the Democrats endorsed most of labor's program.

The Socialist Party hailed the A.F.L.'s hesitant entrance into partisan politics, viewing it as a step toward an independent labor party, such as the English unions had formed after a court had held in 1902 that the Amalgamated Society of Railway Engineers was responsible for business losses to the Taff Vale railway during a strike. Socialist agitation in the A.F.L. had been continuous since 1902, and in Europe a close relationship between the unions and the Socialist parties had always been the rule. The fear that American labor would follow the European example constantly gnawed at the consciousness of Civic Federation leaders. As leaders of American society, the businessmen in the Civic Federation believed that the "great chasm" between capital and labor was "an effect of the imagination, to be regretted and always combatted." They labored so that the "habitual normal sense of social solidarity which is the foundation stone of democracy" might prevail. Yet, Seth Low, then president of the Civic Federation, wrote Gompers that he could "understand, of course, that the question may occur to men identified with the labor union movement, whether, under the circumstances, it might not be better to resort to political agitation all along the line, as the English laboring men did after the Taff Vale decision."

One other aspect of labor's entry into politics bothered businessmen in the Civic Federation, just as it would later alienate many of them from Theodore Roosevelt's Progressive Party. This was the fear that the increasing use of court injunctions against labor would move the A.F.L. to political action designed to limit the independence of the judiciary. "It is a matter of great moment," complained August Belmont at the National Civic Federation's annual meeting in 1906, "when our workmen . . . become imbued with the idea that our courts are used by employers for partisan purposes." Two years later, when Samuel Gompers was appealing the injunction in the Buck Stove and Range Case, Andrew Carnegie contributed funds through the Civic Federation to help pay expenses of the appeal. To Easley, Carnegie warned that he was "one member of the National Civic Federation who will very promptly resign if it gives the slightest countenance to attacks on the Supreme Court." "I am as strong a friend of Labor and I think a wiser one than Mr. Gompers," Carnegie continued, "but if we are to fail to preach and practice implicit obedience to the Law as defined by the final tribunals, you can count me out." In a postscript, Carnegie commanded: "I should like to hear whether Mr. Gompers agrees to acquiesce in the decision, whatever it may be."

At the 1906 Annual Meeting of the National Civic Federation it was clear that business and labor could not agree on the role of the courts. The businessmen flatly denied there was "discrimination or inequality, either in the law or its administration as to labor combinations," and consequently attacked labor's opposition to the use of the Sherman Act against the unions as "class politics." This reflected a growing anxiety on the part of the business members of the Federation and was part of the process of searching for common ground with labor. What was needed was some course of social action "upon which the non-business members would be willing to follow the lead of the business members." Since labor's experience with employer liability legislation was unsatisfactory, workmen's compensation emerged as the ideal program for the Civic Federation. The largest corporations were instituting it in their plants; public agitation for relief had created a good political climate; compensation was paternalistic and would probably reduce somewhat the appeal of unionism to workers, yet the unions could be induced to support it. By 1909 the Civic Federation had convinced Gompers and so was able to commit itself fully to the sponsorship of this reform. In so doing, it took a large stride into its new phase as the leading organization of businessman's reform.

In line with its earlier paternalism, the National Civic Federation had established an Industrial Insurance Commission in 1908, and President Seth Low appointed George W. Perkins of the Steel and Harvester companies as chairman. But the Commission was not very active, and the perspective of the Federation was changing. In 1909, reflecting this change, Low appointed the banker and traction magnate, August Belmont, to head the reorganized Department on Compensation for Industrial Accidents and their Prevention. From this point on, the Federation was at the center of agitation for the workmen's compensation bills. At the annual meeting in 1908 one session was devoted to industrial insurance. Speakers included Louis D. Brandeis; William R. Wilcox, a leading banker; Haley Fiske, a vice president of Metropolitan Life Insurance Company; and Major A. E. Piorkowski, of the Krupp Company in Essen, Germany. Lee K. Frankel of the Sage Foundation Fund reminded his audience that the United States was alone among industrial nations in putting the burden of industrial accidents on the workers. "In Germany," he pointed out, "insurance is no longer a business proposition, but a distinct social program." But Frederick L. Hoffman of Prudential Life argued that although "the German government system was specifically devised to do away with Socialism," in fact "the Socialists never polled as many votes as they do at the present time."

At the next meeting, in 1909, few opposed compensation laws, and only the problem of state versus private insurance remained open: the businessmen generally lined up for private insurance, while the trade unionists favored state insurance. Major Piorkowski was present again and spoke on workmen's insurance in Germany; A. H. Gill, a member of Parliament, discussed workmen's compensation in England. Among the Federation members speakers, George M. Gillette, of the Minneapolis Steel and Machinery Company (and president of the Minnesota Employers' Association), commented that the "reactionary" on workmen's compensation was "in such a hopeless minority that he should not be seriously considered." It was clear, Gillette went on, that the existing system was unsatisfactory because it disturbed the relation of employer to employee, bred perjury, failed to prevent or decrease accidents, and was uncertain and wasteful. In his view, workmen's compensation was emphatically not "a thin entering wedge for socialism." His thinking was endorsed by most of the speakers, including Louis B. Schram, chairman of the Labor Committee of the United States Brewers Association, and by Major J. G. Pangborn of the Baltimore and Ohio Railroad who held that "with a compensation act friction is reduced to a minimum."

When the Civic Federation began to draw up model compensation bills, and to agitate in state legislatures and among state governors, no state had effective compensation legislation. The federal government had passed only a weak act in 1908 at President Roosevelt's insistence. The few attempts to pass compensation acts before 1909 had either failed, or the limited acts were unconstitutional. In 1907, for example, a commission of the state of Connecticut recommended continuation of the employer liability principle and opposed compensation. But beginning in 1909 many states appointed commissions to investigate the feasibility of compensation acts and to propose specific legislation. Three commissions were appointed in 1909; eight in 1910; twelve in 1911; seven in 1912. All these favored some form of compensation act.

Although there was widespread agreement on the need for compensation, the process of drawing up bills was far from smooth. Shortly after Belmont became head of the Federation's compensation department, he appointed a legal committee to draw up a model bill, and as its chairman appointed P. Tecumseh Sherman, a conservative lawyer and former New York Commissioner of Labor. Like most of those engaged in drawing up compensation measures, Sherman looked to Germany and England for guidance. The German system appeared to him to be best, as it was "an intimately interconnected system of compulsory insurance against sickness, accidents, and old age." But Sherman recognized that the paternalistic nature of the German system would raise constitutional problems, as well as hostility from labor. "Eventually," he hoped, "by general recognition of a social necessity, we may work up to some similar system of our own,"—one adapted, of course, to American conditions. Sherman admitted that his proposed bill was "a half-way measure—a mere entering wedge."

Sherman's original draft bill was widely distributed in May 1910. It was sent to the governors and legislators of all states that had appointed commissions to study compensation, and governors of other states were urged to consider such legislation. But both within and outside the Federation, Sherman's draft came under attack. As Sherman admitted to Seth Low, he was "conservative" on workmen's compensation and believed it should be compulsory only in hazardous industries. Raynall C. Bolling, of United States Steel, disagreed. His view was that compensation should be universal and compulsory, that it should include agricultural and domestic workers as well as industrial—so that it could not be condemned as class legislation. A third view, held by a number of middle-class progressives and by Socialists and labor men, favored state insurance rather than private, and emphasized the need for higher benefits than either Bolling or Sherman proposed. Within the Federation,

Hugh V. Mercer was the main opponent of Sherman's draft. Mercer represented Minnesota at a Chicago conference of the National Association of State Commissioners on Compensation in which ten states participated in late 1910. He was chairman of the conference and one of the three-man committee chosen to draw up a model bill. He argued that Sherman's draft was inadequate; and he was supported by George M. Gillette. Stressing the need for uniformity of state laws, a basic concern of the Civic Federation, Gillette suggested that since Mercer's draft would represent the proposals of ten states, the Federation ought not to come forward with a different proposal. But Low and Sherman considered Mercer's bill too radical. They insisted on having their own, and even refused to allow Mercer to present his alternative plan as a minority report of Sherman's committee. As Sherman told Easley: "the most conservative and least expensive scheme which is ours may prove the basis of comparative uniformity. At any rate the Civic Federation owes no apologies or explanations for not circulating the most radical and expensive plan of all—Mr. Mercer's."

Sherman's defense of his plan was a tacit admission of the charges levelled against the Civic Federation by Morris Hillquit, the Socialist leader, in 1911. Hillquit had described the "game played by the National Civic Federation" as "the shrewdest yet devised by the employers of any county." It took "nothing from capital"; it gave "nothing to labor." But it "does it all with such an appearance of boundless generosity" that "some of the more guileless diplomats in the labor movement are actually overwhelmed by it." Hillquit then quoted the Civic Federation's statement to employers on the need for compensation laws to forestall "legislation which will sweep away all the defenses of the employer." What this really means, Hillquit insisted, was that to ignore the movement for compensation would be to face the "danger that this agitation may give rise to a powerful political labor movement along Socialist lines." But Hillquit had no alternative proposals and his attack was used by Easley to assert that while the Socialists could offer nothing to labor short of socialism—which even the Socialist admitted was a long way off—the Civic Federation was providing for labor's real and immediate needs.

By December 1910, the Civic Federation was "getting requests from every part of the country by telegram and letter, from governors and legislators" for copies of the bill and other material. In January 1911, Theodore Roosevelt addressed the Eleventh Annual Meeting of the Federation and emphasized the need for workmen's compensation legislation. In a few years, he said, the Civic Federation's attitude, "while it seemed revolutionary to some very good people of an outworn philosophy," will be "so normal" that people "will be unable to understand how anyone ever took the opposite view." Ten days later, Sherman's bill was approved by the Executive Council of the Civic Federation. Up to this time, no state had passed a general compensation act, except New York, where the 1909 compulsory compensation act was declared unconstitutional in March 1911. But during 1911 compensation or accident insurance laws were passed in twelve states.

Although most corporation leaders and politicians of great prominence, such as Roosevelt and President Taft, had publicly endorsed workmen's compensation, there was a residue of conservative opposition to such "radical" social legislation. This was expressed in the courts, which at that time trailed behind the leaders of the large corporations and those politicians close to them, who were developing the new liberal, or progressive, ideology of the welfare state. The issue came to a head in the spring of 1911, when the New York Court of Appeals unanimously held, in Ives *vs.* South Buffalo Railway Company, that the conservative compensation act of that state was unconstitutional. Viewing the act as "plainly revolutionary" judged by common law standards, the court found it to be contrary to the positive limitations against deprivation of property without due process.

This ruling enraged Theodore Roosevelt, who months later complained to Hiram Johnson that for the past twenty-five years such decisions had served "to absolutely bar the path of social reform," thereby adding "immensely to the strength of the Socialist party." *The Survey*, a progressive magazine with close corporate connections, insisted that the decision would have been different "if a board of broad gauge business men," with "responsibility for vast property interests on their shoulders," had been on the bench, when this question was decided. Suppose, *The Survey* mused, J. Pierpont Morgan, Jacob H. Schiff, E. H. Gary, Andrew Carnegie, and James J. Hill were asked to decide whether compensation deprived them of property without due process. "Can anyone doubt what their answer would be. These men control great industrial enterprises. They know the value of the good will of employees. They know the value of public opinion. They know the wastefulness and the wickedness of the existing common law system. . . . They know the danger of such strained interpretations." These men, *The Survey* concluded, will be "quite as impatient as labor leaders or social reformers at the refusal of the Court of Appeals to pay closer attention to economic facts." This view was confirmed a few months later when Francis Lynde Stetson a lawyer for the International Harvester Company, P. Tecumseh Sherman and William J. Moran, lawyers who were members of the Civic Federation's compensation commission, criticized the Ives decision in a brief submitted to congress in behalf of federal compensation legislation.

When Roosevelt announced his candidacy for President in 1912, the Ives decision still irritated him. Speaking at the Ohio Constitutional Convention in Columbus that spring, Roosevelt supported laws permitting the recall of judicial decisions and recommended that the new constitution include such a provision. But the proposal to allow popular review of judicial decisions was too much even for the many businessmen who supported Roosevelt's position on social reform and the trusts. The effect was twofold: Roosevelt lost a good deal of support on this issue, and conservatives rushed to support compensation legislation and to recall the decision of the New York court by more traditional means. At the January meeting of the New York State legislature an amendment to the state constitution was drawn up to place workmen's compensation legislation outside the reach of the due process clause. The amendment was widely supported as a means to head off the demands of Roosevelt and the Progressive Party for recall of judicial decisions. Urging a vote for the amendment, *The New York Times* told Roosevelt's followers that this was a perfectly "safe, wholesome, proper case of referendum, and in these respects totally different from the revision of judicial decisions advocated by their leader."

In the election, the amendment carried overwhelmingly. *The Nation* hailed this " 'Recall' of the Ives Decision," and it was clear that compensation was no longer a controversial issue. At the Conference of Republicans of the State of New York in 1913, Elihu Root, also an active member of the N.C.F., spoke in favor of compensation, and the resolution in its favor was carried unanimously. Beyond that, the Conference resolved that "changed and changing social and industrial conditions impose new duties on government." It sympathized "with the humanitarian spirit now abroad in the world," and recognized "that there are other social measures besides workmen's compensation, which have been adopted in other countries and states, which must be seriously considered." The Republican Party, the resolution concluded, must "meet industrial and social demands of modern civilization, so far as they are reasonably consistent with our institutions."

Other state courts also adopted a more liberal attitude toward compensation, either in reaction to the agitation over the Ives decision or simply as a result of greater sophistication. In Washington, the state compensation act, which was compulsory and (unlike the New York law) set up a state insurance fund, was upheld as a valid exercise of police power. The courts of Massachusetts, Ohio, and Wisconsin upheld elective laws in 1912. As Clark B. Firestone, of the Firestone National Bank of Lisbon, Ohio, told the Fourteenth Annual meeting of the National Civic Federation: "We see things coming our way all over the field . . . Mr. Dooley has said that if the Constitution does not follow the flag, at least the Supreme Court followed the election returns, and the courts of our country have felt the breath of this new spirit; their later interpretations of the law have modified the rigors of Common Law fabric of employer's liability which gave the workman the stone of litigation instead of the bread of prompt and certain compensation."

Widespread agreement on the need for compensation legislation did not end all conflict over the reform. The Civic Federation, businessmen in general, and insurance companies in particular, still clashed with labor and the Socialists over specific bills and over questions of coverage, waiting periods, and state versus commercial insurance. Senator George Sutherland (Republican of Utah), who served as the chairman of the Civic Federation's Committee on Uniform Legislation Upon Workmen's Compensation, was instrumental in helping draw up legislation both for states and for the federal government. A member of the joint Congressional Commission on Workmen's Compensation, Sutherland was also author of a bill that passed the Senate in May 1912. It had the strong support of the Civic Federation, and of the Brotherhood of Locomotive Engineers, the Order of Railway Conductors, and the Brotherhood of Railway Trainmen. But Senate progressives opposed Sutherland's bill, the *New York American* urged House Democrats to vote against it "until the workmen's side of the case has a more considerate hearing," and the *Atlanta Journal of Labor* thought the maximum damages "grossly and grotesquely inadequate." The *New York World* commented wryly that the theory behind the bill appeared to be that the industrial worker should receive compensation for his injuries "corresponding to the soldier's pension for wounds incurred in battle."

A similar debate occurred in 1913 over legislation to replace the bill invalidated by the Ives decision. Three bills were introduced in the New York legislature in the wake of the Ives ruling. One of them, known as the Jackson bill, was supported by the State Federation of Labor. It provided for exclusive state insurance, for payments of two-thirds of weekly wages, with a $15.00 maximum weekly payment and ten years payment in case of death. The Foley Bill, supported by the administration, provided for commercial or mutual insurance. The McClelland, or National Civic Federation Bill, authorized company or state insurance at the option of the employer. Both the McClelland and the Foley bills provided one-half weekly wages, with a maximum of $10.00 per week. In the hearings on these bills, the Civic Federation took no public position because of the disagreement with its position by the labor members. The State Insurance Department opposed state insurance, and the labor men accused the State Superintendent of Insurance of acting for the insurance companies. Finally, a compromise was agreed upon. The act allowed private insurance companies, as in the Foley and McClelland bills, but provided for payments of two-thirds weekly wages, up to $15.00 per week. The businessmen and their allies in Albany conceded on the amount of money to be given injured workmen, but held out on the principle of private insurance. The business unionists sacrificed the principle of state insurance in return for immediately higher benefits. It was not the last time trade unionists and big business would reach a compromise of this kind.

Socialists continued to criticize many of the bills passed, and insurance companies continued to exert pressure against state insurance—attacking it as "socialistic." The Socialists drew up a model bill for introduction by Party legislators in several states; it provided for state insurance coverage of all industrial, agricultural, domestic, and office workers, and one hundred percent of wages for total disability. Their pressures tended to keep rates above fifty percent, but the debate in each state was different and the specific legislation varied widely in details. Despite Socialist and labor criticism, the movement was clearly a success. In 1911, after the Ives decision invalidated the New York law, no state had an effective compensation law; yet by 1920 every state but six in the South had one, and the federal government had amended the Act of 1908 to include all civil employees. This sweeping achievement was made possible by the concerted activity of the National Civic Federation, with the strong support of its big business affiliates. It represented a growing maturity and sophistication on the part of many large corporation leaders who had come to understand, as Theodore Roosevelt often told them, that social reform was truly conservative.

Chapter 10 PROTECTING IMMIGRANTS

The object of welfare concern, a half century and more ago, were poor immigrants in the cities. Who cared about them and why? In the following essay, which received the Organization of American Historians' Pelzer Award for 1971, ROBERT L. BUROKER *(1945-) answers that the people who cared were not so much businessmen as members of an emerging professional class. A member of Pitzer College's History Department, Professor Buroker is preparing for publication a book on the origins of the welfare state during the Progressive Era.*

With the decline in recent years of the welfare state as a major political issue, it is perhaps now time to trace its administrative history. American historians, fascinated by the partisan and ideological struggles of American liberalism, have produced a substantial literature on the intellectual and political movements which culminated in the New and Fair Deal. They know much less, however, about the social and technological changes which made a national welfare state possible, and they have little knowledge of earlier state and local contributions. This was a crucial phase in the modernization of American government, and social scientists and public officials as well as historians might profit from examining how bureaucracies began and what experiences prior to 1933 made such innovations possible.

Robert L. Buroker, "From Voluntary Association to Welfare State: The Illinois Immigrants' Protective League, 1908-1926," *Journal of American History*, LVIII (December 1971), 643-660. Reprinted with the permission of the Organization of American Historians and the author.

What happened in early twentieth-century America to spur the development of public welfare bureaucracies? Modernization, after all, implies that certain types of change have made other types of changes much more probable. Before a welfare state is feasible a society must have at least the following: (1) a permanent group of people who are continually occupied with social problems and who develop the expertise to deal with them; (2) provisions for the expansion and transmission of such expertise; (3) organization and techniques to integrate that expertise into public recognition and state action. While not exhaustive, these three criteria are necessary conditions for the development of a modern welfare state. How were they fulfilled during the Progressive era?

The years between 1900 and 1920 saw an enormous proliferation of voluntary associations to assist a variety of disadvantaged groups, including the impoverished immigrant with his unique set of problems. The history of the Illinois Immigrants' Protective League (IPL) during the Progressive era suggests how progressive movements contributed to the welfare state in America. What kinds of people were involved and why? How successful were their efforts to fulfill the three necessary conditions for a welfare state? What was the relationship between voluntary associations and subsequent government agencies?

Illinois, and Chicago in particular, experienced a massive influx of immigrants between 1890 and 1910 (see Tables 1 and 2). In 1910 there were 974,013 foreign born in Illinois. Between 1910 and 1919 there were 362,756 new arrivals from abroad. The League was organized in 1908 in response to the problems encountered by immigrants in the Chicago area. The idea for such a league came from a committee of a women's trade union group, which was formed to visit immigrant girls and women. One of the first efforts of IPL was to take over that work.

Table 1
Foreign Born in Illinois between 1910 and 1919*

Nationality	*Foreign Born in Illinois, 1910*	*Admitted Aliens Giving Illinois as Their Destination, 1910-1919*
German	311,680	45,875
Scandinavian	166,812	34,561
English, Irish, Scotch, and Welsh	214,161	44,207
Greek	10,487	24,088
Italian	73,085	77,489
Lithuanian and Lett	32,662	22,920
Polish	148,809	86,910
Russian	2,595	15,199
Slovak	13,722	11,507

*Grace Abbott, "Memorandum as to Work to be Immediately Undertaken by the Immigrants Commission (March 19th, 1920)," 1, Supplement II, Box 58, Records of the Illinois Immigrants' Protective League.

Table 2
Immigrant Aliens Admitted to, Emigrant Aliens Departed from, Illinois, and Net Increase or Decrease in Population, from 1892 to 1928*

Year	*Immigrant Aliens Admitted*	*Emigrant Aliens Departing*	*Net Increase or Decrease*
1892	46,012		
1893	45,686		
1894	22,783		
1895	16,798		
1896	22,093		
1897	12,067		
1898	12,129		
1899	18,795		
1900	27,118		
1901	30,509		
1902	45,845		
1903	63,378		
1904	57,457		
1905	72,770		
1906	86,539		
1907	104,156		
1908**	58,733	28,725	+30,008
1909	63,379	14,485	+48,894
1910	93,340	13,165	+80,175
1911	76,565	21,157	+55,408
1912	67,118	28,355	+38,763
1913	107,060	24,178	+82,882
1914	105,811	23,637	+82,174
1915	19,062	11,682	+7,380
1916	418	6,612	-6,194
1917	10,690	2,182	+8,508
1918	2,748	3,488	-740
1919	3,951	4,638	-687
1920	16,964	17,951	-987
1921	48,358	17,652	+30,706
1922	22,410	14,039	+8,371
1923	35,612	4,582	+31,030
1924	46,254	3,977	+42,277
1925	20,382	4,557	+15,825
1926	20,176	4,377	+15,799
1927	20,723	3,911	+16,812
1928	19,165	3,802	+15,363

*"Immigrant Aliens Admitted to, Emigrant Aliens Departed from Illinois," Main Collection, Box 47. Records of the Illinois Immigrants' Protective League.

**No departure figures are available before 1908.

Each year about 20 percent of the women and girls leaving Ellis Island destined for Chicago were unaccounted for at their destinations. Most were never found. Women and girls who did arrive often had incorrect addresses; some were taken to saloonkeepers or houses of prostitution by cabbies and expressmen. Many were picked up by policemen and "placed" in the homes of Chicago residents who had contacted the police department for just that purpose. Quite a few officers were involved in the racket, and many girls never reached their families. In 1910 Jane Addams wrote of the heartbreak these abuses caused:

> Every year we have heard of girls who did not arrive when their families expected them, and although their parents frantically met one train after another, the ultimate fate of the girls could never be discovered; we have constantly seen the exploitation of the newly arrived immigrant by his shrewd countrymen in league with the unscrupulous American; from time to time we have known children detained in New York and even deported whose parents had no clear understanding of the difficulty.

A related problem was the protection of all immigrants upon arrival at Chicago's railroad stations. Unscrupulous cabbies and expressmen used official-looking costumes and badges and a stock of foreign phrases to lure immigrant families into their vehicles, usually to charge them exorbitant fares, but often to transport them to labor camps in the Chicago area. The League planned to assist immigrants at the railroad stations and to support proposals for a federal protective bureau for immigrants in Chicago.

There were also flagrant malpractices by employment agencies which specialized in immigrant workers. Charging exorbitant rates, they often delivered men and women to employers in seasonal labor camps, many as far away as Wisconsin and Iowa. The immigrant was later discharged without any way of returning to Chicago. The League decided to investigate the situation and to recommend appropriate city and state legislation.

In general IPL tried to help the immigrant adjust to American life. As an article in the by-laws of the League stated:

> The objects of this organization shall be to apply the civic, social and philanthropic resources of the city to the needs of foreigners in Chicago, to protect them from exploitation, to cooperate with the Federal, State and local authorities and with similar organizations in other localities, and to protect the right of asylum in all proper cases.

Time and time again the League lamented its own and the public's colossal ignorance of immigrant life. One purpose from the beginning was to collect as much information as possible on the problems of various immigrant groups in Chicago. In this respect IPL was starting to develop the expertise necessary to manage a social problem. Acting on its information, according to the first *Annual Report*, the League would welcome newcomers and see that they reached their destination; guard them against wrongs at railroad stations, labor camps, and employment agencies; assist them in finding work; advise and encourage them to take advantage of the many co-operating educational facilities furnished by night schools, settlements, churches, YMCA, and others; supplement these when necessary; protect women and girls from prostitution and the white slave trade; personally visit to assist newcomers and to follow up assistance; confer with local, state, and national authorities, and especially with police.

Among IPL's founders were Margaret Dreier Robbins, social economist, suffragette, educator, and wife of the prominent progressive politician Raymond Robbins; Ernst Freund, University of Chicago law professor and later president of the American Political Science Association; Julius Rosenwald, chairman of the board of Sears, Roebuck and Company; Julian Mack, a judge on federal circuit court of appeals; and Samuel N. Harper, professor of Russian language and literature of the University of Chicago and son of William Rainey Harper, president of the University of Chicago. The most active members were the social workers. Addams was instrumental in getting IPL started, although after that her other duties kept her from being more directly involved. Sophonisba P. Breckinridge, a social worker and professor of social economy at Chicago, was active as an advisor to the League. Grace Abbott, later to become director of the Federal Children's Bureau, was the moving force behind the League. As executive secretary throughout most of its first twenty years, her professional approach to social work, her valuable experience, and her influential contacts in Illinois and throughout the country were indispensable to the League's operation.

These eight people were the most famous League leaders, but they represent only a small portion of the total leadership. Between 1908 and 1917 there were sixty trustees, officers, and executive committee members. Enough biographical information is available for forty of them to reveal definite patterns of occupation, age, religion, politics, education, and geographic backgrounds. A majority were members of a profession or the wives of members of a profession (see Table 3). The businessmen all worked for large-scale enterprises. Most were high-level managers in corporations, and not one worked in or owned a small business. The lawyers either had successful private practices in commercial law or worked in corporate legal departments.

Of those whose politics are known, nine were Republicans and four were Democrats. They ranged in age from twenty-six to sixty-seven, the mean age being forty-five. In leadership this was not a young organization, although several young women worked on the staff throughout this period. Of the twenty-one leaders whose religious preferences are known, fourteen were Protestants, five were Jews, and two were Catholics. Among those whose place of birth is known, there were thirty native Americans and only five foreign born. Those who had been born in the United States came from a variety of geographic backgrounds. Seven had been born in Chicago, eleven in other large cities, four in rural or small-town Illinois and seven in rural areas or small towns outside Illinois. It was a highly educated group (see Table 4). Almost two-thirds of them had a college degree, and over one-third of them had doctorates.

Table 3
Occupations of Forty League Leaders, 1908-1917

Occupation	*Number*	*Percentage*
Lawyer	7†(1)*	20.0†
Businessman	8 (1)	22.5
Professor	8 (1)	22.5
Social Worker	5	12.5
Physician	1 (2)	7.5
Journalist	3 (1)	10.0
Public School Administrator	1	2.5
Politician	(1)	2.5
Total	40	100.0

*Parentheses include the number of wives whose husbands practiced each profession.
†Total number and percentages include occupations of the husbands whose wives served as League leaders.

Table 4
Highest Educational Level Achieved by Thirty-Three League Leaders

Level	*Number*	*Percentage*
High School Only	10	30.3
Some College	2	6.1
Bachelor's Degree	7	21.2
Master's Degree	3	9.1
Doctorate	11	33.3
Total	33	100.0

A leader of the League was thus likely to be a Protestant, well-educated, middle-class, native-stock American. This is a familiar portrait of progressive reform, but while it discloses something about the people who participated in organizations like IPL, it does not explain why they chose to do so. Indeed, the most troublesome question for progressive historiography is simply raised again. Why, beginning around 1900, did so many of the American middle class decide that their country needed urgent reform? By most standards those were prosperous times, and materially the middle class was doing well. Discontent among workers, farmers, and immigrants seems logical, but not within the ranks of the relatively well-to-do.

The traditional and most enduring explanation is that progressivism was their response to industrialism. Through the state they wanted to remove the evils of the city and factory, aid the underprivileged, to regulate a capitalist economy, and democratize the American political system. It is a testament to the power of this thesis that over the years historians of widely divergent perspectives have reasserted it. Still, a crucial question remains unanswered. Why did some members of the middle class participate in progressive movements while others continued to support McKinley-Taft conservatism? An adequate explanation should be able to tell historians the relevant differences between these two groups. Moreover, the precise connections between aspects of industrialism and the responses to them are often left undefined. Several historians, including Samuel Hays, Robert Wiebe, Gabriel Kolko, and James Weinstein, have explored those linkages for businessmen in the new corporate economy, but other dimensions of progressivism (and especially social welfare movements) have yet to receive such explicit treatment.

In 1955 Richard Hofstadter offered a persuasive interpretation. According to Hofstadter, anxiety over declining status often motivated progressives to reform efforts.

> [T]he United States was a nation with a rather broad diffusion of wealth, status, and power, in which the man of moderate means, especially in the many small communities, could command much deference and exert much influence. The small merchant or manufacturer, the distinguished lawyer, editor, or preacher, was a person of local eminence in an age in which local eminence mattered a great deal. In the absence of very many nation-wide sources of power and prestige, the pillars of the local communities were men of great importance in their own right.

After the Civil War this began to change, and the result was a severe sense of dislocation on the part of the social groups which had traditionally provided community leadership.

> The newly rich, the grandiosely or corruptly rich, the masters of great corporations, were bypassing the men of the Mugwump type—the old gentry, the merchants of long standing, the small manufacturers, the established professional men, the civic leaders of an earlier era. . . . [T]he American [of the traditional groups] they knew did not lack opportunities, but it did seem to lack opportunities of the highest sort for men of the highest standards. In a strictly economic sense these men were not growing poorer as a class, but their wealth and power were being dwarfed by comparison with the new eminences of wealth and power. They were less important, and they knew it.

The status revolution thesis explains the behavior of many progressives. It is not so applicable to people like those who founded and directed the League. For one thing the status anxious progressives often resented the immigrant because he was a source of political power for the corrupt city machine. Moreover, it is unlikely that the people participating in IPL were experiencing status anxiety. The majority were well-educated professionals, and many were the first of their families to receive a college education. Several, instead of being replaced by the new plutocracy, were active participants in it. All but one of the lawyers worked for large corporations. Among the businessmen there was not a single small merchant or manufacturer. To a man they were part of the élite of the new economic order, and, in addition, several of them were self-made men, stock boys who became corporation presidents. The university professors and the social workers were members of professions which were rapidly growing as distinctive occupational groups. Thus, far from resenting the changes which industrialization and urbanization had brought to American society since the Civil War, the leaders of the League had every reason to feel self-confident since they were riding the crest of those changes. They represented the new occupations of corporate management and professional skill which were to become the élite strata of twentieth-century America.

Recent investigations of professionalism and bureaucratization during the Progressive era suggest another social basis for reform movements. The growing post-Civil War professional middle class is the subject of an important chapter in Wiebe's *The Search for Order: 1877-1920.* During this period most modern professional associations were organized, and those which practiced specialized skills became an integral part of urban-industrial America. Their self-awareness further accentuated rural-urban differences, and living primarily in the larger cities they understandably tried to focus increasing political attention on the problems of the city environment. Roy Lubove's *The Professional Altruist* describes the growth of social work as a profession. After using recent refinements of the sociological literature on bureaucracy and professions to explain the history of both social work and the public welfare agency, he concluded:

> Specialization and the idealization of expertise, the growth of an occupational subculture, and bureaucratization were instrumental in shaping the character of twentieth-century social work. These typical features of an urban-industrial society have affected not only the professions but most spheres of life, and their controlling influence will undoubtedly remain potent.

Hays discovered an important political result of these developments when he analyzed the social bases of municipal reform movements. Professionals as well as businessmen dominated these groups, and Hays found that what distinguished these reformers from their less active colleagues in business and the professions was their relatively recent arrival on the social and political scene. The businessmen came from large-scale industries which were but a half century old, and the professionals were "in the vanguard of professional life, seeking to apply expertise more widely to public affairs."

These insights suggest a more adequate explanation for why so many ostensibly comfortable people became at least social welfare progressives. By 1900 a social class based on specialized expertise had become numerous and influential enough to come into its own as a political force. Educated to provide rational answers to specific problems and oriented by training if not by inclination toward public service, they sensed their own stake in the stability of the new society, which increasingly depended upon their skills, and quite predictably turned attention to the misery of the urban lower classes. In this sense they were responding to the evils of industrialism and urbanism. They were themselves, however, as much a part of the modernization process as the sweat shop and the tenement.

The history of the League is consistent with this interpretation. Clearly IPL was concerned primarily with integrating the immigrant into American society. The leaders were not fundamentally dissatisfied with the American system, and they urged no radical changes. They were trying to solve problems of limited scope. Social theorists have often commented on the stabilizing influence which professionals seem to exercise. Indeed, as Talcott Parsons noted, "The development and increasing strategic importance of the professions probably constitute the most important change that has occurred in the occupational system of modern societies." A professional class can prevent serious conflict in a modernizing social system with glaring inequalities in wealth, status, and power. Professionals become experts at alleviating problems and adjudicating conflicts which might otherwise develop into significant disruptions.

Prior to the Progressive era the professions had been growing at an unprecedented rate. Between 1870 and 1900 the number of professionals per 100,000 population almost doubled. The professional labor force increased 245 percent in contrast to a 125 percent rate of growth for the total labor force. The expansion was greatest in architecture, teaching, and journalism. Most League leaders were members of the professional classes, and the plight of immigrants became a focus for their expertise. Whatever their differences, the social science professor, the journalist, the corporation lawyer, and even the corporate executive shared a belief that American society needed their special skills.

Another dimension to IPL leadership deserves special consideration. Thirteen among the forty IPL leaders were women, and most of the staff workers were young women in their twenties. Abbott was the moving force behind the League in its first two decades. A social worker, Marion Schibsby, directed the staff work throughout much of this period and stayed with her work during the financial crisis years of the early 1920s. The participation of women in reform movements is nothing new to progressive historiography.

Indeed, the suffragette and the female social worker had already become classic American types. One historian, however, has put these women in a most interesting perspective. Arthur Mann notes something fundamentally different between Addams' generation and generations of earlier female reformers. By 1900 the legal emancipation of women was almost completed, and a new social type was emerging. The career woman was replacing the feminist. Speaking of Vida D. Scudder, Addams, and their contemporaries, Mann states, "All these women the modern American will recognize as completely modern, whereas the feminists, whether Lucy Stone or Alice Stone Blackwell, Julia Ward Howe or Elizabeth Stuart Phelps, savor of an age unlike our own."

Addams recalled in *Twenty Years at Hull House* how, when she graduated from Rockford College, her first concern was to find a useful purpose for her training. She went to Europe, discovered the settlement house concept, returned to Chicago, and found her role at Hull House. With minor variations, her story is the story of many of these women. They were the first American generation of their sex to leave the household in large numbers and contribute significantly to the society outside the home. Women like Breckinridge and Abbott became highly competent social scientists and adminstrators. Like the corporation lawyer, the industrial executive, and the university professor, they were, as Mann suggests, part of the first generation of modern America. Far from being anxious to preserve their traditional roles, they were assertive career women, a new and permanent type in American society. In Boston, Scudder spoke for all such women when she wrote:

> Into this world . . . life with bewildering and contradictory theories, yet bent, as no other age has ever been, in the analysis of social evil and the right of social wrong–into this world we are born–we, the first generation of college women. In a sense, we represent a new factor in the social order. . . . Surely, I may at least say, that we make ourselves significant if we will.

In Chicago, the organizers of IPL were part of the larger search by an emerging professional class for the expertise to direct the advance of the new order.

How successfully did the League translate its objectives into results? The evidence indicates that between 1908 and 1926 it managed an impressive quantity of private and public social work. Operating with a staff which rarely exceeded ten or twelve people, it collected information on Illinois immigrant groups, established a case work service, aided new arrivals, improved the employment agency situation, and pressed for state and federal legislation. Its work went a long way toward fulfilling many of the functions of a modern welfare state agency.

The League began in 1908 to locate lost immigrant girls. It obtained their names through private agencies in New York and later through the United States Immigration Service. Representatives of IPL who were familiar with the language and European backgrounds of newcomers made regular visits. It helped to locate missing family members. Girls who needed assistance were put in touch with night schools and various available social agencies. From 1909 to 1915 the League contacted and helped 19,512 immigrant girls.

To protect all immigrants upon arrival in Chicago the League worked closely with newspapers to publicize the problem. In July 1910, the Chicago and Western

Indiana Railroad donated a small building across the street from the Dearborn station. There the League established offices, reception rooms, bedrooms, and baths. For the next eighteen months it was a well-matched battle between the female IPL workers and the cabbies and expressmen. There were numerous altercations, but the women won out, and the number of people aided by the League at the Dearborn station increased steadily through 1913. Between July and December 1910, the League helped 1,903 people. In 1911 the number increased to 5,204. The next year it tripled to 15,537, and in 1913 it increased to 41,322.

Throughout this period IPL negotiated with federal officials in an effort to obtain a federal bureau to protect immigrants in the Chicago railroad stations. In this effort they received the support of a number of influential Chicago civic associations, including the prestigious Commercial Club. In 1913 Congressman Adolph J. Sabath of Illinois introduced a bill to establish federal bureaus at stations like Dearborn. It became law in July 1913. The government rented a building near the station which was equipped with reception rooms, baths, laundry, and beds. These facilities, however, were rarely used. The government's most frequent excuses were the decline in immigration beginning in August 1914 and the fact that there were no provisions for getting people from the station to the federal building. The League offered to transport the immigrants, but in the end it had to carry on most of the station work itself. Congress failed in later years to appropriate sufficient funds, and IPL continued as the sole protector of new arrivals from abroad.

One of the first League projects was a thorough study of Chicago employment agencies. Abbott's research team discovered that of 289 licensed agencies in Chicago in 1908, there were 110 which specialized in immigrant workers. On the basis of the published reports of malpractices by many of these agencies, the legislature in 1909 passed amendments to the employment agency licensing laws which provided for stricter standards and better enforcement.

Besides these major activities, the League carried on a number of other projects designed to help immigrants adjust to American life. For several years, for example, until it persuaded the Bureau of Immigration to take over the task, IPL compiled a list of all children, aged six through sixteen, who came to Illinois by way of Ellis Island. These lists were furnished to truant officers and school superintendents in Illinois communities. During American participation in World War I the League handled 2,840 draft cases involving immigrant men. League members explained to alien registrants their rights and obligations under the laws and acted as interpreters in communications with draft boards. Beginning in the autumn of 1918 the League began to assist aliens in connection with the new income tax laws. There were a number of ambiguities in the laws relating to non-citizens, and IPL was able to get some of the regulations clarified. Case workers also assisted immigrants in filing their forms.

In 1918, at a time when the League was experiencing severe financial difficulty resulting from the war, the Illinois state legislature established the Immigrants

Commission within the State Department of Registration and Education. The League had been publicizing the need for such a commission for some time. On July 1, 1919, the new agency began its work. Abbott was named director, and, for all practical purposes, the staff of the League became the staff of the new Immigrants Commission. According to the authorizing statute, the new Commission was to:

> Make a survey of the Immigrant, alien born, and foreign-speaking people of the State, and of their distribution, conditions of employment, and standards of housing and living. Examine into their economic, financial and legal customs, their provisions for insurance, and other prudential arrangements, their organization, and their education needs; keeping in friendly and sympathetic touch with alien groups and co-operating with State and Local officials, and with immigrant or related authorities of other States and of the United States.

The Commission operated on a budget of $15,000 for the biennium. This sum did not compare favorably with the budgets for similar commissions in three other large states. For equal periods the California commission had $140,000; the New York commission had $51,200; and the Massachusetts commission had $56,000. In the following two years, however the Commission was surprisingly active. Under Abbott's direction two massive studies were completed and well-publicized by the press in 1921. One involved the educational needs of immigrants in Illinois, and the other reported the results of investigations on the immigrant and the coal mining communities in Illinois. Both studies prompted a variety of state actions. One, the attack on adult illiteracy, was especailly productive.

Abbott's study of the immigrants' education first brought to light the problem of illiteracy in Illinois. The report noted that Illinois ranked twenty-third among the states in the amount of money spent on schools for each $100 of taxable wealth. As a result, Abbott commented, "It was not surprising that the commission found that 96.9 percent of the women and 88.6 of the men interviewed in the course of its investigation . . . were not able to read and write English, and that 53.5 per cent of the women and 24.2 per cent of the men could not speak English.

Following the Commission's report, both the Commission and the League, now just a paper organization, made a concerted effort to collect as much data as possible on the problem of illiteracy in the state. They compiled a memorandum, "Startling Statistics on Illiteracy in Illinois," which did, indeed, include some startling findings. Illinois, it was discovered, ranked twenty-second among the states in the percentage of illiteracy and twenty-fifth in the percentage of native white illiterates. In 1910 there had been 168,294 illiterates in the state, and by 1920 the number had increased to about 174,000.

The most serious obstacle was a state law which forbade local communities from providing educational facilities for people over the age of twenty-one. The Commission, the League, and a number of other voluntary organizations including the Illinois League of Women Voters began a publicity campaign to amend the statute. Six years later they were successful. The legislature passed a bill that gave the communities of the state the power "to establish classes for the instruction of persons over twenty-one years of age, and to pay the necessary expenses of the same out of the school funds of the district." At the end of the decade there was significant improvement. By 1930 the number of persons ten years of age and over unable to read and write English had decreased to 153,507. The percentage of illiteracy in Illinois had been 3.4 percent in 1920. In 1930 it was 2.4 percent.

The illiteracy studies were only one example of the skill with which the League and the Commission collected statistics on social problems in Illinois. Abbott and her co-workers in IPL had long been known for their ability to conduct massive survey research. In 1914 Abbott and some other Chicago social workers were invited by the state of Massachusetts to conduct a statewide survey of immigrant problems. Their efforts were instrumental in the success of the Massachusetts Immigration Commission. It would have been impossible for a national welfare system to develop without the now commonplace tools of social statistics. Their refinement was primarily a nineteenth-century development, and IPL leaders were no exceptions among social workers in Europe and America in recognizing the usefulness of the innovations in applied mathematics. The Chicago School of Civics and Philanthropy, founded in 1903 by Addams, Abbott, Breckinridge, and others, offered regular courses to those wishing to join the new profession of social service administration. From the very first year one of the required courses was "Methods of Social Investigation," a class taught by Abbott and Breckinridge. It dealt with a variety of social research techniques including "the application of statistical methods to social problems, the collection and tabulation of data, the use and misuse of averages, index numbers and weighting." Since many IPL staff members were trained at this school, it is not surprising that the League and the Commission were able to ascertain both the quality and the magnitude of immigrants' problems in Illinois.

The Illinois Commission maintained a large and growing load of case work, primarily in the Chicago area. The Commission case load for a three month period increased from 332 in January-March 1920, to 874 during the same three months of the next year. The Commission also carried on IPL's work in supervising the assistance of immigrants at railroad stations. In the last three months of 1920, 942 people received assistance, and 1,218 received Commission aid at Chicago railroad stations in the first quarter of 1921.

Despite the Commission's successes, its functions were terminated by Governor Lennington Small's veto of its next biennial appropriation on June 30, 1921. In his farewell address the previous governor, Frank Lowden, had urged that the legislature continue to support the work of the Commission. The lawmakers had responded by voting a $58,000 budget for the years of 1921 to 1923. Small's veto was part of a last minute economy move which included vetoes or appropriations for a number of state agencies.

The Commission and League members were stunned on the evening of June 30, when they received word through the press that as of the next day, the beginning of a new fiscal year, the Illinois Immigrants Commission would cease to exist. At that time the Commission was working on about 500 cases, but it had to vacate its offices in Springfield and Chicago within a few hours. On July 2, the trustees of the League met to decide what to do in the face of the veto crisis. There was enough money to pay two people to finish the existing case load. The Girls' Protective Bureau at Hull House donated office space, and through July 118 cases and 117 new ones were either handled or referred. After August 1, Abbott and Schibsby handled case work themselves, and together during the next month they helped 145 new clients.

The trustees decided to try to raise about $5,000 each year for casework and to wait for the state to reactivate the Commission which still retained its legal existence. They had trouble raising the money, but by 1924 they were able to add four new case workers to the staff, making a total of six. During the next two years the League handled about 4,000 new cases. Finally, after five years of waiting and lobbying, the League decided to reconstitute itself as a private organization, a status which it has maintained to this day.

What can be concluded about the work of the League and the Commission through 1926? The evidence suggests that IPL, in both its private and public capacities, fulfilled the necessary conditions for a modern welfare state agency. It constituted a group of people who were continually concerned with social problems and who became experts on such matters. Through the Chicago School of Civics and Philanthropy, several League members laid the groundwork for the growth of an expertly trained profession of welfare administration. They collected and analyzed mass data. They publicized problems and thereby facilitated public recognition and state action. Finally, they actually performed welfare service work on a surprisingly large scale. They set an example of the type of organization which was necessary to administer a modern welfare system.

The League was only one of hundreds of voluntary associations founded between 1900 and 1920. There is no reason to believe that its experience was unique within its own reform era or throughout the history of American reform. Alexis de Tocqueville wrote of Jacksonian America that, "Wherever, at the head of some new undertaking, you see the government in France, or a man of rank in England, in the United States you will be sure to find an association." This perceptive observer captured something essential to the growth of American government. In a country where decision-making was highly decentralized and where the natural impulse was always toward local autonomy and a suspicion of government, the voluntary association assumed a crucial role in developing the expertise and the organization necessary to manage social problems. When the state finally acted, the minimum requirements of knowledge, personnel, and procedure were already available in the experience of private groups.

Mann has noted the absence of thorough histories of a number of important voluntary associations. Closer study of these groups might substantiate the thesis that in the United States voluntary organizations formed the basis not only for the welfare state but for the whole development of modern public bureaucracies. One can think of numerous examples of people involved in private organizations who assumed newly created government positions in areas where they possessed special skills. Perhaps this is only part of a larger pattern involving a characteristic if not unique American system of public administration, a system in which the voluntary association has usually laid the necessary foundation.

If this is so, the Progressive era deserves reinterpretation as a key transition period in American history. Historians have overemphasized the extent to which progressive reform was a reaction against industrialization and urbanization. Granted it was a response to the more severe evils of the city and the factory, but many progressive leaders were themselves a part of the emerging system. The corporation lawyer, the business executive, the social science professor, the career woman—all were the results of forces transforming a nineteenth-century nation.

If the experience of the League holds true generally, there were many influential progressives who were quite at home in urban-industrial America. They formed associations, and within those associations they developed and professionalized new skills. Max Weber saw professionalization and technical efficiency as two characteristics of the ideal type bureaucracy. Perhaps the Progressive era was among other things the era of the proto-bureaucratic association, a necessary link between agrarian, town meeting America and the America of the managed metropolis.

Part Five RACE

Chapter 11 WILSON DRAWS THE COLOR LINE

Of all the underprivileged groups in American society during the Progressive era, none was more scorned than black Americans. One would have thought that Progressives, as believers in social justice, would have been the last persons to make things even harder for blacks. But that is what the Wilson administration did, as NANCY J. WEISS *(1944-) shows below. Why did they do it? A specialist both in ethnic and twentieth-century history, Professor Weiss teaches at Princeton University.*

If broadened opportunities, political democracy, and social justice describe Wilsonian Progressivism, the man on the furthest fringe of that movement was surely the American Negro. Woodrow Wilson's first administration inaugurated officially-sanctioned segregation in the federal departments and witnessed ill-concealed moves to cut into already meager Negro patronage.

White liberals and Negroes alike worried the same question: how could Progressivism find room for race discrimination? Or, how could one explain the introduction of official shackles on the black man at a time when America was legislating the liberation and protection of the individual? The President, liberal publicist Oswald Garrison Villard declared, "fails utterly to see that to discriminate in his

Nancy J. Weiss, "The Negro and the New Freedom: Fighting Wilsonian Segregation." Reprinted with permission from the *Political Science Quarterly*, 84, (March 1969), 61-79 and the author.

democracy against anyone, is to bring his whole carefully reared edifice crashing to the ground."

Yet, federal segregation was less a new departure than the logical culmination of a decisive Southern—and national—trend. Moreover, despite the anomaly of a New Freedom bringing a new bondage, Progressivism and racism were in many respects interdependent. The early years of the Progressive era coincided with widespread Negro disfranchisement and the birth of full-scale, state-level Jim Crow legislative discrimination. Accustomed by imperial design and judicial decision to thoughts of racial superiority, white America linked Progressive democracy and equality to greater separation from Negroes.

I

By the election of 1912 most Southern states had succeeded in purging their political systems of Negro voters and office-holders. Those Negroes retaining the franchise generally aligned themselves as a bloc with the party of emancipation. But 1912 marked a turning point in national Negro political participation. Angry at Theodore Roosevelt's "lily white" Progressivism and alienated by incumbent William Howard Taft's concessions to racism, Negroes were fair game for Democratic efforts to split the solidarity of the bloc vote.

Democratic candidate Woodrow Wilson was a Southerner who concurred in his wife's outspoken belief in social separation of the races, a college president who barred Negroes from Princeton (and who later told darky stories in Cabinet meetings). Prominent Negroes faced the issue squarely: "We do not believe that Woodrow Wilson admires Negroes," W. E. B. Du Bois wrote with considerable understatement. And yet, he told readers of the NAACP's magazine *Crisis*, Negroes might well expect such a "cultivated scholar" to treat them with "farsighted fairness." Leaders of the race secured a much-publicized campaign pledge "to see justice done them in every matter, and not mere grudging justice, but justice executed with liberality and cordial good feeling." "Should I become President of the United States," Wilson promised in 1912, "[Negroes] may count upon me for absolute fair dealing and for everything by which I could assist in advancing the interests of their race in the United States." Even Villard proclaimed himself "quite delighted" with the candidate's position.

Thus, the election of 1912 saw the curious spectacle of the champions of the Negro lining up, albeit hesitantly, behind a symbol of Southern Democracy. "We sincerely believe," the *Crisis* intoned,

> that even in the face of promises disconcertingly vague, and in the face of the solid caste-ridden South, it is better to elect Woodrow Wilson President of the United States and prove once for all if the Democratic party dares to be Democratic when it comes to black men.

Although there is no way of measuring the Negro vote, observers speculated that roughly half a million black men would exercise the franchise in 1912. Du Bois has written that Wilson won the votes of nearly 100,000 Negroes in the North alone. While many Negroes voted for Roosevelt, Professor Arthur Link states that Wilson got "more [Negro votes], probably, than any other Democratic presidential candidate had ever received." In any event, it appears that influential Negro leaders and a significant part of the rank and file did break away from their traditional Republican affiliations.

After Wilson took office Negroes quickly discovered that their support packed little bargaining power. By the summer of 1913 segregated toilets, lunchroom facilities, and working areas had been ordered in the Departments of the Treasury and the Post Office, among others. Job segregation was especially evident in cases where Negro men had previously supervised white women. Some construed the new policies as a backhanded way of phasing out all Negro civil service employes, and pointed to cases where Negroes were shifted into separate departmental divisions later slated for dissolution. For the first time photographs were required on all civil service applications. The impact was so great that Booker T. Washington could write of an August visit to the nation's capital: "I have never seen the colored people so discouraged and bitter as they are at the present time."

Secretary of the Navy Josephus Daniels relates that the question of federal segregation was first introduced in high administration circles at a Cabinet meeting in April 1913, when Postmaster General A. G. Burleson brought up complaints over integration in the railway mail service. Burleson, a Southerner like Daniels, "was anxious to segregate white and negro employees in all Departments of the Government . . . he believed segregation was best for the negro and best for the Service." Secretary of the Treasury William Gibbs McAdoo (another Southerner) especially seemed to agree with him. Then, Daniels recalls, the Cabinet discussed the general question of Negro appointments. "The President said he made no promises in particular to Negroes, except to do them justice, and he did not wish to see them have less positions than they now have; but he wished the matter adjusted in a way to make the least friction." Although no action was taken, the Cabinet certainly made no effort to halt the beginnings of deliberate segregation.

Departmental segregation was a conspicuous reversal of a fifty year tradition of integrated civil service. With racism having infiltrated state and local systems, easily-delineated pressures pushed the Wilson administration toward federal discrimination. The administration, itself obviously Southern, paid considerable attention to senatorial influence from the James K. Vardamans, Benjamin R. Tillmans, and Hoke Smiths. Moreover, organizations like the National Democratic Fair Play Association worked as powerful lobbies for a racist outlook on the civil service. And the capital itself, as the New York *Evening Post's* Washington correspondent wrote, was "essentially a Southern city," where "the great majority of the white people . . . hold the Southern view of the negro. . . . " "The white men and women in the Government service," he continued, "have resented being compelled to associate with the negroes. *Never before has there been an Administration that dared to cater to this feeling, except in surreptitious ways.* . . . There has always been . . . a *wish* to do it, but not the *courage*." Forces defending racial equality finally gave way to long-latent desires for discrimination.

While segregation orders were conceived and issued by subordinates, it is clear that Wilson made little or no effort to stop them. He summed up his own attitude in a letter to the editor of the *Congregationalist*:

> . . . I would say that I do approve of the segregation that is being attempted in several of the departments. . . . I certainly would not . . . have . . . if I had not thought it to their [Negroes'] advantage and likely to remove many of the difficulties which have surrounded the appointment and advancement of colored men and women.

Federal appointment policy, on the other hand, initiated directly from the White House. Certain federal positions—like Register of the Treasury, Recorder of Deeds and Customs Collector for the District of Columbia, and Auditor of the Navy Department—as well as diplomatic assignments to black nations, were traditionally held by Negroes. Given their support for the Democrats in 1912, Negro leaders expected increased patronage. When Wilson took office the *Negro Year Book* reported that Negroes held thirteen significant federal offices and filled eleven posts in the diplomatic and consular service. By the end of 1915 nine of the former (plus four officials not listed in the original account) and three of the latter had "retired from office and white men . . . [had] been appointed to fill their places." Three years later just six diplomatic representatives and one judge were left. Wilson made only two key Negro appointments: Minister to Liberia and Municipal Court Judge of the District of Columbia. Negroes were especially incensed when the black Register of the Treasury was replaced by an Indian. Wilson lamely noted the difficulty of pushing Negro nominations past a Vardaman-Tillman-Smith Senate, but failed to explain his predecessors' perseverance in pursuing the same end. Negro leaders underlined the irony of an administration preaching social separation of the races, but sending a white envoy to a black nation.

Executive discrimination found considerable sympathy on Capitol Hill. During the first Wilson administration nearly two dozen anti-Negro measures were introduced in the House and Senate, "the greatest flood of bills proposing discriminatory legislation against Negroes" ever to come before the Congress. They ran the gamut from Jim Crow transportation regulations and armed forces enlistment to prohibition of miscegenation, civil service segregation, and repeal of the Fifteenth Amendment. Their sponsors were Southerners, and they made little or no progress, with only the miscegenation bill being reported by a committee.

II

Incorporating a remarkable ethnic, social, and occupational diversity, the youthful

National Association for the Advancement of Colored People seemed the logical forum for liberals of every cast who challenged the thinking of those supporting segregation. As chairman of its executive committee, Oswald Garrison Villard, grandson of famed abolitionist William Lloyd Garrison, led off with a steady letter-writing campaign designed to clarify the administration's stand on the race issue. He urged the President to repudiate a disastrous policy, due, he hoped, "to the individual initiative of department heads without your knowledge and consent." But Wilson insisted that departmental segregation was "in the interest of the negroes. . . ." "My own feeling," he wrote, "is, by putting certain bureaus and sections of the service in the charge of negroes we are rendering them more safe in their possession of office and less likely to be discriminated against." This gave spokesmen for the Negro grounds for open attack. On August 15, 1913, the NAACP filed an official protest at the White House against the "drawing of caste lines." Negroes "desire a 'New Freedom,' too, Mr. President." they asserted. The organization called for public response to their appeal for social justice.

Villard mobilized his liberal *Nation* and New York *Evening Post*; Boston *Guardian* editor William Monroe Trotter led off the Negro press reaction; and the NAACP's branches organized nationwide protest meetings. The press, both Northern and Southern, white and Negro, answered the call. Responding to suggestions for a letter-writing marathon, countless citizens flooded the White House mailbags. Hundreds of letters bore the signatures of Negroes of every station. More notably, however, the NAACP's appeal brought forth vocal support from white clergymen, professors, social workers, philanthropists, Progressive politicians, and leaders of other minority groups like Jews and women. The "harsh and humiliating discrimination," they wrote, was "an insult and an outrage upon American citizenship," "violating the spirit of the Constitution and opposed to the teachings of Jesus Christ." From all corners there arose cries of dismay over the "unjust and disheartening" measures instituted "in plain derogation of the policy favored by our fundamental law."

Beyond letters and editorials, white liberals exerted little, if any, more active pressure. Some appealed to their spokesmen in Congress to influence the President, and touched off critical communications from Capitol Hill to the White House. Congressman John J. Rogers of Massachusetts introduced resolutions urging investigation of treatment of Negro employes in the Treasury and Post Office Departments, but both measures died on committee calendars without gaining so much as a hearing. Some whites debated arranging a peaceful protest at the White House by representatives of the segregated employes, but nothing ever materialized. In short, white liberals spoke up vociferously for the Negro cause, but the issue never packed enough political leverage to evoke more effective tactics.

Negroes appealed to Wilson not only on grounds of humanitarianism, campaign pledges, constitutionalism, and plain American decency, but also on the basis of political expediency. The precarious Democratic strength established among members of their race in 1912 crumbled rapidly in the face of the President's policies, so that Negro Democratic politicians found themselves "in a political wilderness of dispair [*sic*]." The men who decried segregation were fighting for their very political lives. "We are constantly being called traiters [*sic*] and being threatened with bodily harm," the secretary of the National Colored Democratic League wrote to presidential secretary Joseph P. Tumulty. "We are publically [*sic*] and frequently charged with having sold the Race into slavery. . . ."

But these men were talking about more than their own careers. What they saw was a fast-disappearing opportunity to capitalize on Negro disaffection from the Republican fold. They continually emphasized that Wilsonian discrimination would mean political suicide for any vestiges of Negro Democracy in 1916. And Wilson countered just as consistently by insisting that segregation was not a matter of politics, but of humanitarianism. Certainly the size of the Negro vote, and the political leverage it wielded, were small, so that the immediate political benefits of courting Negroes were limited. But the chances for constructive reconciliation and for a useful precedent were not insignificant.

The future, and not only the political future, was very much on the minds of those who cried for a change in policy. What were the implications of the new caste system for future generations? There was no telling, protesters noted, what measures others might justify on the basis of the Wilsonian precedent. "Should the National Government adopt this seemingly simple provision," a prominent Negro professor wrote, "it would thereby sanction all of the discriminatory legislation on the statute books of the several states and would suggest and justify all such enactment in the future." Hand in hand with this caution went a curiously ambivalent attitude toward the President himself. Carefully noting Wilson's sincerity and highmindedness, many tried to rationalize his program as the work of underlings unbeknownst to him. What they feared more than anything, however, was the future election of a less scrupulous, less principled chief executive who would tailor Wilsonian segregation policies to more disastrous, far-reaching ends, affecting not only Negroes but possibly other minority groups like Jews.

With the public "campaign of making the White House just as uncomfortable as possible" gaining in momentum, Villard continued his own efforts at private persuasion. Finding Tumulty sympathetic to his arguments, he nevertheless had great difficulty in establishing any real understanding with the President on the race issue. While justifying departmental segregation, Wilson admitted that "in several instances the thing has been managed in a way which was not sufficiently thoughtful of their feelings . . . ," which provoked Villard to retort: "Believe me, it is not a question of handling segregation awkwardly or tactfully, or otherwise, it is a question of right and wrong." The interchange ended temporarily with the President pleading for time and tolerance:

> I hope . . . that by the slow pressure of argument and persuasion the situation may be changed and a great many things done eventually which now seem impossible. . . . I appeal to you most earnestly to aid at holding things at a just

> and cool equipoise until I can discover whether it is possible to work out anything or not.

Shifting focus from the White House to the departments proved no more rewarding. Villard informed Treasury Secretary McAdoo of a speech he intended to give concerning segregation instituted under McAdoo's jurisdiction. The ambivalence of the Secretary's reply summed up the sheer frustration encountered by those who tried to reverse the discriminatory policies. "There is no 'segregation issue' in the Treasury Department," McAdoo insisted. "It has always been a mischievous exaggeration." And yet, in the same letter he confessed,

> . . . I shall not be a party to the enforced and unwelcome juxtaposition of white and negro employees when it is unnecessary and avoidable without injustice to anybody, and when such enforcement would serve only to engender race animosities detrimental to the welfare of both races and injurious to the public service.

From the Negro's point of view, departmental segregation was anything but a "mischievous exaggeration." In November 1913 a group of prominent Negroes representing the National Independent Political League and sponsored by Massachusetts congressmen went to the White House to deliver a petition of protest against discrimination in the government service. Wilson seemed impressed by the protest and surprised at the conditions they mentioned. He assured the delegation that "segregation had not been decided upon as an administration policy," and promised further investigation. The protests reputedly made some impact, so that in December the New York *Evening Post* could write, "it seems plain that the word has gone forth that the segregationists must take the back track. . . . it appears that a return to former conditions is underway all along the line."

III

Despite token efforts, like removal of some signs on toilets, there seems to have been little concrete evidence of actual reversal of policies. In November 1914 the delegation of Negro leaders called again at the White House to discuss the situation. Headed by Boston *Guardian* editor Trotter, the group detailed instances of continued segregation, charged certain officials with race prejudice, asked for investigation and redress by executive order, and predicted Negro opposition to the Democrats in 1916. Wilson, dismissing any political considerations, "said that the policy of segregation had been enforced for the comfort and best interests of both races in order to overcome friction." The President ended the interview abruptly, announcing that he was insulted by Trotter's approach, and warning that any future meetings would have to be conducted by another Negro spokesman. The so-called Trotter incident provoked a new flurry of editorials and correspondence; even those who found Trotter's conduct objectionable agreed on the positive results of reintroducing the segregation issue into public discussion. Whether Trotter actually did anything out of order is open to doubt; Tumulty told Villard that the Negro's speech was "one of the most eloquent he had ever heard," and the President later admitted privately to Tumulty that "he was very sorry he had lost his temper as he had made a great mistake."

As the controversy over the Trotter interview died down another issue arose to take its place on Negro and white liberal editorial pages. President Wilson and his Cabinet had attended a private White House showing of "The Birth of a Nation," the controversial D. W. Griffith film based on Thomas Dixon's *The Clansman*. Featuring vicious distortions of Negro activities during the Reconstruction era, the movie was a potent weapon for inflaming white hatred of blacks. Indignant at this so-called "work of art, " Negroes organized nationwide protests calling either for censorship of particularly offensive scenes or for total banning of the film. In only a smattering of communities were they at all successful. The movie's producers delighted in justifying its value by noting that it had been screened without objection before the President and his Cabinet. Wilson, driven into a corner by persistent inquiries, lamely directed Tumulty to explain that "the President was entirely unaware of the character of the play before it was presented, and has at no time expressed his approbation of it. Its exhibition at the White House was a courtesy extended to an old acquaintance."

While "The Birth of a Nation" and federal segregation bred loud public protest, a private effort in behalf of the Negro was also taking shape. Largely unsuccessful at curbing Wilson's negative policies, white liberals and Negro leaders put forth a constructive suggestion of their own to grapple with the Negro's place in an expanding American democracy. The idea of a National Race Commission was first developed by R. H. Leavell, professor of economics at Texas A & M, and later taken up by Villard and the NAACP. The plan called for a presidentially-appointed, privately-financed, biracial, multi-sectional commission to investigate every phase of Negro life in the country, "with particular reference to his economic situation." Hopefully, the inquiry might ease racial tensions and provoke legislative recommendations from the White House. Moreover, the investigation would be in the best tradition of Progressive concern for social justice; it "would be of great service to the white South as well as to Negroes," for "a situation in which millions of people were living on the border line of destitution in the slums . . . ought to be intolerable in civilized communities. . . ."

The Race Commission plan spoke the purest language of Progressivism. Its primary objective—"to promote realization of democracy in America"—could be attained "by providing adequate opportunity for self-realization by all individuals of all classes or all races in ways beneficial both to the individual and to society." Those who drafted the proposal fully understood the American reform tradition of widening avenues of opportunity for the disadvantaged.

Villard took the plan to the White House in May 1913. He left the interview enthusiastic over Wilson's reaction; the President, he wrote to Professor Leavell, was "wholly sympathetic," promising to consider the proposal in the light of "his relations with the Senate and Congress, and what it will mean to him to antagonize the reactionary Southern politicians. As to the necessity of some such inquiry he was quite clear. . . . " Wilson postponed subsequent interviews throughout the summer, insisting that the Mexican crisis kept him too preoccupied for other considerations. Villard repeatedly sought authorization to proceed with the fund-raising; "I am particularly urging this upon you now," he wrote in August, "because of the intense dissatisfaction of the colored people at the treatment by your Administration thus far."

A few days later Wilson rejected the suggestion. With the balance of his legislative program still awaiting congressional action, he shrank from alienating powerful Southern congressional leaders. An investigation, he maintained, inevitably implied an indictment. Recalling his earlier receptivity, he admitted, "I never realized before the complexity and difficulty of this matter in respect of every step taken here."

Strikingly, the President's stand on the Race Commission sparked absolutely no public protest. Villard had purposely avoided any publicity of the negotiations, fearing that outside pressure might force Wilson's hand. At the same time, departmental segregation and appointments more than occupied the efforts of those championing the Negro cause. Indeed, the Race Commission "lobby" consisted of only one man—Villard himself. Various professionals and NAACP leaders made comments on the original draft, but the organization itself remained officially silent. The only recriminations after Wilson's refusal came in bitter letters from Villard. "Frankly, I feel very sorry that you find yourself 'absolutely blocked by the sentiment of senators,' " he wrote. "I believe that like your most immediate predecessors, the time will come when you will find it necessary to go ahead and do what is right without considering their feelings. . . . " But "[bowing] down to the god Expediency," Villard warned, ought not to demand continued segregation and non-appointment of Negroes. Unless Wilson faced squarely the place of the Negro in his New Freedom, the liberal editor predicted, "the feeling of bitterness among colored people towards your Administration and the Democratic party shall steadily increase."

Villard was right. The election of 1916 justified warnings that segregation policies spelled the end of an unusual opportunity to convert Negroes to the Democratic party. Unfortunately, there are no satisfactory statistics to indicate just how many Negroes broke away to vote for Wilson in 1912, or how many deserted the Democrats in 1916. Beyond just holding their own, the Democrats seemed unable to absorb any significant portion of the Negro voters who had defected from Republicanism to support the Progressive ticket in 1912. General contemporary comment indicates that Negroes "returned en masse to the party of liberation." In Negro Harlem, for instance, the Democratic vote slipped from 23.29 to 20.23 per cent, while the Republican share jumped from 17.67 to 77.99 per cent, undoubtedly including the 56.63 per cent who had voted for Roosevelt in 1912. More important than the overall tallies, leaders of the race who stumped for the Democrats in 1912 faced the 1916 election with nothing but distaste for Wilson. Their continued allegiance, promising future Democratic dividends of large-scale Negro support, would have been especially valuable.

Surely, Negroes in general found in their press little reason to stick with the Democrats. The New York *Age*, expressing the philosophy of Booker T. Washington and a supporter of Taft in 1912, declared for Charles Evans Hughes, as did the Washington *Bee*. The NAACP solicited explicit statements on the race question from both candidates. Tumulty responded for Wilson with a noncommital "he stands by his original assurances. He can say with a clear conscience that he has tried to live up to them, though in some cases his endeavors have been defeated." Hughes never answered the NAACP's letter, and left himself to be judged on the basis of a Nashville campaign pledge of "equal and exact justice to all. I stand for the maintenance of the rights of all American citizens, regardless of race or color." At first Association leaders reluctantly found Hughes "practically the only candidate for whom Negroes can vote." The *Crisis* eventually urged Negroes to disown both major party candidates, suggesting formation of an all-Negro party and ultimately advising abstention or a vote for the Socialist candidate.

In sum, in 1916 Negro leaders found their race courted by neither party. Despite years of agonizing controversy over their place in Progressivism, the political establishment was again trying its best to ignore the Negro question. Looking back on the election the *Crisis* summed up best of all the frustrating lack of progress toward enlisting those in power in the cause of a democracy not limited by the color line. By the peak of the Progressive era the President had proven "satisfactory as a reducer of the tariff, a promoter of currency reform, and as a man of Peace." "But," the editors wrote, "he was still the representative of the southern Negro-hating oligarchy, and acknowledged its leadership." By the same token, "Mr. Hughes was the author of several of the best decisions in favor of the Negro that the reluctant Supreme Court has ever handed down. At the same time, on specific Negro problems he was curiously dumb."

IV

Why were Negroes and white liberals unsuccessful in extending the boundaries of a Progressivism limited "to whites only"? Wilson argued that his sentiments were on the side of the protesters, but that courting Southern senatorial support for his Progressive legislative package made it impossible for him to act in their behalf. Yet he straightforwardly advocated "separate but equal" as mutually beneficial to both races.

It is too easy, however, to attribute the stalemate to executive inhibitions alone.

The key still seems to lie in the nature of the protest. Negro groups lacked a cohesive, tightly organized program. Gaining the right to vote, and fighting lynching, preoccupied much of their effort. This was the decade of landmark Supreme Court decisions striking down the Grandfather Clauses in state voting requirements and levelling an initial blow at residential segregation. For many, these struggles were much more important than gaining political positions. But Negroes disagreed over more than just priorities affecting their race alone. Looking at the national scene, many played down their grievances; "we believe," a North Carolina cleric told Wilson after Trotter's White House demands, "that he should not have approached you with a minor domestic protest when you are filled with graver responsibilities. . . ."

These disavowals were well calculated to cripple the effectiveness of any organized protest. The Negroes who wrote to the President claiming that "Mr. Trotter does not represent the Negroes of the United States," or that "the more thoughtful" members of the race "don't approve of Mr. Trotter's insult to you," may honestly have been ashamed of his reported disrespect. But they also testified to the exceptional fragmentation of Negro leadership. Theirs was largely the fading gasp of a Washingtonian theory of Negro conduct, reflecting the growing split in Negro philosophies of self-advancement.

In previous Republican administrations Booker T. Washington had been recognized as "the office broker for the race," or chief consultant on Negro patronage and policies. Publicly conciliatory toward the white South, the Tuskegee educator subordinated eventual attainment of political and civil rights to the more immediate goals of moral and economic progress through self-help and vocational training. The Wilson administration found Washington newly out of favor not only in official circles, but also among the ranks of leading Negroes. New expectations and new spokesmen came to prominence with the Democrats. Seriously challenging the old, more accommodating outlook, fathers of the Niagara Movement, like Du Bois and Trotter, stressed immediate equality–social, economic, *and* political–and urged agitation to reach these goals. The inability of these men to agree among themselves contributed to a proliferation of loose factions and formal groups all in the same fight without meaningful coordination of efforts.

The protest movements petered out, too, because they eventually lost even their divided leadership. Villard, certainly their most influential white spokesman, became preoccupied with keeping the United States out of World War I. Washington died early in 1915, and Bishop Alexander Walters ("the new political leader of his race for the incoming Democratic administration at Washington") was dead before Wilson's second inaugural. Discredited (however unfairly) among Negroes and whites alike after the White House incident, Trotter quickly began to "slip . . . out of the main current of the protest movement." A foe of accommodation, he nonetheless divorced himself from the activist Du Boisian camp, and never took full advantage of cooperation with white liberals. Du Bois, too, had already generated considerable friction with white NAACP leaders. In 1916 he decisively curbed his effectiveness when he told Negroes, in effect, to throw away their votes and abandon the regular political process, surely their best hope for any kind of influence on the status of the race in Wilsonian Progressivism.

Even if we accept this analysis of deficiencies in the protest movement, it is still important to ask whether we may not be overstating the case. In short, could Negroes have been expected to make much of a dent in Wilsonian segregation policies? The national apotheosis of Jim Crow militated strongly against any possible hope of success for the champions of the Negro cause. But the generation of the current Negro revolution may still wonder over the striking lack of militancy in the protests of the Progressive era. The afflicted exercised unusual restraint and self-discipline, engaging in thoroughly polite, deferential opposition. In the second decade of this century, hardly more than a generation removed from the demise of Reconstruction, Negroes were in considerable part an ex-slave population. Their educational level and political consciousness were still barely above a minimum. It is a commonly accepted principle of social science that a submerged group must reach a certain plateau before it can even begin to rebel, and most Negroes of the Wilson era were still struggling toward that level. The birth of the NAACP, fusing white liberal strength into the Niagara Movement, was barely three years past when Wilson took office. The transition in Negro thinking from a Washingtonian to a Du Boisian approach was an important one, and one whose earliest stages coincided with the birth of the New Freedom. Negro protest, symbolized and centralized chiefly in the NAACP, was a very new, highly improvised instrument in the Wilson era—an instrument which took nearly forty years to impress upon the nation the gravity and sincerity of its purpose.

Chapter 12 PROGRESSIVES FOR EQUAL RIGHTS

Contrast the racism just described with the movement for equal rights depicted below. Founded in New York City a few years before World War I, the NAACP and the National Urban League are a vital part of the Progressive legacy, as GILBERT OSOFSKY *(1935-   ) reminds us. His essay is a further reminder, if read in conjunction with Nancy Weiss', that the Progressive mind was not of a single piece. The author of an important history of Harlem, Professor Osofsky has been teaching since 1963 at the University of Illinois, Circle Campus.*

From the 1890s through the first World War there was a significant migration of southern Negroes to northern cities. It was the migration of Negroes in these years, in fact, which laid the foundations for the development of large, segregated Negro communities in New York City, Chicago and Philadelphia. As the Negro populations of these areas increased rapidly, the dominant reaction of the majority of white Northerners was one of heightened racial hostility. There was an overall hardening in patterns of social and residential segregation, and occasional outbreaks of racial violence, in every city to which Negroes came in large numbers. "One of the striking developments of very recent years," wrote one northern commentator in 1906, "is the recrudescence of prejudice against people of African descent. . . ."

Gilbert Osofsky, "Progressivism and the Negro: New York, 1900-1915," *American Quarterly*, XVI (Summer 1964), 153-168. Reprinted with the permission of the *American Quarterly*, the author, and the University of Pennsylvania as publisher.

The emergence of racial violence and antagonism, and the increasing number of varied social problems brought on by Negro migration, created a need for reform in the North in the early twentieth century. The movement for social and economic reform in northern cities, a vital part of the national Progressive movement, was deeply concerned with the welfare of the Negro People. In the years preceding World War I there was a revitalization of interest in Negro life among Progressives in every major northern city. These reformers, were, in the words of a Negro businessman, the "doers" not the "talkers" of American society.

The white people involved in this movement were primarily social workers and urban reformers who had established settlement houses or tried in other ways to improve living conditions in the industrial and tenement-house areas of northern cities. They also established settlement houses for Negroes in the North–many of them branches of parent organizations founded for immigrants in the 1890s. In the first decade of the twentieth century Progressives organized the Frederick Douglass Center in Chicago, the Robert Gould Shaw House in Boston, the Eighth Ward Settlement in Philadelphia, the Stillman House and two Lincoln Settlements in New York. Frances Bartholomew, Carl Kelsy and R. R. Wright Jr., in Philadelphia; Isabel Eaton in Boston; Celia Parker Wooley, Sophinisba Breckinridge and Louise DeKoven Bowen in Chicago; Mary White Ovington, Victoria Earle Matthews and William Lewis Bulkley in New York City were all actively engaged in social work among Negroes. Perceptive studies of Negro society were undertaken as well in these years. In typical Progressive fashion, volumes of facts and statistics were gathered in order to learn how best to improve living conditions. "We must not forget," wrote W. E. B. Du Bois in 1903, "that most Americans answer all queries regarding the Negro *a priori*, and that the least that human courtesy can do is to listen to evidence." Between 1899 and 1915 such works as Du Bois' *Philadelphia Negro* (1899), Ray Stannard Baker's *Following the Color Line* (1908), R. R. Wright Jr.'s *The Negro in Pennsylvania* (1908), Mary White Ovington's *Half A Man: The Status of the Negro in New York* (1911), George Edmund Haynes' *The Negro at Work in New York City* (1912), Louise DeKoven Bowen's *The Colored People of Chicago* (1913), Frank U. Quillin's *The Color Line in Ohio* (1913), William A. Crossland's *Industrial Conditions Among Negroes in St. Louis* (1914), John Daniel's *In Freedom's Birthplace: A History of the Boston Negro* (1914), and Frances Blascoer's *Colored School Children in New York* (1915) were published. Numerous articles on Negro life also appeared in contemporary periodicals. In 1909-11 the first national Negro defense and improvement societies were founded–the NAACP and the National League on Urban Conditions Among Negroes. Both were founded in New York City. The general movement to improve the status of the Negro in the North in the first decade of the twentieth century was led by persons, Negro and white, who responded in a positive manner to the same problems that produced increased alienation among the majority of Northerners.

Concern for the welfare of Negroes among the white people of New York City had traditionally been associated with religious groups, and more particularly with the Society of Friends. Quakers were leading abolitionists in New York and played an important part in founding free schools for Negro children. After the Civil War, the only white organization that continued its works among the city's Negroes was the New York Colored Mission. There were a few Negro churches in these years, however, that gave some assistance "to needy persons who find themselves in the great city without a home for a few days."

The "Friends' Mission," as some contemporaries called it (more vituperative observers named it the "Nigger school"), was founded primarily as a religious institution which did missionary work among Negroes and offered them "Christian Fellowship." It distributed religious tracts, temperance literature and Bibles by the thousands to New York's Negro population. Prior to its incorporation in 1971, the society had been called the "African Sabbath School Association." When it was incorporated it conceived of its task basically as a religious one: "To conduct in the city of New York a Sabbath School for Religious Instruction," and hold "Social, Religious Meetings." Whatever practical assistance the organization would give Negroes was to be secondary to its religious obligation. The City Mission and Tract Society contributed enough money to the Colored Mission to permit it to purchase a building of its own in the Tenderloin, the midtown area of Manhattan in which the majority of the city's Negroes then lived. "Inasmuch as ye have done it unto one of the least of these my brethren, ye have done it unto me," was the motto of the organization.

In reality, however, as the Negro population of Manhattan increased, slightly in the 1870s and 1880s, more rapidly in the 1890s, the Colored Mission was slowly transformed into a social service agency. It conducted an employment bureau, provided temporary housing and inexpensive meals for migrants (a "Sunday bowl of soup and slice of bread"), opened a small "infant school" which cared for and fed Negro children for five cents a day, and bought glasses for Negroes who wanted to learn how to read (most wished to read the Bible). Destitution was so widespread in the depression winter of 1893-94 that the Colored Mission distributed tons of coal and barrels of food to Negro families—flour, corn meal, oatmeal, hominy, rice, bread, beans, pork, milk. "The records of those months are so sad that one shrinks from recurring to them," wrote the society's missionary. "No fire, no food, dispossession inpending, illness, death . . . confronted us." Between the Civil War and the 1890s, with this one modest exception, there were no organizations in New York City concerned with the welfare of Negroes. By 1915 there were more than a dozen.

Increasing interest in Negro life emerged in the 1890s and the first decade of the twentieth century among white and Negro reformers. The movement was widespread and involved some people who disagreed with one another on the overall methods of improving the position of the Negro in American society. Some were avid supporters of the gradualism of Booker T. Washington, others were followers of W. E. B. Du Bois. Whatever theoretic differences may have existed among them, there was basic agreement on the need for solid, practical reforms which would immediately improve the generally harsh lives of Negroes in the city. Reformers were primarily concerned with finding jobs and decent homes for Negro migrants, opening playgrounds for Negro children, breaking down the color barrier in employment opportunities, improving health and sanitary conditions in the Tenderloin, San Juan Hill and Harlem (two other areas of Negro concentration), protecting Negro domestics from the exploitation of employment agents.

The first organization that this new spirit of social welfare produced was the White Rose Industrial Association. The "White Rose Working Girls' Home" (as the sign which hung over its door read) was founded in 1897. Its organizer was a Negro, Mrs. Victoria Earle Matthews.

Mrs. Matthews was the youngest daughter of a Georgia slave. She was born into slavery herself just one month after the Civil War began, but came to New York with her mother and family in the 1870s. When she arrived in the city Victoria was young enough to attend the Negro public schools, and after graduation she became a writer. Her stories and articles were published in white and Negro journals. She thought of herself as an emancipated woman, founded a Negro protest and women's rights society in the city (the "Women's Loyal Union of New York and Brooklyn"), and delivered lectures on "The Awakening of the Afro-American Woman." When she learned of the "unscrupulous employment agents who deceive the unsuspecting girls desiring to come North," Mrs. Matthews decided to "check the evil." She established a home which provided lodgings and meals for women until they were able to find work. The society kept agents at piers in Norfolk as well as New York City to answer questions, escort women to their places of employment or, instead, to the White Rose Home. Aside from this, its major function, Mrs. Matthews and her fellow workers extended their activity to the general Negro population of New York City. The White Rose Home became a settlement house as well as a temporary lodging place for migrants. The classes that were presented there in domestic training and "race history," the library of books on Negro life, and the facilities for recreation were all open to the public as well as to residents of the home. The Home continued its work among Negroes even after Mrs. Matthews' death in 1907, and finally moved to larger quarters in Harlem in 1918.

The same fear of exploitation of Negro women by "intelligence agents" that motivated Victoria Earle Matthews led to the founding of an organization which attempted to do on a national scale what the White Rose Home did for Negro migrants who came to New York City. The initiator of this movement was the white reformer Frances A. Kellor. She also spent a good part of her early crusading career attacking the corruptions of private employment bureaus. In 1903, sponsored by the Woman's Municipal League of New York, she was given the responsibility of collecting as much data on the problem as a thorough investigation could produce. She gathered information from 732 private employment agencies, published her findings in 1904 in *Out of Work: A Study of Employment Agencies* and bombarded municipal officials with the information she had uncovered. Her criticisms and prodding resulted in the creation of the Office of Commissioner of Licenses in New York City, and were also influential in establishing the first state-controlled employment bureau in New York in 1911.

The underlying concern that seemed to motivate Frances A. Kellor and other municipal reformers in this area was not only that many employment agents were dishonest and treated their clients in a shoddy manner, but that many agencies were used as guises which subtly tried to draw women into the arms of "the alluring procuresses of the city." Some Negro women were given jobs as maids and cooks in what Miss Kellor called "sporting houses." "They are often threatened until they accept positions in questionable places and are frequently sent out without knowing the character of their destination," she wrote in *Out of Work*. The recruiting of women for "immoral purposes" by "intelligence agents" was the first point the Commissioner of Licenses listed in a memorandum which explained why the office had been created. "The southern states, especially Virginia and Georgia, are honeycombed with the slick agents of these employment bureaus," Miss Kellor said in 1905. ". . . good wages, easy work . . . and good times, are promised. . . . To them, going to Philadelphia or to New York seems like going to Heaven, where the streets will be paved with gold, all will be music and flowers!"

The disparity between image and reality led Miss Kellor to establish a society for the protection of Negro women—the National League for the Protection of Colored Women. The League had offices in New York City and Philadelphia and agents in many southern port cities. It distributed literature to southern Negro pastors and schools urging them to "educate the women of these conditions." Like the White Rose Home, and sometimes in conjunction with it, the League stationed its workers at the major depots within the city and offered general fellowship and advice to country strangers who came to town for the first time: "It is the aim of the League to furnish helpful information to colored girls who are intending to come North, to protect them during the journey . . . and to find work or friends or homes for them" when they arrive. The National League for the Protection of Colored Women continued this work until 1911 when it became one of three Negro reform agencies which consolidated into the National League on Urban Conditions Among Negroes.

Victoria Earle Matthews and Frances A. Kellor were reformers who concentrated primarily on a single problem—the exploitation of Negro domestic workers. The first prominent New Yorker to fully devote her energy to improving all aspects of Negro life in New York City, and eventually in the entire nation, was Mary White Ovington.

Miss Ovington's background was similar to that of many other urban reformers of her generation. She grew up in comfort and gentility, the daughter of a well-to-do New York merchant. Her home in an exclusive section of Brooklyn was geographically not too distant from the working-class districts, but it was as separate from them in spirit as two distinct worlds could have been: "In my youth," she recalled in an autobiographical sketch, "no place was more remote than the section of the city in which persons of different caste lived."

The patrician's daughter had the typical education of a young woman of refinement. As a child she studied exclusively in private schools, and when she was ready for college, Miss Ovington was sent to Radcliffe. After her graduation the family expected her to take her proper place in society—"what we called 'going into society,' " she said. But the quiet, secure and stable world into which Miss Ovington was born seemed too remote in the America of the 1880s and 1890s. Industrialization had created major social problems on a scale unequaled in the previous history of the nation. It had created slums, and the immigrants who lived in them often experienced poverty, distress, illness and a sense of hopelessness which was difficult to overlook: "I found out about conditions in my own city of which I was utterly ignorant," she remembered.

Miss Ovington's reaction to these new conditions, similar to the responses of other Progressives, was positive and optimistic. Involvement in a movement for social reform also gave added meaning and fulfillment to her own life. There was, she recalled, a "fervor for settlement work in the nineties, for learning working-class conditions by living among the workers and sharing to some small extent in their lives. . . . The desire for such knowledge was in the air—hope was in the air." In 1896 Miss Ovington opened a settlement house "among white working-class people" in Greenpoint, Brooklyn. Her five-room home grew into a forty-room settlement in the seven years she remained there. "That I should later work for the Negro never entered my mind," she wrote.

Her first awareness of the seriousness of Negro conditions in the city came at a lecture given by Booker T. Washington. The "Social Reform Club," of which she was a member, invited Washington to speak before it. He apparently described in detail many of the restrictions on Negro equality in New York City and Miss Ovington was shocked to hear about them: "To my amazement I learned that there was a Negro problem in my city. I had honestly never thought of it before." She decided at that time to find out more about these conditions and, from 1904 till her death in 1951, devoted her life to trying to improve them.

Although Washington's descriptions may have appeared new and shocking to her as an adult, Mary White Ovington had heard similar stories as a child. The Ovington family had originally come from New England. William Lloyd Garrison had been a friend of her grandmother's. Miss Ovington was born in 1865 and grew up when memories of the Great Rebellion were very much alive. She listened attentively to her grandmother's tales of abolitionism, the Underground Railroad, anti-abolitionist rioting in Boston, and the preaching of Garrison's close friend and follower, the Rev. Samuel J. May. She was taught to despise Daniel Webster and Henry Clay for compromising on the slavery issue. When Frederick Douglass came to speak at

Plymouth Congregational Church, Miss Ovington went to see one of her idols. "I was," she wrote, "a sympathetic listener." Garrison "was my childhood's greatest hero."

Mary White Ovington's parents were abolitionists too. Her father told her that he severed connections with Plymouth Congregational Church because Henry Ward Beecher dealt with a missionary association which had contact with a slaveholder. He joined a Unitarian congregation (and his daughter continued in this religion) led by an abolitionist "of the strictest brand." "Ours was an abolition family," she recalled.

The Ovington family, similar to other supporters of abolitionism, lost contact with Negro life after the Civil War. Slavery had been the great evil and it was destroyed. The Thirteenth, Fourteenth and Fifteenth Amendments were passed and Negroes were legally made equal American citizens. It seemed to them that there was nothing left to be done: "Slavery was ended," she said. "That was the great point."

Booker T. Washington reawakened Miss Ovington's interest in the Negro people. She decided to open a settlement house for Negroes in New York City and asked Mary Kingsbury Simkovitch of Greenwich House for advice. They both decided that the first thing to be done was to gather as much specific information as possible on Negroes in New York City. Miss Ovington was made a Fellow of Greenwich House in 1904 and began the studies which led to the publication of *Half A Man* seven years later.

The difficulties Negroes faced in finding decent and inexpensive living accommodations impressed her as a most important problem. Henry Phipps, steel magnate and philanthropist, had previously constructed model tenement houses for immigrants in the city. The City and Suburban Homes Company managed them and Phipps accepted the modest profit of 4 per cent on his investment. Miss Ovington and Phipps had a mutual friend, John E. Milholland, whom she went to see. Milholland was convinced of the need for the project and he, in turn, persuaded Phipps to construct a model tenement for the Negroes of San Juan Hill. When the Tuskegee Apartments were completed on West 63rd Street in 1907 they seemed an incongruity in the neighborhood. This fireproof, steam-heated, roof-gardened, six-story house stood out against the older rundown tenements on the West Side. (The Phipps apartment houses have survived a half-century of construction and can still be seen today.) Miss Ovington also hoped that Phipps would support a settlement house for Negroes in the building and decided to live there herself: "I hoped by quietly renting on my own account, to persuade him to add social work."

She moved into the Tuskegee Apartments, the only white person in the entire house, in January 1908. There she gathered information for her book, became a close friend of the Rev. Dr. George H. Sims of Union Baptist Church on the block, attended his services occasionally, and read "Peter Rabbit" and other stories to the Negro youngsters who knocked at her door. (She later published stories for Negro children.) Miss Ovington lived on West 63rd Street for eight months, but was unable to get the philanthropist to support a Negro settlement house there. In September 1908, as is well known, she read an article in *The Independent* which diverted her attention to broader Negro problems and changed the course of her life. William English Walling's "The Race War in the North" attacked the growing racial antipathy and apathy that were developing in the North and called for a revival of "the spirit of the abolitionists. . . . " Miss Ovington responded to this appeal and called a small meeting of her friends to discuss what could be done to counteract this burgeoning racism. A National Negro Conference met in 1909 at the Henry Street Settlement House. The NAACP was born of the National Negro Committee that was established at this conference, and Mary White Ovington spent the rest of her career working within this organization.

Although her main energies were channeled into the NAACP (she was called "Mother of the New Emancipation"), Miss Ovington continued to be active in social work among New York Negroes. She was an executive of the Committee for Improving the Industrial Condition of the Negro in New York City, chairman of its "Neighborhood Work" subcommittee, president and main fund-raiser of the Lincoln Settlement which she helped found for Negroes in Brooklyn, and organizer of the West End Workers' Association which was active among the Negroes of San Juan Hill. The Negro woman who was her private secretary from 1905 till her death remembers Miss Ovington as a person who was totally dedicated to the struggle for Negro rights and honestly devoid of any racial prejudice. "No white woman's life in America has been colored more by the clash of color and race," editorialized a Negro newspaper. "That the sincerity of my friendship has never been doubted," wrote Miss Ovington when she resigned as Chairman of the Board of Directors of the NAACP, "has been my greatest joy."

The reforming zeal that was evident in Mary White Ovington reached a high point in 1906 when the Committee for Improving the Industrial Condition of the Negro in New York (CIICN) was founded. The primary motivation that led to the organization of the CIICN was the desire to broaden employment opportunities for the city's Negroes. Its members, supporters, directors and subcommittee chairmen were the most important reformers in New York City in the Progressive era. Many of them were later active in the NAACP and other areas of municipal reform. The CIICN was interracial in structure and was composed of social workers, philanthropists, educators, clergymen, writers, publishers, physicians, supporters of Hampton and Tuskegee, businessmen. The founder of the CIICN was a Negro principal in the New York City school system, Dr. William Lewis Bulkley. Bulkley was motivated to organize this Committee, he said in 1906, after seeing Negro students leaving his school "to open doors, run bells or hustle hash for the rest" of their lives.

Dr. Bulkley was the leading Negro educator in New York City in the early twentieth century. He was a bright, idealistic and ambitious man who had risen from the slavery into which he was born in South Carolina in 1861 to earn a doctorate in ancient languages and literature from Syracuse University. As a boy he attended the local log cabin school and finally graduated from Claflin University, in his home state, in 1882. He came north to continue his studies at Wesleyan University in Connecticut and at Syracuse. In 1893, after completing his master's degree, he earned the Ph.D.

For a time, Dr. Bulkley was a professor of Latin and Greek at Claflin University. During his student days, however, he had taken a variety of odd jobs to support himself. At different times he worked as a janitor, a steward, a cook and a salesman. To save the little money he did earn in this way he scrimped wherever he could. His meals often consisted of oatmeal and water; he washed and darned his own clothing, and pressed his socks and handkerchiefs between the pages of his books or under the mattresses on which he slept. William Lewis Bulkley, in the language of his day, achieved "Success Under Difficulties." The "Slave Boy Now a Professor" was "A Noble Example of the Triumph of Perserverance."

Bulkley thought of himself as a Southerner who had been driven from his home by racism: "There is not one of us who would not gladly go back home if we did not know that every right dear to any full man has been ruthlessly torn from our grasp," he said in 1909. He longed to share the "soul-refreshings that only a [southern] Negro revival can give." Dr. Bulkley came to New York City in the 1890s and was appointed seventh grade teacher in a lower Manhattan public school. In 1899 he became principal of P. S. 80 on West 41st Street in the Tenderloin. This school, in the heart of the Negro district, had formerly been an all-Negro institution which was made a ward school as a result of the city's integration policy which went into effect in 1884. In 1909, despite protest meetings and petitions of the teachers in P. S. 125, Bulkley was appointed the first Negro principal of a predominantly white school in city history.

William Lewis Bulkley insisted that Negroes be given full equality in American society immediately. He supported the demands made by W. E. B. Du Bois along these lines, and became a founder of the NAACP. During his summer vacations he was a temporary expatriate who lived in Switzerland and France with his wife and children. His family sometimes remained there when he returned to resume his duties in the fall. On retiring from the New York City school system in 1923 he left the country and established a private school in Nice. He died there in 1934. That a supporter of Du Bois should have founded an organization that tried to find practical, industrial employment for the Negroes of the city seemed the height of inconsistency to Booker T. Washington's supporters. "You will see that this opponent of industrial education is not practicing what he preaches," wrote one of them. "This is inconsistency with a vengeance." White social workers, like Mary White Ovington, Jane Addams and Julia Richman, on the other hand, thought highly of Bulkley's work.

Bulkley was a pragmatist who met conditions in the city as he saw them and tried to improve them as best he could. One of the first things he did after becoming principal of P. S. 80, for example, was to open a kindergarten class to relieve the working mothers of the neighborhood. In 1903 Bulkley established an evening school in the building which specialized in classes offering industrial and commercial training to its students. Some of the most diligent students in the school were elderly Negro men and women, some in their seventies and eighties, who had no opportunity for education as young people, and now wanted to learn to read and write. Bulkley invited friends and associates to visit the school. On one occasion, when members of the Board of Education made an inspection tour, they stated "that it was the most successful evening school that ever was established in New York. . . ."

The idea for a permanent industrial organization to assist Negroes in New York City had apparently originated with William H. Baldwin. Baldwin, president of the Long Island Railroad and philanthropist, was one of Booker T. Washington's key financial supporters. It was Dr. Bulkley, however, who initiated the movement which led to the creation of the CIICN.

Since 1902 Bulkley had agitated for the need of an organization to do on a broad scale what he had attempted to do as an individual at his school: "With an Afro-American population in New York increasing yearly at a very great, I had almost said alarming rate," he said in one speech, "it behooves every thoughtful man and woman in this city to stop long enough to think what it may mean to us and to them."

Early in 1906 the Negro educator initiated a series of local meetings to discuss the subject. He, Mary White Ovington and others lectured these gatherings on the harsh facts of life that each Negro in New York City was forced to experience. Finally, in May, 1906, at a meeting of some sixty Negro and white New Yorkers, Bulkley's hope became reality. The CIICN was founded and issued a public statement on its goals. "Here at home," the report maintained, "conditions are piling up which must be met . . . at once." The Committee would endeavor to provide equal "economic opportunities" for all citizens: "A square deal in the matter of getting livelihood is held to be fundamental." William Jay Schieffelin, philanthropist, urban reformer, heir to the Jay family abolitionist tradition, and president of the Board of Trustees of the Armstrong Association, was appointed chairman. Schieffelin immediately began to contact his friends to mobilize support for the new organization. With "seventy thousand Negroes in New York," he wrote in one letter, "we ought to feel a responsibility concerning them."

The CIICN was divided into subcommittees, each headed by an eminent specialist in a particular area of work—"Employment," "Neighborhood Work," "Craftsmen," "Publication," "Trade Schools," "Social Centers," "Legal Affairs," "Public Meetings." Negro streets in the city were canvassed to gather information on social problems which seemed most pressing. Regular public meetings were held in Negro churches to stimulate interest in the Committee's work and provide a sounding board for local discontent. An employment bureau was established to locate and help create jobs for Negroes. The names of skilled Negro workers were collected and these craftsmen were organized into small trade units. Such associations were created for dressmakers, printers, mechanics, waiters, carpenters. A slight dent was made in the policies of racial restriction normally adhered to by unions when, under prodding from the CIICN, the Grand United Brotherhood of Carpenters and Joiners of America issued a charter to a Negro local in the city. Jobs were found for plumbers, construction workers, painters, bricklayers, masons, decorators. Subway companies were contacted and asked to hire Negro motormen. The subcommittee on Trade Schools, headed by a New York City school superintendent, collected a thousand names on a petition for new night schools in the Negro districts. Two more evening schools were created primarily for Negroes in these years. The City and Suburban Homes Company was encouraged to build additional model tenements for Negroes.

The CIICN also cooperated with the other Negro reform agencies in the city. In 1908, for example, it began to send people to the docks to assist Frances A. Kellor's organization with the always increasing numbers of migrants who came to town. When the Committee on Urban Conditions Among Negroes was established in New York in 1910, the CIICN sent spokesmen to the new organization to map out lines of cooperation with it. The problems which emerged from Negro migration grew more complex each year. It was obviously wasteful to have a number of separate bodies which defined their spheres as particular aspects of what was one broad and interrelated problem. In 1911 a general agreement for consolidation was reached among the CIICN, the National League for the Protection of Colored Women and the Committee on Urban Conditions Among Negroes. All three organizations merged into a new and stronger society which is still operating today, the National League on Urban Conditions Among Negroes (National Urban League).

The founding of the two most prominent national Negro organizations, the NAACP and the National Urban League was, therefore, a culmination and fulfillment of individual local reforming efforts that had begun in the North in the first decade of the twentieth century. The serious revitalization of concern in the Negro people that this demonstrated was evident in New York City in a variety of other ways as well. Spontaneously, each year brought to life some new Negro welfare institution. Two settlement houses, one of which was a branch of the Henry Street Settlement, were founded for Negroes in 1904 and in 1907. In 1911 they consolidated into one large unit, the Lincoln Settlement House. Lillian D. Wald sent Negro nurses into the Tenderloin, San Juan Hill and Harlem to help these communities with their medical problems. A Negro Music School Settlement, numerous free nurseries and kindergartens, homes for delinquent girls and two new Negro Y's were established. The NAACP opened an office in Harlem to provide help for Negroes who were discriminated against in any way. The National Urban League organized a housing bureau which tried to clean up the streets of Negro areas and locate clean, respectable and inexpensive homes for Negro families. Tuberculosis was an ever-present disease among Negroes and the New York City Board of Health conducted special evening classes for colored people on its prevention. Some migrants, fresh from the country, were given rudimentary lessons in the use of modern sanitary and plumbing devices. Playgrounds and summer camps were opened for Negro children. A Negro Fresh Air Committee was established in 1905.

When the new century began the prevailing attitude toward the Negro in New York City was one of hositility and increasing alienation. As far as the majority of the population was concerned, this continued to be the dominant reaction of the city to the Negro people. The racial antagonism of the majority made necessary the creation of segregated communities like Harlem. A sense of renewed promise and hopefulness among Negroes, however, was born of the important reform movements that were established to cope with the problems which resulted from the settlement of southern Negroes in New York City. In 1900 Booker T. Washington and W. E. B. Du Bois would have agreed that the Progressive movement seemed to overlook the Negro. Ten years later, both recognized a new "awakening" of interest in Negro life. This general reform movement was, in the words of a Negro New Yorker, "a veritable godsend to the colored people."

Part Six

WAR AND AFTERMATH

Chapter 13 FAREWELL TO REFORM

The untimely death of RICHARD HOFSTADTER *(1916-1971) deprived the historical profession of a fertile and original mind. A prolific writer long associated with Columbia University, where he took his doctorate in 1942, Professor Hofstadter's interests spanned the whole of American history. In the following fragment from his influential* Age of Reform, *he argues that the Progressive movement came to an end because of World War I. The logic is compelling, but is there supporting evidence for it?*

Participation in the war put an end to the Progressive movement. And yet the wartime frenzy of idealism and self-sacrifice marked the apotheosis as well as the liquidation of the Progressive spirit. It would be misleading to imply that American entrance into the war was in any special sense the work of the Progressives, for the final movement toward war was a nationwide movement, shared by the majority of Americans in both major parties. What is significant, however, is that the war was justified before the American public—perhaps had to be justified—in the Progressive rhetoric and on Progressive terms; and that the men who went to work for George Creel (himself a crusading journalist) in the Committee on Public Information, whose job it was to stimulate public enthusiasm for the war, were in so many instances the same men who had learned their trade drumming up enthusiasm for the Progressive reforms and providing articles for the muckraking magazines. By

1912 the Progressive spirit had become so pervasive that any policy—whether it was entrance into the war as rationalized by Wilson or abstention from the war as rationalized by La Follette—could be strengthened if a way could be found to put it in Progressive language. In the end, when the inevitable reaction came, the Progressive language itself seemed to have been discredited.

In the course of the long struggle over neutrality Wilson is the key figure, not merely because of the central power of leadership he exercised but because he was, on this issue, a representative American and a good Progressive citizen who expressed in every inconsistency, every vacillation, every reluctance, the predominate feelings of the country. He embodied, too, the triumph of the Progressive need to phrase the problems of national policy in moral terms.[1] At first, while sharing the common reluctance to become involved in the struggle, he eschewed the "realistic" formula that the whole struggle was none of America's business and that the essence of the American problem was to stay out at all costs. Even his plea for neutrality was pitched in high moral terms: the nation must stay out in order to be of service, to provide a center of sanity uncorrupted by the strains and hatreds of belligerence. It must—the phrase was so characteristic—maintain "absolute self-mastery" and keep aloof in order that it might in the end bring a "disinterested influence" to the settlement.

Then, as the country drew closer to involvement under the pressure of events, Wilson again chose the language of idealism to formulate the American problem—the problem not only whether the United States should intervene, but what might be the valid reasons for intervening. One view—a view widely shared within the Wilson administration and among thoughtful men in the country at large—rested chiefly upon the national interest and cool calculations of the future advantage of the United States. According to this view, a victory for imperial Germany would represent a threat to the long-term interests of the United States in some sense that a victory for the Allies would not. It was expected that a victorious Germany would be more aggressive, more formidable, more anti-American, and that after the defeat of the Allies and the surrender of the British fleet it would either turn upon the United States at some future time or at least present so forceful and continuous a threat as to compel this country to remain a perpetual armed camp in order to protect its security. Therefore, it was argued, it was the business of the United States, as a matter of self-interest, to see to it that the Allies were not defeated—acting if possible as a nonbelligerent, but if necessary as a belligerent. Another view was that intervention in the war could not properly be expressed in such calculating and self-regarding terms, but must rest upon moral and ideological considerations—the defense of international law and freedom of the seas, the rights of small nations, the fight against autocracy and militarism, the struggle to make the world safe for democracy.[2] To be sure, the argument from self-preservation and national interest and the argument from morals and ideals were not mutually contradictory, and both tended to have a place in the course of public discussion. But Wilson's course, the characteristically Progressive course, was to minimize and subordinate the self-regarding considerations, and to place American intervention upon the loftiest possible plane. He committed himself to this line of action quite early in the game when he rested so much of his diplomacy on the issue of the conduct of German submarine warfare and the freedom of the seas. This was quixotically formulated because it linked the problem of American intervention or non-intervention to an issue of international law—though one entirely congenial to the Progressive concern over lawlessness. To Wilson's critics it seemed hypocritical because in purely formal terms British violations of maritime law were about as serious as German violations. American concern over them could never be pressed so vigorously because such a course of action would trip over the more urgent desire to do nothing to impair the chances of Allied victory.

Our experience after the second World War suggests that in the long run there was nothing Wilson could have done to prevent a reaction against both the war itself and the Progressive movement that preceded the war. But this too seems almost certain: that by pinning America's role in the war so exclusively to high moral considerations and to altruism and self-sacrifice, by linking the foreign crusade as intimately as possible to the Progressive values and the Progressive language, he was unintentionally insuring that the reaction against Progressivism and moral idealism would be as intense as it could be. For he was telling the American people, in effect, not that they were defending themselves, but that as citizens of the world they were undertaking the same broad responsibilities for world order and world democracy that they had been expected, under the Yankee ethos of responsibility, to assume for their own institutions.[3] The crusade for reform and for democratic institutions, difficult as it was at home, was now to be projected to the world scene.[4]

Wilson turned his back on the realistic considerations that might be offered as reasons for intervention, and continually stressed the more grandiose idealistic reasons. He did more than ignore the self-regarding considerations: on occasion he repudiated them. "There is not a single selfish element, so far as I can see, in the cause we are fighting for," he told the people shortly after American entry. "We are fighting for what we believe and wish to be the rights of mankind and for the future peace and security of the world."[5] Again: "We have gone in with no special grievance of our own, because we have always said that we were the friends and servants of mankind. We look for no profit. We look for no advantage."[6] "America," he said, all too truthfully, during the debate over the treaty, ". . . is the only idealistic Nation in the world."[7]

What takes the sting of chauvinism out of this extraordinary assertion is that Wilson justified it by going to the peace conference without a single distinctively nationalist demand to make, without a single claim for territory, indemnities, or spoils, with no more self-regarding national object than to restrain his allies, make a durable and just peace, and form a League that would secure such a peace for an incalculable future. It was an amazing episode in the history of diplomacy, an episode that repeated with ironic variations the themes of American domestic Progressivism: for here was Wilson, the innocent in the presence of the interests, the reformer among such case-hardened "bosses" of Europe as Lloyd George and Clemenceau, the spokesman of the small man, the voiceless and unrepresented masses, flinging his well-meaning program for the reform of the world into the teeth of a tradition of calculating diplomacy and an ageless history of division and cynicism and strife. But it was not merely upon Europe that Wilson was making impossible demands: he had pushed the idealism and the resolution of his own people—and even, among his own people, of those who were closest to him—beyond the breaking-point. The vein of idealism he was trying to mine was there; but the demands he made upon it assumed that it would be inexhaustible, and his effort to give to the idealism of America an internationalist form reckoned without the fact that his country was not, even in the remotest sense, a country with an internationalist outlook. The traditional American idea had been not that the United States was to lead, rescue, or redeem Europe, but that it was to take its own people in a totally different direction which Europe was presumably incapable of following. The United States was to be a kind of non-Europe or anti-Europe.[8] Where European institutions were old, static, decadent, and aristocratic, American institutions were to be modern, progressive, moral, and democratic. This undercurrent of feeling was as strong in the native American as the uplifting passions of Progressivism, and far stronger than the ephemeral passions of the war period. For a moment the Western Allies might be thought of as exempt from these charges, but before long they would again be considered, as England for instance so characteristically was in the populistic mind, as the embodiment of them.[9]

It was remarkable that Wilson should have succeeded even for a moment in uniting behind him as large a part of the country as he did in an enterprise founded upon the notion of American responsibility for the world. But it is in no way surprising that he should have been resoundingly repudiated in the election of 1920—more resoundingly than any administration before or since. Not long after they began to pay the price of war, the people began to feel that they had been gulled by its promoters both among the Allies and in the United States. In this respect the historical revisionists of the postwar period were merely tardy in catching up with them. The war purged the pent-up guilts, shattered the ethos of responsibility that had permeated the rhetoric of more than a decade. It convinced the people that they had paid the price for such comforts of modern life as they could claim, that they had finally answered to the full the Progressive demand for sacrifice and self-control and altruism. In repudiating Wilson, the treaty, the League, and the war itself, they repudiated the Progressive rhetoric and the Progressive mood—for it was Wilson himself and his propagandists who had done so much to tie all these together. Wilson had foreseen that the waging of war would require turning the management of affairs over to the interests the Progressives had been fighting—but this was hardly the change that he had imagined it to be, for only on limited issues and in superficial respects had the management of affairs ever been very far out of those hands. The reaction went farther than this: it destroyed the popular impulse that had sustained Progressive politics for well over a decade before 1914. The pressure for civic participation was followed by widespread apathy, the sense of responsibility by neglect, the call for sacrifice by hedonism. And with all this there came, for a time, a sense of self-disgust. By 1920, publishers were warning authors not to send them manuscripts about the war—people would not hear of it. When at last they were willing to think about it at all, they thought of it as a mistake, and they were ready to read books about the folly of war.

NOTES

1. Although T. R. prided himself on his "realism," I do not think the case was much different with him. He too was a moralist, except that where Wilson invoked pacifist moral considerations. T. R. was constantly crying for the hairy-chested Darwinian virtues, attacking "cowardice," "ease and soft living," "the pleasures of material well-being," and the like, and dealing with international relations in terms of the "timidity" of a man whose wife has been slapped and who will not fight, and similar juvenile comparisons. "The just war," he once wrote, "is a war for the integrity of high ideals. The only safe motto for the individual citizen of a democracy fit to play a great part in the world is service—service by work and help in peace, service through the high gallantry of entire indifference to life, if war comes on the land." Osgood, , p. 140. Osgood concludes (ibid., p. 143) that "for more than two years before the United States entered the war Roosevelt's appeals to the American people were couched in terms of saving civilization and the national honor rather than the United States itself. . . . His influence . . . was not, after 1914, directed toward arousing a realistic appraisal of the imperatives of self-preservation."

2. This is not to say that the conception of a German invasion of the United States played no part in pre-intervention discussions of the subject. Fantasies about such an invasion were common in the press. (Osgood, ibid., pp. 132-3.) In its issues from May 1915 to February 1916, *Mc Clure's* ran two series of articles about an imaginary German invasion of the United States in 1921, under the titles "The Conquest of America," and "Saving the Nation." In the end, after the assassination of the President, Theodore Roosevelt, Herman Ridder the German-American, William Jennings Bryan, and Charles Edward Russell the Socialist, all join hands to lead the American people in a spiritual awakening. Much of the discussion of preparedness in this period was in the Rooseveltian vein. Cf. Porter Emerson Browne, "We'll Dally 'round the Flag, Boys!" *Mc Clure's*, Vol. XLIX (October 1916), p. 81: "Here we are, the richest nation in the world, and the most supine and the fattest, both in body and in head. Wallowing in physical luxury, we have become spiritually so loose, so lax and so lazy that we have almost lost the capacity to act."

3. Daniel J. Boorstin has pointed out that while Americans had previously hoped on occasion to encourage the growth of representative institutions abroad, as in the period after the revolutions in 1848, it was not until the time of Wilson that there was in this country any serious expectation that this could be done, much less that Americans could be considered to have any responsibility to see to it. The prevailing notion had been, rather, that American institutions were distinctive and that Europe was incapable of adopting them. It was Wilson who first urged Americans to be "citizens of the world" and insisted that their principles were "not the principles of a province or of a single continent . . . [but] the principles of a liberated man-

kind." "*L'Europe vue par l'Amérique du Nord*," in Pierre Renouvin et al., eds.: *L'Europe du XIXe et du XXe siècles: problèmes et interprétations historiques* (Milan, 1955).

4. And quite literally too. Cf. Bryan as late as 1923: "Our Nation will be saloonless for evermore and will lead the world in the great crusade which will drive intoxicating liquor from the globe." "Prohibition," *Outlook*, Vol. CXXIII (February 7, 1923). p. 265.

5. *The Public Papers of Woodrow Wilson* (New York, 1925-7), Vol. V, p. 22.

6. Ibid., p. 33.

7. Ibid., Vol., VI, p. 52. It is worth noting, by way of contrast, that F. D. R. suggested that the second World War be designated simply the War for Survival.

8. Cf. Boorstin, op. cit., *passim.*

9. Note La Follette's objection to Wilson's argument that it was impossible for democratic America to remain friendly with Prussian autocracy: "But the President proposes alliance with Great Britain which . . . is a hereditary monarchy . . . with a . . . House of Lords, with a hereditary landed system, with a limited . . . suffrage for one class." *Congressional Record*, 65th Congress, 1st Sess., p. 228.

Chapter 14 SPUR TO SOCIAL JUSTICE

As ALLEN F. DAVIS *(1931-) points out below, Hofstadter was hardly alone in believing that the war killed Progressivism. Davis does not merely question that belief--he turns it upside down, claiming that the war effort pumped new life into the Progressive quest for social justice. His evidence is persuasive, but in his concluding paragraphs does he not come close to Hofstadter's position? The author of a superb book on the settlement-house movement, Professor Davis teaches at Temple University and has recently completed an important biography of Jane Addams.*

Only a decade ago historians were satisfied with the simple generalization that World War I killed the progressive movement, or that the crusade to make the world safe for democracy absorbed the reforming zeal of the progressive era and compounded the disillusionment that followed. "Participation in the war put an end to the Progressive movement," Richard Hofstadter announced. "Reform stopped dead," Eric Goldman decided. It is now obvious that the relationship between social reform and World War I is more complex. Henry May has demonstrated that some of the progressive idealism had cracked and begun to crumble even before 1917, while Arthur Link and Clarke Chambers have discovered that a great deal of

Allen F. Davis, "Welfare, Reform and World War I," *American Quarterly,* XIX (Fall 1967), 516-533. Reprinted with permission of the *American Quarterly*, the author, and the University of Pennsylvania as publisher.

progressivism survived into the 1920s. At the same time several historians have shown that for the intellectuals associated with the *New Republic* the war seemed something of a climax to the New Nationalism. And William Leuchtenburg has argued that the economic and social planning of World War I was a much more important model for the New Deal than anything that happened during the progressive era.

It is an overworked truism that there were many progressive movements, but one of the most important and interesting was the social justice movement. Led by social workers, ministers and intellectuals, the social justice movement, in broadest terms, sought to conserve human resources and to humanize the industrial city. The social justice reformers tried to improve housing, abolish child labor, limit the hours of work for both men and women, build parks and playgrounds and better schools. Like all progressives they believed that by altering the environment it was possible to reconstruct society. They conbined optimism and a large amount of moral idealism with an exaggerated faith in statistics, efficiency and organization. Of course the social justice reformers did not always agree among themselves; prohibition, immigration restriction and the war itself caused divisions within the group.

The optimism and the idealism of the social justice reformers had been tempered before 1917. In a real sense the formation of the Progressive Party with its platform of industrial minimums had seemed the climax to their crusade. The collapse of the Progressive Party coming almost simultaneously with the outbreak of war in Europe led to shock and disillusionment and to many pronouncements that the war had ended social reform. The shock wore off quickly, though some of the disillusionment remained. Many reformers continued to promote social welfare legislation. They lobbied for the La Follette Seaman's bill, and early in 1916 helped to force a reluctant Wilson into supporting a national child labor law. Most of the social justice reformers voted for Wilson in 1916 but without a great deal of enthusiasm. The specter of war hung over them as it hung over all Americans, but for many of them the acceptance or rejection of war was an especially difficult, and in some cases, a shattering experience. A few, like Jane Addams, Lillian Wald and Alice Hamilton, were consistent pacifists. Most of them opposed the preparedness movement and America's entry into the war, and they played important roles in organizations like the American Union Against Militarism. But when the United States declared war most of them went along with the decision, with fear and trembling but with loyalty. They feared that the crisis of war would cancel the victories they had won, that civil liberties would be abridged, that education and recreation and health standards would be neglected, that child labor and long hours for men and women would be resumed in the name of national need. Yet gradually, to their own surprise, many of them came to view the war, despite its horror and its dangers, as a climax and culmination of their movement for social justice in America.

Few of the reformers saw the war as a great crusade to make the world safe for democracy, at least in the beginning, but they were soon caught up in the feverish activity and enthusiasm for action that marked the first months of the war. Part of the excitement came from the thrill of being listened to after years of frustration, of plotting and planning and lobbying. "Enthusiasm for social service is epidemic . . . ," Edward T. Devine, the General Secretary of the New York Charity Organization Society, wrote in the summer of 1917, "a luxuriant crop of new agencies is springing up. We scurry back and forth to the national capital; we stock offices with typewriters and new letterheads; we telephone feverishly, regardless of expense, and resort to all the devices of efficient 'publicity work'. . . . It is all very exhilarating, stimulating, intoxicating." The reformers went to Washington; they also joined the Red Cross or the YMCA and went to France. For a time during the war the capital of American social work and philanthropy seemed to have been transferred from New York to Paris. Devine, who in 1918 was in Paris working for the Red Cross, wrote:

> We have moved our offices to 12 Boissy d'Anglas, the Children's Bureau is on the ground floor; the Tuberculosis Bureau with the Rockefeller Foundation was already on the third . . . , the rest of the Department of Civil Affairs is on the first floor, Bureau Chiefs and Associate Chiefs being marshalled along the street side in an imposing array, with Mr. [Homer] Folks and Mr. [John] Kingsbury at one end and Miss Curtis and myself at the other.

John Andrews, Secretary of the American Association for Labor Legislation, surveyed the new kind of administrator being employed by the government, many of them social workers and college professors, and decided that "Perhaps aggressive competition with Germany is having a beneficial effect on bureaucratic Washington." Andrews had gone to Washington in October 1917 to try to get the House to pass a bill, already approved by the Senate, providing workmen's compensation for longshoremen. With Congress ready to adjourn everyone assured him there was no chance for passage. But he went to see President Wilson, and the next day the bill passed the House under the unanimous consent rule. Andrews was amazed and found himself with a great stack of unused facts and statistics. "Usually before our bills are passed, we wear our facts threadbare," he remarked. "Perhaps this is not the most democratic way to secure urgently needed labor laws, but it is effective."

Not everyone of course shared the enthusiasm for war, not the confidence that war would lead to great social gain. There was some truth in Randolph Bourne's charge that the intellectuals who saw so much good coming out of war were deceiving themselves and falling victim to the worst kind of chauvinism and rationalization. "It is almost demonical," Helena Dudley, a Boston settlement worker, wrote to Jane Addams, "the sweep toward conscription and these enormous war loans which Wall Street is eager to heap on: and labor so passive and the socialists broken up, and the social workers lining up with the bankers." Another woman reported from Seattle that there "the men who feel 'the call to arms' and the women who feel 'the call to knit' for the Red Cross are the men and women generally opposed to labor legislation and all progressive movements to increase the rights and well being of the many." But these were minority views.

Most of the social justice reformers joined John Dewey, Thorstein Veblen and the *New Republic* progressives and applauded the positive action of the Wilson administration in taking over the railroads, mobilizing industry and agriculture. They looked forward to sweeping economic reforms and contemplated the "social possibilities of war." "Laissez-faire is dead," one of them wrote, "Long live social control: social control, not only to enable us to meet the rigorous demands of the war, but also as a foundation for the peace and brotherhood that is to come." Some of them, inspired by the promise of the Russian Revolution and wartime socialism in England, looked forward to a kind of "democratic collectivism."

But the social justice reformers were concerned with more than an extension of the New Nationalism, and their primary interest was not in economic planning. They wanted to continue their crusade for social justice. Nothing was more important to them than the rights of the workingman, and the working woman and child. More than most progressives they had supported the cause of organized labor, and they were cheered by the rights won by labor during the war. The National War Labor Policies Board, the United States Employment Service and other wartime agencies recognized collective bargaining, the minimum wage and the eight-hour day, improved conditions of work and reduced the exploitation of women and children in industry. "One of the paradoxes of the war is the stimulus it is giving to human conservation," a writer in *The Survey* noted. The social justice reformers spent a large amount of time making sure labor standards were not weakened, and that women and children were not exploited during the war. Yet even the invalidation of the National Child Labor Law by the Supreme Court failed to dim their enthusiasm. The National Child Labor Committee set to work to design another and better law, and Congress responded by passing a bill that levied a 10 per cent tax on products produced by children under fourteen. A Supreme Court decision did not seem very important when Secretary of War Newton Baker and other members of the Wilson administration were saying publicly: "We cannot afford, when we are losing boys in France to lose children in the United States at the same time . . . , we cannot afford when this nation is having a drain upon the life of its young manhood . . . , to have the life of women workers of the United States depressed."

The crisis of war also stimulated the movement to improve urban housing. The housing movement was central to the social justicc movement and intertwined with all other reforms from child labor legislation to progressive education. Much of the prewar movement, led by men like Lawrence Veiller, was devoted to passing restrictive legislation, but the war brought the first experiment with public housing. Borrowing something from the English example and spurred to action by the crucial need for housing war workers, the Federal Government, operating through the

United States Shipping Board and the Department of Labor, built or controlled dozens of housing projects during the war. For many who had been working to improve urban housing for decades the government experiments seemed like the climax to the movement. Lawrence Veiller himself drew up the "Standards for Permanent Industrial Housing Developments." that were followed by the government agencies. The result was that the projects were much better designed and safer than those built by commercial builders. In addition the architects of the developments, influenced by the English Garden City Movement and by the settlement ideal of neighborhood unity, experimented with row houses, curved streets, recreation and shopping areas. Thus the public housing experiment of World War I was clearly the product of the city planning as well as of the housing movement of the progressive era.

The war also provided a climax to the social insurance movement, which had won very little support in the United States before 1910. Many states had passed workmen's compensation laws by 1917, but they were inadequate and filled with loopholes, and the philosophy of the movement was only gradually being accepted by many reformers, let alone the general public, when the United States became involved in World War I. Consequently the Military and Naval Insurance Act, which became law October 6, 1917, was hailed as a great victory by the leaders of the movement. The act, which was drawn up by Judge Julian Mack with the aid of experts like Lee Frankel and Julia Lathrop, required each enlisted man to make an allotment to his family, which the government supplemented. It also provided compensation in case of death or disability, and re-education in case of crippling injury. The architects of the plan hoped that it would prevent the demands for pensions and bonuses that had followed every American war, but more important to those who had fought for social insurance was the fact that the government had assumed the extra hazard involved in military service and guaranteed a minimum standard of subsistence to the soldier's family. The act was slow to get into operation, indeed some families did not receive their allotments until after the Armistice. It also put a heavy burden on the Red Cross, which tried to advance the money to needy families, but at the time the act seemed to mark a victory for an important progressive measure.

Health insurance had made even less progress in the United States before 1917 than had workmen's compensation laws, but a group of social workers in 1915 picked it as the next great reform. "Health Insurance—the next step in social progress," became their slogan. A few states had amended their workmen's compensation laws to include industrial diseases, and New York, New Jersey, Massachusetts and a few other states were investigating the possibility of compulsory, contributory workmen's health insurance when the war came. The war seemed to increase the need. The New Jersey commission on old age insurance, in urging the government to enact a health insurance law, declared that "health protection . . . has been raised by the war from a position deserving of humanitarian consideration to one demanding action if we are to survive as a nation." But compulsory health insurance quickly aroused the opposition of the insurance companies and the medical profession, as well as of other groups who denounced it as "Prussianism." Not even the reminder that most of the British troops were protected by government health insurance could stop the opposition.

While health insurance fell victim to the war, or perhaps more accurately to a combination of circumstances, the movement to improve the nation's health was stimulated by the conflict. "War makes sanitation a common cause," Alice Hamilton announced. "We suddenly discovered that health is not a personal matter, but a social obligation," Owen Lovejoy remarked. Early fears that the war, by drawing doctors and nurses into the Army, would lead to a rise in infant mortality, tuberculosis and other diseases proved groundless as a variety of agencies, volunteers and the Federal Government rallied to the cause. Lillian Wald, who opposed American participation in the war, served on the Red Cross Advisory Committee, traveled frequently to Washington as a consultant on health matters, and labored long and hard to keep the district nurses in New York functioning at top efficiency even during the influenza epidemic at the end of the war. Part of the stimulus to the health movement during the war came from the massive attempt to control venereal disease, part came from shock, especially over the rejection of 29 per cent of those drafted as physically unfit for service. But it was more than shock. As one social worker expressed it: "far from arresting public health progress, the war has suddenly defined America's public health problem. And the aroused public conscience has promptly enacted measures which a few months ago would have been tabled by leisurely officials and classed as visionary schemes. Into a year has been packed the progress of a decade."

Other reform movements seemed to make great strides during the war. The use of industrial education in rehabilitation work pleased the supporters of progressive education, while the mental hygiene movement approved the use of psychiatrists and psychiatric tests by the Army. The use of schools as community centers by the Council of National Defense led to the climax of the school social center movement, and the development of community councils and war chests stimulated community organization and led to acceptance of the federated fund drive.

Women also profited from the war. Out of necessity they achieved a measure of equal rights. They entered hundreds of occupations formerly barred to them, and their presence led to the establishment of the Women in Industry Service and ultimately to the Women's Bureau of the Department of Labor. "Wonderful as this hour is for democracy and labor—it is the first hour in history for the women of the world," Mrs. Raymond Robins, the President of the National Women's Trade Union League, announced in 1917. "This is the woman's age! At last after centuries of disabilities and discriminations, women are coming into the labor and festival of life on equal terms with men." The war also seemed to accelerate the movement for woman suffrage. Eight additional states gave women the vote, at least on some issues, during 1917. Wilson, after years of opposition, came out in favor of women voting, and the House of Representatives passed a woman suffrage amendment in January 1918.

The Negro and the immigrant often fell victim to racist hysteria during the war and did not gain as much as other groups. But the war seemed to hold hope even for the disadvantaged. Negroes were drafted and enlisted in the Army in great numbers and often served with distinction. All the training camps, recreation facilities and even the YMCA buildings were segregated, and there were many incidents of progressives, who had always been more sympathetic to the Negro's plight than had most reformers, hoped that the Negro's willingness to serve and what he learned in the Army would help lead to better conditions after the war. They were cheered by the appointment of Emmett J. Scott, Secretary of Tuskegee Institute, as Special Assistant to the Secretary of War, and by the emergence of a number of young leaders within the Negro community. "We may expect to see the walls of prejudice gradually crumble before the onslaught of common sense and racial progress," a writer in *The Crisis* predicted.

It was hard to forget the bloody battle of East St. Louis and the race riot in Houston for which thirteen Negro soldiers were executed. It was easy to dwell on a thousand incidents of prejudice and on the lynchings that continued during the war, but many agreed with William E. B. Du Bois when he called in July 1918 for the Negro to close ranks, support the war effort and put aside special grievances. "Since the war began we have won: Recognition of our citizenship in the draft; One thousand Negro officers; Special representation in the War and Labor Departments; Abolition of the color line in railway wages; Recognition as Red Cross Nurses; Overthrow of segregation ordinances; A strong word from the President against lynching. . . . Come fellow black men," Du Bois urged his critics, "fight for your rights, but for god's sake have sense enough to know when you are getting what you fight for."

The war did not end the grievances, but it seemed to improve the Negro's lot. It also stimulated a massive migration. A large number of Negroes had moved north even before 1914 but the war and the lure of jobs increased the flow. Many Negroes did find employment, but they also encountered prejudice and hate. Social workers and a few other reformers continued to struggle against increasing odds to aid the Negro. Yet during the war the problems and the prejudice seemed less important than the promise for the future. The migration north and the large numbers who joined the Army also seemed to create improved wages and better treatment for Negroes in the South. The story of the migration might be told in terms of crime and corruption, of drift and hate, a writer in *Survey* noted but "Against it, there is a story of careful adjustment to new circumstances, of stimulation to self-help, of education . . . , of job findings and vocational guidance. . . ."

The story of the treatment of the immigrant and alien during the war was also not entirely bleak. German-Americans were attacked as radicals, pacifists and traitors, and wartime hysteria led to the development of super-patriotism and the decline of civil liberties. Yet at the time the patriotic enthusiasm seemed in some cases to accelerate the process of Americanization. The sight of many different ethnic groups joining enthusiastically to support Liberty Bond drives and other war activities led one observer to predict that the war would "weld the twenty-five or thirty races which compose our population into a strong, virile and intelligent people . . . ," into "a splendid race of new Americans." The war also strengthened the movement to restrict immigration. In February 1917, a bill requiring a literacy test for the first time passed Congress and became law. There had always been disagreement among social justice progressives on the matter of restriction; some had argued that to help those already here it was necessary to reduce the flow, but the war seemed to end the debate. Not all reformers greeted the new law as a victory for progressivism, but no one, not even the Immigrant Protective League, launched an effective protest against the bill. The National Committee for Constructive Immigration Legislation, formed in 1918, and supported by a great variety of reformers, tried only to soften and define the restrictive legislation.

Despite occasional setbacks reform seemed to triumph in many areas during the war, but perhaps the most impressive victory came with the progressive take-over of the training camps. The Commission on Training Camp Activities was a product of the minds of Newton Baker and Raymond Fosdick. Baker, of course, had been a municipal reformer, and progressive mayor of Cleveland before becoming Secretary of War. Fosdick had been a settlement worker and Commissioner of Accounts in New York and an expert on American and European police systems. As Chairman of the Commission Fosdick picked men like Joseph Lee of the Playground Association, Lee Hanner of the Russell Sage Foundation and John Mott of the YMCA to serve with him. With the aid of several other private agencies the Commission on Training Camps set out to apply the techniques of social work, recreation and community organization to the problem of mobilizing, entertaining and protecting the American serviceman at home and abroad. They organized community singing and baseball, post exchanges and theaters, and even provided university extension courses for the troops. They moved out into the communities near the military bases and in effect tried to create a massive settlement house around each army camp. No army had seen anything like it before, but it provided something of a climax to the recreation and community organization movement and a victory for those who had been arguing for creative use of leisure time, even as it angered most of the career army men.

The Commission on Training Camp Activities also continued the progressive crusades against alcohol and prostitution. Clearly a part of the progressive movement, both crusades sought to preserve the nation's human resources, and were stimulated by a mixture of moral indignation and the latest medical knowledge. The prohibition movement had a long history, of course, but in its most recent upsurge it had been winning converts and legislative victories since the 1890s. The fight was led by the Anti-Saloon League and the Woman's Christian Temperance Union, but was supported by many social workers and social justice reformers who saw prohibition as a method of improving social conditions in the cities. But many of them had refused to go all the way with the crusade against alcohol. In New York a group of settlement workers had agitated against the Sunday closing of saloons; they appreciated that the saloon served as a social center. The most successful municipal reformers, including Newton Baker in Cleveland, carefully avoided enforcing some of the liquor laws, realizing how easy it was to antagonize the urban masses. The war stimulated the movement and brought it to a climax; it also ended the lingering doubts among many reformers. It became patriotic to support prohibition in order to save the grain for food, and for the first time in 1917 the National Conference of Social Work came out in favor of prohibition. But it was more than patriotism, for temperance was one key to social advance. Edward T. Devine announced after returning from Russia in 1917 that "the social revolution which followed the prohibition of vodka was more profoundly important and more likely to be permanent than the political revolution which abolished autocracy." Robert Woods, who had long supported prohibition, predicted in 1919 that the 18th amendment would reduce poverty, nearly wipe out prostitution and crime, improve labor organization and "substantially increase our national resources by setting free vast, suppressed human potentialities.

The progressive era also saw a major attack on prostitution, organized vice and the white slave trade, which seemed closely allied with the liquor traffic. Although the progressive vice reformer concentrated his attack on the madams and pimps and business interests which exploited the natural sex instincts of others, he also denied the time-honored defense of the prostitute, that it was necessary for the unmarried male to "sow his wild oats." Using the latest medical statistics, he argued that continence was the best defense against the spread of venereal disease.

Progressive attitudes toward alcohol and prostitution were written into sections twelve and thirteen of the Military Draft Act. They prohibited the sale of liquor to men in uniform and gave the President power to establish zones around all military camps where prostitution and alcohol would be outlawed. There was opposition from a few military commanders, a number of city officials and from at least one irate citizen who protested that red-light districts were "God-provided means for prevention of the violation of innocent girls, by men who are exercising their 'God-given passions.' " But Raymond Fosdick, with the full cooperation of the government, launched a major crusade to wipe out sin in the service; "Fit to Fight" became the motto. It was a typical progressive effort—a large amount of moral indignation combined with the use of the most scientific prophylaxis. Josephus Daniels, the Secretary of the Navy, disapproved of Fosdick's methods. He believed that urging the men to avoid sexual contact was the best and only way to reduce disease; "Men must live straight if they would shoot straight," he told the sailors on one occasion. But when the disease rate in the Navy became the highest in the service he gave in to Fosdick's demand that science as well as moralism be used. The crusade was successful, for by the end of 1918 every major red-light district in the country had been closed, and the venereal disease rate had been lowered to produce what the man called, "the cleanest Army since Cromwell's day."

To protect the health of the soldiers was not enough, however; "We must make these men stronger in every sense, more fit, morally, mentally and physically than they have ever been in their lives . . . ," one recreation worker announced. "These camps are national universities–training schools to which the flower of American youth is being sent." When the boys go to France, "I want them to have invisible armour to take with them," Newton Baker told a conference on War Camp Community Service. "I want them to have armour made up of a set of social habits replacing those of their homes and communities."

France provided a real test for the "invisible armour" of the American soldier. He was forbidden to buy or to accept as gifts any alcoholic beverage except light wine and beer. Despite hundreds of letters of protest from American mothers, Fosdick and Baker decided it would be impossible to prevent the soldiers from drinking wine in France. But sex posed a more serious threat, for both the British and French armies had tried to solve the problem of venereal disease by licensing and inspecting prostitutes. Clemenceau could not understand the American attempt to outlaw prostitution and even accused the American Army of spreading disease among the French civilian population. He graciously offered to provide the Americans with licensed prostitutes. General Pershing considered the offer "too hot to handle" and gave it to Fosdick. When Fosdick showed it to Baker, the Secretary of War remarked, "For God's sake, Raymond, don't show this to the President or he'll stop the war." The Americans never accepted Clemenceau's invitation and he continued to be baffled by the American progressive mind.

One of the overriding assumptions of those who sought to protect the American soldier at home and abroad was that he would learn from his experience and return to help make a better America after the war. Indeed one of the major reasons for the optimism of the social justice reformers was their confidence that the experiments and social action of the war years would lead to even greater accomplishments in the reconstruction decade ahead. Robert Woods surveyed the positive actions of the federal government during wartime in the spring of 1918 and asked, "Why should it not always be so? Why not continue in the years of peace this close, vast, wholesome organism of service, of fellowship, of constructive creative power?" Even Jane Addams, who saw much less that was constructive about war than did many of her colleagues, lectured for Herbert Hoover's Food Administration, and looked ahead with confidence and hope for the future. Paul Kellogg, editor of *The Survey*, also mirrored some of the hope for continuing the reform that the war had accelerated when he wrote to his subscribers in September 1918:

With hundreds of people for the first time shaken out of their narrow round of family and business interests and responding to public service as a patriotic call, with American help going out to the far ends of the earth as at no time since the early stages of the missionary movement; with federal action affecting housing, labor relations, community life, as never before; with reconstruction plans afoot in England and France . . . we feel that *The Survey* has never before faced such a great obligation and such a great opportunity.

Of course the enthusiasm for the present and optimism for the future was sometimes tempered by doubts. There was the occasional glimpse of the horror of war, especially by those who went overseas. There was the abridgment of the freedom of speech and the persecution of radicals and aliens and pacifists. There was the fear that opposition or apathy would arise after the war to strike down the gains, and that the American labor movement, led by Gompers, was too conservative to take advantage of the opportunity for labor advance. There was even a lingering worry about the very enthusiasm for reform that made the war years exciting, concern over the disappearance of the opposition and even the decline of debate over immigration restriction, prohibition and other measures. But the doubts were few and far between. Most of the social justice reformers surveyed the success of social reform at home and looked confidently toward the future. For them the war was not so much a war to make the world safe for democracy as it was a war that brought to a climax their crusade for reform at home.

Yet the progressives deluded themselves. They were the victims of their own confidence and enthusiasm, for the social reforms of the war years were caused more by the emergency situation than by a reform consensus. Quickly after the war, the Wilson administration abandoned public housing and social insurance, and withdrew the government from positive participation in many areas. The gains for labor and the Negro proved ephemeral, and the dream that the newly enfranchised women, together with a generation of young men educated on the battlefields and in the training camps, would lead a great crusade to reconstruct America turned out to be idealistic in the extreme.

By 1920 there was little left from wartime social reform except prohibition, immigration restriction and racist hysteria. The disillusionment that followed can be explained in part by the false hopes raised by the war. Many social justice progressives had been discouraged by the failure of the Progressive Party, then rescued by the excitement of the wartime social experiments. The collapse of the dreams fostered by the war changed American reformers irrevocably. They would never again be quite as optimistic and enthusiastic. Their faith in statistics and their confidence that the American people really wanted reform were shattered. Yet the despair was not complete—it never reached the depths that marked the group of young intellectuals which Ernest Hemingway came to symbolize. Their disillusionment was tempered by a lingering vision of social justice, a vision of government action to protect the rights of labor, and especially the working woman and child, of public housing and social insurance, of equal opportunity for the Negro and other minorities.

A number of social justice progressives worked quietly and sometimes forlornly during the twenties preparing to battle for the success of some of their plans in the 1930s and after. Very often their point of reference was World War I. It is no longer possible to say simply that the war ended the progressive movement. It was not the war itself which killed reform, but rather the rejection afterward of the wartime measures which seemed at the time to constitute the climax to the crusade for social justice. Yet scholars interested in the collapse and survival of progressivism should examine the war years, for here were raised some of the hopes that were later dashed and some of the dreams that were later fulfilled.

Chapter 15 SPLINTERED BUT ALIVE IN THE 1920's

ARTHUR S. LINK *(1920-   ), the leading Wilson scholar of our day and Edwards Professor of American History at Princeton University, has an unparalleled knowledge of Progressivism. In the following article, he traces the course of the Progressive movement from the beginning of World War I to just before the Great Depression. Unlike many historians, including Allen F. Davis, Professor Link refuses to believe that Progressivism was "defunct" in the 1920s. Does his evidence satisfy you?*

If the day has not yet arrived when we can make a definite synthesis of political developments between the Armistice and the Great Depression, it is surely high time for historians to begin to clear away the accumulated heap of mistaken and half-mistaken hypotheses about this important transitional period. Writing often without fear or much research (to paraphrase Carl Becker's remark), we recent American historians have gone on indefatigably to perpetuate hypotheses that either reflected the disillusionment and despair of contemporaries, or once served their purpose in exposing the alleged hiatus in the great continuum of twentieth-century reform.

Stated briefly, the following are what might be called the governing hypotheses

Arthur S. Link, "What Happened to the Progressive Movement in the 1920s?" *American Historical Review*, LXIV (July 1959), 833-851. Copyright Arthur S. Link; used by permission of the author.

of the period under discussion: The 1920's were a period made almost unique by an extraordinary reaction against idealism and reform. They were a time when the political representatives of big business and Wall Street executed a relentless and successful campaign in state and nation to subvert the regulatory structure that had been built at the cost of so much toil and sweat since the 1870's, and to restore a Hanna-like reign of special privilege to benefit business, industry, and finance. The surging tides of nationalism and mass hatreds generated by World War I continued to engulf the land and were manifested, among other things, in fear of communism, suppression of civil liberties, revival of nativism and anti-Semitism most crudely exemplified by the Ku Klux Klan, and in the triumph of racism and prejudice in immigration legislation. The 1920's were an era when great traditions and ideals were repudiated or forgotten, when the American people, propelled by a crass materialism in their scramble for wealth, uttered a curse on twenty-five years of reform endeavor. As a result, progressives were stunned and everywhere in retreat along the entire political front, their forces disorganized and leaderless, their movement shattered, their dreams of a new America turned into agonizing nightmares.

To be sure, the total picture that emerges from these generalizations, is overdrawn. Yet it seems fair to say that leading historians have advanced each of these generalizations, that the total picture is the one that most of us younger historians saw during the years of our training, and that these hypotheses to a greater or lesser degree still control the way in which we write and teach about the 1920's as a reading of textbooks and general works will quickly show.

This paper has not been written, however, to quarrel with anyone or to make an indictment. Its purposes are, first, to attempt to determine the degree to which the governing hypotheses, as stated, are adequate or inadequate to explain the political phenomena of the period, and, second to discover whether any new and sounder hypotheses might be suggested. Such an effort, of course, must be tentative and above all imperfect in view of the absence of sufficient foundations for a synthesis.

Happily, however, we do not have to proceed entirely in the dark. Historians young and old, but mostly young, have already discovered that the period of the 1920's is the exciting new frontier of American historical research and that its opportunities are almost limitless in view of the mass of manuscript materials that are becoming available. Thus we have (the following examples are mentioned only at random) excellent recent studies of agrarian discontent and farm movements by Theodore Saloutos, John D Hicks, Gilbert C. Fite, Robert L. Morlan, and James H. Shideler; of nativism and problems of immigration and assimilation by John Higham, Oscar Handlin, Robert A. Devine, and Edmund D. Cronon; of intellectual currents, the social gospel, and religious controversies by Henry F. May, Paul A. Carter, Robert M. Miller, and Norman F. Furniss; of left-wing politics and labor developments by Theodore Draper, David A. Shannon, Daniel Bell, Paul M. Angle, and Matthew Josephson; of the campaign of 1928 by Edmund A. Moore; and of political and judicial leaders by Alpheus T. Mason, Frank Freidel, Arthur M.

Schlesinger, Jr., Merlo J. Pusey, and Joel F. Paschal. Moreover, we can look forward to the early publication of studies that will be equally illuminating for the period, like the biographies of George W. Norris, Thomas J. Walsh, and Albert B. Fall now being prepared by Richard Lowitt, Leonard Bates, and David Stratton, respectively, and the recently completed study of the campaign and election of 1920 by Wesley M. Bagby.

Obviously, we are not only at a point in the progress of our research into the political history of the 1920's when we can begin to generalize, but we have reached the time when we should attempt to find some consensus, however tentative it must now be, concerning the larger political dimensions and meanings of the period.

In answering the question of what happened to the progressive movement in the 1920's, we should begin by looking briefly at some fundamental facts about the movement before 1918, facts that in large measure predetermined its fate in the 1920's, given the political climate and circumstances that prevailed.

The first of these was the elementary fact that the progressive movement never really existed as a recognizable organization with common goals and a political machinery geared to achieve them. Generally speaking (and for the purposes of this paper), progressivism might be defined as the popular effort, which began convulsively in the 1890's and waxed and waned afterward to our own time, to insure the survival of democracy in the United States by the enlargement of governmental power to control and offset the power of private economic groups over the nation's institutions and life. Actually, of course, from the 1890's on there were many "progressive" movements on many levels seeking sometimes contradictory objectives. Not all, but most of these campaigns were the work of special interest groups or classes seeking greater political status and economic security. This was true from the beginning of the progressive movement in the 1890's; by 1913 it was that movement's most important characteristic.

The second fundamental fact—that the progressive movements were often largely middle class in constituency and orientation—is of course well known, but an important corollary has often been ignored. It was that several of the most important reform movements were inspired, staffed, and led by businessmen with very specific or special-interest objectives in view. Because they hated waste, mismanagement, and high taxes, they, together with their friends in the legal profession, often furnished the leadership of good government campaigns. Because they feared industrial monopoly, abuse of power by railroads, and the growth of financial oligarchy, they were the backbone of the movements that culminated in the adoption of the Hepburn and later acts for railroad regulation, the Federal Reserve Act, and the Federal Trade Commission Act. Among the many consequences of their participation in the progressive movement, two should be mentioned because of their significance for developments in the 1920's: First, the strong identification of businessmen with good government and economic reforms for which the general public also had a lively concern helped preserve the good reputation of middle-class business community (as opposed to its alleged natural enemies, monopolists, malefactors of great wealth, and railroad barons) and helped to direct the energies of the progressive movement toward the strengthening instead of the shackling of the business community. Second, their activities and influence served to intensify the tensions within the broad reform movement, because they often opposed the demands of farm groups, labor unions, and advocates of social justice.

The third remark to be made about the progressive movement before 1918 is that despite its actual diversity and inner tensions it did seem to have unity; that is, it seemed to share common ideals and objectives. This was true in part because much of the motivation even of the special-interest groups was altruistic (at least they succeeded in convincing themselves that they sought the welfare of society rather than their own interests primarily); in part because political leadership generally succeeded in subordinating inner tensions. It was true, above all, because there were in fact important idealistic elements in the progressive ranks–social gospel leaders, social justice elements, and intellectuals and philosophers–who worked hard at the task of defining and elevating common principles and goals.

Fourth and finally, the substantial progressive achievements before 1918 had been gained, at least on the federal level, only because of the temporary dislocations of the national political structure caused by successive popular uprisings, not because progressives had found or created a viable organization for perpetuating their control. Or, to put the matter another way, before 1918 the various progressive elements had failed to destroy the existing party structure by organizing a national party of their own that could survive. They, or at least many of them, tried in 1912; and it seemed for a time in 1916 that Woodrow Wilson had succeeded in drawing the important progressive groups permanently into the Democratic party. But Wilson's accomplishment did not survive even to the end of the war, and by 1920 traditional partisan loyalties were reasserting themselves with extraordinary vigor.

With this introduction, we can now ask what happened to the progressive movement or movements in the 1920's. Surely no one would contend that after 1916 the political scene did not change significantly, both on the state and national levels. There was the seemingly obvious fact that the Wilsonian coalition had been wrecked by the election of 1920, and that the progressive elements were divided and afterward unable to agree upon a program or to control the national government. There was the even more "obvious" fact that conservative Republican presidents and their cabinets controlled the executive branch throughout the period. There was Congress, as Eric F. Goldman had said, allegedly whopping through pro-corporation legislation, and the Supreme Court interpreting the New Freedom laws in a way that harassed unions and encouraged trusts. There were, to outraged idealists and intellectuals, the more disgusting spectacles of Red hunts, mass arrests and deportations, the survival deep into the 1920's of arrogant nationalism, crusades against the teaching of evolution, the attempted suppression of the right to drink, and myriad other manifestations of what would now be called a repressive reaction.

Like the hypotheses suggested at the beginning, this picture is overdrawn in some particulars. But it is accurate in part, for progressivism was certainly on the downgrade if not in decay after 1918. This is an obvious fact that needs explanation and understanding rather than elaborate proof. We can go a long way toward answering our question if we can explain, at least partially, the extraordinary complex developments that converge to produce the "obvious" result. For this explanation we must begin by looking at the several progressive elements and their relation to each other and to the two major parties after 1916. Since national progressivism was never an organized or independent movement (except imperfectly and then only temporarily in 1912), it could succeed only when its constituent elements formed a coalition strong enough to control one of the major parties. This had happened in 1916, when southern and western farmers, organized labor, the social justice elements, and a large part of the independent radicals who had heretofore voted the Socialist ticket coalesced to continue the control of Wilson and the Democratic party.

The important fact about the progressive coalition of 1916, however, was not its strength but its weakness. It was not a new party but a temporary alliance, welded in the heat of the most extraordinary domestic and external events. To be sure, it functioned for the most part successfully during the war, in providing the necessary support for a program of heavy taxation, relatively stringent controls over business and industry, and extensive new benefits to labor. Surviving in a crippled way even in the months following the Armistice, it put across a program that constituted a sizable triumph for the progressive movement—continued heavy taxation, the Transportation Act of 1920, the culmination of the long fight for railroad regulation, a new child labor act, amendments for prohibition and woman suffrage, immigration restriction, and water power and conservation legislation.

Even so, the progressive coalition of 1916 was inherently unstable. Indeed, it was so wracked by inner tensions that it could not survive, and destruction came inexorably, it seemed systematically, from 1917 to 1920. Why was this true?

First, the independent radicals and antiwar agrarians were alienated by the war declaration and the government's suppression of dissent and civil liberties during the war and the Red scare. Organized labor was disaffected by the administration's coercion of the coal miners in 1919, its lukewarm if not hostile attitude during the great strikes of 1919 and 1920, and its failure to support the Plumb Plan for nationalization of the railroads. Isolationists and idealists were outraged by what they thought was the President's betrayal of American traditions of the liberal peace program at Paris. These tensions were strong enough to disrupt the coalition, but a final one would have been fatal even if the others had never existed. This was the alienation of farmers in the Plains and western states produced by the administration's refusal to impose price controls on cotton while it maintained ceilings on the prices of other agricultural commodities, and especially by the administration's failure to do anything decisive to stem the downward plunge of farm prices that began in the summer of 1920. Under the impact of all these stresses, the Wilsonian coalition gradually disintegrated from 1917 to 1920 and disappeared entirely during the campaign of 1920.

The progressive coalition was thus destroyed, but the components of a potential movement remained. As we will see, these elements were neither inactive nor entirely unsuccessful in the 1920's. But they obviously failed to find common principles and a program, much less to unite effectively for political action on a national scale. I suggest that this was true, in part at least, for the following reasons:

First, the progressive elements could never create or gain control of a political organization capable of carrying them into national office. The Republican party was patently an impossible instrument because control of the GOP was too much in the hands of the eastern and midwestern industrial, oil, and financial interests, as it had been since about 1910. There was always the hope of a third party. Several progressive groups–insurgent midwestern Republicans, the railroad brotherhoods, a segment of the AF of L, and the moderate Socialists under Robert M. La Follette–tried to realize this goal in 1924, only to discover that third party movements in the United States are doomed to failure except in periods of enormous national turmoil, and that the 1920's were not such a time. Thus the Democratic party remained the only vehicle that conceivably could have been used by a new progressive coalition. But that party was simply not capable of such service in the 1920's. It was so torn by conflicts between its eastern, big city wing and its southern and western rural majority that it literally ceased to be a national party. It remained strong in its sectional and metropolitan components, but it was so divided that it barely succeeded in nominating a presidential candidate at all in 1924 and nominated one in 1928 only at the cost of temporary disruption.

Progressivism declined in the 1920's, in the second place, because, as has been suggested, the tensions that had wrecked the coalition of 1916 not only persisted but actually grew in number and intensity. The two most numerous progressive elements, the southern and western farmers, strongly supported the Eighteenth Amendment, were heavily tinged with nativism and therefore supported immigration restriction, were either members of, friendly to, or politically afraid of the Ku Klux Klan, and demanded as the principal plank in their platform legislation to guarantee them a larger share of the national income. On all these points and issues the lower and lower middle classes in the large cities stood in direct and often violent opposition to their potential allies in the rural areas. Moreover, the liaison between the farm groups and organized labor, which had been productive of much significant legislation during the Wilson period, virtually ceased to exist in the 1920's. There were many reasons for this development, and I mention only one–the fact that the preeminent spokesmen of farmers in the 1920's, the new Farm

Bureau Federation, represented the larger commercial farmers who (in contrast to the members of the leading farm organization in Wilson's day, the National Farmers' Union) were often employers themselves and felt no identification with the rank and file of labor.

It was little wonder, therefore (and this is a third reason for the weakness of progressivism in the 1920's), that the tension-ridden progressive groups were never able to agree upon a program that, like the Democratic platform of 1916, could provide the basis for a revived coalition. So long as progressive groups fought one another more fiercely than they fought their natural opponents, such agreement was impossible; and so long as common goals were impossible to achieve, a national progressive movement could not take effective form. Nothing illustrates this better than the failure of the Democratic conventions of 1924 and 1928 to adopt platforms that could rally and unite the discontented elements. One result, among others, was that southern farmers voted as Democrats and western farmers as Republicans. And, as Professor Frank Freidel once commented to the author, much of the failure of progressivism in the 1920's can be explained by this elementary fact.

A deeper reason for the failure of progressives to unite ideologically in the 1920's was what might be called a substantial paralysis of the progressive mind. This was partly the result of the repudiation of progressive ideals by many intellectuals and the defection from the progressive movement of the urban middle classes and professional groups, as will be demonstrated. It was the result, even more importantly, of the fact that progressivism as an organized body of political thought found itself at a crossroads in the 1920's, like progressivism today, and did not know which way to turn. The major objectives of the progressive movement of the prewar years had in fact been largely achieved by 1920. In what direction should progressivism now move? Should it remain in the channels already deeply cut by its own traditions, and, while giving sincere allegiance to the ideal of democratic capitalism, work for more comprehensive programs of business regulation and assistance to disadvantaged classes like farmers and submerged industrial workers? Should it abandon these traditions and, like most similar European movements, take the road toward a moderate socialism with a predominantly labor orientation? Should it attempt merely to revive the goals of more democracy through changes in the political machinery? Or should it become mainly an agrarian movement with purely agrarian goals?

These were real dilemmas, not academic ones, and one can see numerous examples of how they confused and almost paralyzed progressives in the 1920's. The platform of La Follette's Progressive party of 1924 offers one revealing illustration. It embodied much that was old and meaningless by this time (the direct election of the president and a national referendum before the adoption of a war resolution, for example) and little that had any real significance for the future. And yet it was the best that a vigorous and idealistic movement could offer. A second example was the plight of the agrarians and insurgents in Congress who fought so hard all through the 1920's against Andrew Mellon's proposals to abolish the inheritance tax and to make drastic reductions in the taxes on large incomes. In view of the rapid reduction of the federal debt, the progressives were hard pressed to justify the continuation of nearly confiscatory tax levels, simply because few of them realized the wide social and economic uses to which the income tax could be put. Lacking any programs for the redistribution of the national income (except to farmers), they were plagued and overwhelmed by the surpluses in the federal Treasury until, for want of any good arguments, they finally gave Secretary Andrew Mellon the legislation he had been demanding. A third and final example of this virtual paralysis of the progressive mind was perhaps the most revealing of all. It was the attempt that Woodrow Wilson, Louis D. Brandeis, and other Democratic leaders made from 1921 to 1924 to draft a new charter for progressivism. Except for its inevitable proposals for an idealistic world leadership, the document that emerged from this interchange included little or nothing that would have sounded new to a western progressive in 1912.

A fourth reason for the disintegration and decline of the progressive movement in the 1920's was the lack of any effective leadership. Given the political temper and circumstances of the 1920's, it is possible that such leadership could not have operated successfully in any event. Perhaps the various progressive elements were so mutually hostile and so self-centered in interests and objectives that even a Theodore Roosevelt or a Woodrow Wilson, had they been at the zenith of their powers in the 1920's, could not have drawn them together in a common front. We will never know what a strong national leader might have done because by a trick of fate no such leader emerged before Franklin D. Roosevelt.

Four factors, then, contributed to the failure of the progressive components to unite successfully after 1918 and, as things turned out, before 1932; the lack of a suitable political vehicle, the severity of the tensions that kept progressives apart, the failure of progressives to agree upon a common program, and the absence of a national leadership, without which a united movement could never be created and sustained. These were all weaknesses that stemmed to a large degree from the instability and failures of the progressive movement itself.

There were, besides, a number of what might be called external causes for the movement's decline. In considering them one must begin with what was seemingly the most important—the alleged fact that the 1920's were a very unpropitious time for any new progressive revolt because of the ever-increasing level of economic prosperity, the materialism, and the general contentment of the decade 1919 to 1929. Part of this generalization is valid when applied to specific elements in the population. For example, the rapid rise in the real wages of industrial employment and spread of so-called welfare practices among management, certainly did much to weaken and avert the further spread of organized labor, and thus to debilitate one of the important progressive components. But to say that it was prosperity per se that created a climate unfriendly to progressive ideals would be inaccurate. There was little prosperity and much depression during the 1920's for the single largest economic group, the farmers, as well as for numerous other groups. Progressivism, moreover, can flourish as much during periods of prosperity as during periods of discontent, as the history of the development of the progressive movement from 1901 to 1917 and of its triumph from 1945 to 1956 prove.

Vastly more important among the external factors in the decline of progressivism was the widespread, almost wholesale, defection from its ranks of the middle classes—the middling businessmen, bankers, and manufacturers, and the professional people closely associated with them in ideals and habits—in American cities large and small. For an understanding of this phenomenon no simple explanations like "prosperity" or the "temper of the times" will suffice, although they give some insight. The important fact was that these groups found a new economic and social status as a consequence of the flowering of American enterprise under the impact of the technological, financial, and other revolutions of the 1920's. If, as Professor Richard Hofstadter had claimed, the urban middle classes were progressive (that is, they demanded governmental relief from various anxieties) in the early 1900's because they resented their loss of social prestige to the *nouveaux riches* and feared being ground under by monopolists in industry, banking, and labor—if this is true, then the urban middle classes were not progressive in the 1920's for inverse reasons. Their temper was dynamic, expansive, and supremely confident. They knew that they were building a new America, a business civilization based not upon monopoly and restriction but upon a whole new set of business values—mass production and consumption, short hours and high wages, full employment, welfare capitalism. And what was more important, virtually the entire country (at least the journalists, writers in popular magazines, and many preachers and professors) acknowledged that the nation's destiny was in good hands. It was little wonder, therefore, that the whole complex of groups constituting the urban middle classes, whether in New York, Zenith, or Middletown, had little interest in rebellion or even in mild reform proposals that seemed to imperil their leadership and control.

Other important factors, of course, contributed to the contentment of the urban middle classes. The professionalization of business and the full-blown emergence of a large managerial class had a profound impact upon social and political ideals. The acceleration of mass advertising played its role, as did also the beginning disintegration of the great cities with the spread of middle- and upper-middle-class suburbs, a factor that diffused the remaining reform energies among the urban leaders.

A second external factor in the decline of the progressive movement after 1918 was the desertion from its ranks of a good part of the intellectual leadership of the country. Indeed, more than simple desertion was involved here; it was often a matter of a cynical repudiation of the ideals from which progressivism derived its strength. I do not mean to imply too much by this generalization. I know that what has been called intellectual progressivism not only survived in the 1920's but actually flourished in many fields. I know that the intellectual foundations of our present quasi-welfare state were either being laid or reinforced during the decade. Even so, one cannot evade the conclusion that the intellectual-political climate of the 1920's was vastly different from the one that had prevailed in the preceding two decades.

During the years of the great progressive revolt, intellectuals–novelists, journalists, political thinkers, social scientists, historians, and the like–had made a deeply personal commitment to the cause of democracy, first in domestic and then in foreign affairs. Their leadership in and impact on many phases of the progressive movement had been profound. By contrast, in the 1920's a large body of this intellectual phalanx turned against the very ideals they had once deified. One could cite, for example, the reaction of the idealists against the Versailles settlement; the disenchantment of the intellectuals with the extension of government authority when it could be used to justify the Eighteenth Amendment or the suppression of free speech; or the inevitable loss of faith in the "people" when en masse they hounded so-called radicals, joined Bryan's crusade against evolution, or regaled themselves as Knights of the Ku Klux Klan. Whatever the cause, many alienated intellectuals simply withdrew or repudiated any identification with the groups they had once helped to lead. The result was not fatal to progressivism, but is was serious. The spark plugs had been removed from the engine of reform.

The progressive movement, then, unquestionably declined, but was it defunct in the 1920's? Much, of course, depends upon the definition of terms. If we accept the usual definition for "defunct" as "dead" or "ceasing to have any life or strength," we must recognize that the progressive movement was certainly not defunct in the 1920's; that on the contrary at least important parts of it were very much alive; and that it is just as important to know how and why progressivism survived as it is to know how and why it declined.

To state the matter briefly, progressivism survived in the 1920's because several important elements of the movement remained either in full vigor or in only slightly diminished strength. These were the farmers, after 1918 better organized and more powerful than during the high tide of the progressive revolt; and politically conscious elements among organized labor, particularly the railroad brotherhoods, who wielded a power all out of proportion to their numbers; the Democratic organizations in the large cities, usually vitally concerned with the welfare of the so-called lower classes; a remnant of independent radicals, social workers, and social gospel writers and preachers; and finally, an emerging new vocal element, the champions of public power and regional developments.

Although they never united effectively enough to capture a major party and the national government before 1932, these progressive elements controlled Congress from 1921 to about 1927 and continued to exercise a near control during the period of their greatest weakness in the legislative branch, from 1927 to about 1930.

Indeed, the single most powerful and consistently successful group in Congress during the entire decade from 1919 to 1929 were the spokesmen of the farmers. Spurred by an unrest in the country areas more intense than at any time since the 1890's, in 1920 and 1921 southern Democrats and midwestern and western insurgents, nominally Republican, joined forces in an alliance called the Farm Bloc. By maintaining a common front from 1921 to 1924 they succeeded in enacting the most advanced agricultural legislation to that date, legislation that completed the program begun under Wilsonian auspices. It included measures for high tariffs on agricultural products, thoroughgoing federal regulation of stockyards, packing houses, and grain exchanges, the exemption of agricultural cooperatives from the application of the antitrust laws, stimulation of the export of agricultural commodities, and the establishment of an entirely new federal system of intermediate rural credit.

When prosperity failed to return to the countryside, rural leaders in Congress espoused a new and bolder plan for relief—the proposal made by George N. Peek and Hugh S. Johnson in 1922 to use the federal power to obtain "fair exchange" or "parity" prices for farm products. Embodied in the McNary-Haugen bill in 1924, this measure was approved by Congress in 1927 and 1928, only to encounter vetoes by President Calvin Coolidge.

In spite of its momentary failure, the McNary-Haugen bill had a momentous significance for the American progressive movement. Its wholesale espousal by the great mass of farm leaders and spokesmen meant that the politically most powerful class in the country had come full scale to the conviction that the taxing power should be used directly and specifically for the purpose of underwriting (some persons called it subsidizing) agriculture. It was a milestone in the development of a comprehensive political doctrine that it was government's duty to protect the economic security of all classes and particularly depressed ones. McNary-Haugenism can be seen in its proper perspective if it is remembered that it would have been considered almost absurd in the Wilson period, that it was regarded as radical by nonfarm elements in the 1920's, and that it, or at any rate its fundamental objective, was incorporated almost as a matter of course into basic federal policy in the 1930's.

A second significant manifestation of the survival of progressivism in the 1920's came during the long controversy over public ownership or regulation of the burgeoning electric power industry. In this, as in most of the conflicts that eventually culminated on Capitol Hill, the agrarian element constituted the core of progressive strength. At the same time a sizable and well-organized independent movement developed that emanated from urban centers and was vigorous on the municipal and state levels. Throughout the decade this relatively new progressive group fought with mounting success to expose the propaganda of the private utilities, to strengthen state and federal regulatory agencies, and to win municipal ownership for distributive facilities. Like the advocates of railroad regulation in an earlier period, these proponents of regulation or ownership of a great new natural monopoly failed almost as much as they had succeeded in the 1920's. But their activities and exposures (the Federal Trade Commission's devastating investigation of the electric power industry in the late 1920's and early 1930's was the prime example) laid secure foundations for movements that the 1930's would reach various culminations.

Even more significant for the future of American progressivism was the emergence in the 1920's of a new objective, that of committing the federal government to plans for large hydroelectric projects in the Tennessee Valley, the Columbia River watershed, the Southwest, and the St. Lawrence Valley for the purpose, some progressives said, of establishing "yardsticks" for rates, or for the further purpose, as other progressives declared, of beginning a movement for the eventual nationalization of the entire electric power industry. The development of this movement in its emerging stages affords a good case study in the natural history of American progressivism. It began when the Harding and Coolidge administrations attempted to dispose of the government's hydroelectric and nitrate facilities at Muscle Shoals, Alabama, to private interests. In the first stage of the controversy, the progressive objective was merely federal operation of these facilities for the production of cheap fertilizer–a reflection of its exclusive special-interest orientation. Then, as new groups joined the fight to save Muscle Shoals, the objective of public production of cheap electric power came to the fore. Finally, by the end of the 1920's, the objective of a multipurpose regional development in the Tennessee Valley and in other areas as well had taken firm shape.

In addition, by 1928 the agrarians in Congress led by Senator George W. Norris had found enough allies in the two houses and enough support in the country at large to adopt a bill for limited federal development of the Tennessee Valley. Thwarted by President Coolidge's pocket veto, the progressives tried again in 1931, only to meet a second rebuff at the hands of President Herbert Hoover.

All this might be regarded as another milestone in the maturing of American progressivism. It signified a deviation from the older traditions of mere regulation, as President Hoover had said in his veto of the second Muscle Shoals bill, and the triumph of new concepts of direct federal leadership in large-scale development of resources. If progressives had not won their goal by the end of the 1920's, they had at least succeeded in writing what would become perhaps the most important plank in their program for the future.

The maturing of an advanced farm program and the formulation of plans for public power and regional developments may be termed the two most significant progressive achievements on the national level in the 1920's. Others merit only brief consideration. One was the final winning of the old progressive goal of immigration restriction through limited and selective admission. The fact that this movement was motivated in part by racism, nativism, and anti-Semitism (with which, incidentally, a great many if not a majority of progressives were imbued in the 1920's) should not blind us to the fact that it was also progressive. It sought to substitute a so-called scientific and a planned policy for a policy of laissez faire. Its purpose was admittedly to disturb the free operation of the international labor market. Organized labor and social workers had long supported it against the opposition of large employers. And there was prohibition, the most ambitious and revealing progressive experiment of the twentieth century. Even the contemned anti-evolution crusade of Bryan and the fundamentalists and the surging drives for conformity of thought and action in other fields should be mentioned. All these movements stemmed from the conviction that organized public power could and should be used purposefully to achieve fundamental social and so-called moral change. The fact that they were potentially or actively repressive does not mean that they were not progressive. On the contrary, they superbly illustrated the repressive tendencies that inhered in progressivism precisely because it was grounded so much upon majoritarian principles.

Three other developments on the national level that have often been cited as evidences of the failure of progressivism in the 1920's appear in a somewhat different light at second glance. The first was the reversal of the tariff-for-revenue-only tendencies of the Underwood Act with the enactment of the Emergency Tariff Act of 1921 and the Fordney-McCumber Act of 1922. Actually, the adoption of these measures signified, on the whole, not a repudiation but a revival of progressive principles in the realm of federal fiscal policy. A revenue tariff had never been an authentic progressive objective. Indeed, at least by 1913, many progressives, except for some southern agrarians, had concluded that it was retrogressive and had agreed that the tariff laws should be used deliberately to achieve certain national objectives—for example, the crippling of noncompetitive big business by the free admission of articles manufactured by so-called trusts, or benefits to farmers by the free entry of farm implements. Wilson himself had been at least partially converted to these principles by 1916, as his insistence upon the creation of the Federal Tariff Commission and his promise of protection to the domestic chemical industry revealed. As for the tariff legislation of the early 1920's, its only important changes were increased protection for aluminum, chemical products, and agricultural commodities. It left the Underwood rates on the great mass of raw materials and manufactured goods largely undisturbed. It may have been economically shortsighted and a bad example for the rest of the world, but for the most part it was progressive in principle and was the handiwork of the progressive coalition in Congress.

Another development that has often been misunderstood in its relation to the progressive movement was the policies of consistent support that the Harding and Coolidge administrations adopted for business enterprise, particularly the policy of the Federal Trade Commission in encouraging the formation of trade associations and the diminution of certain traditional competitive practices. The significance of all this can easily be overrated. Such policies as these two administrations executed had substantial justification in progressive theory and in precedents clearly established by the Wilson administration.

A third challenge to usual interpretations concerns implications to be drawn from the election of Harding and Coolidge in 1920 and 1924. These elections seem to indicate the triumph of reaction among the mass of American voters. Yet one could argue tht both Harding and Coolidge were political accidents, and beneficiaries of grave defects in the American political and constitutional systems. The rank and file of Republican voters demonstrated during the preconvention campaign that they wanted vigorous leadership and a moderately progressive candidate in 1920. They got Harding instead, not because they wanted him, but because unusual circumstances permitted a small clique to thwart the will of the majority. They took Coolidge as their candidate in 1924 simply because Harding died in the middle of his term and there seemed to be no alternative to nominating the man who had succeeded him in the White House. Further, an analysis of the election returns in 1920 and 1924 will show that the really decisive factor in the victories of Harding and Coolidge was the fragmentation of the progressive movement and the fact that an opposition strong enough to rally and unite the progressive majority simply did not exist.

There remains, finally, a vast area of progressive activity about which we yet know very little. One could mention the continuation of old reform movements and the development of new ones in the cities and states during the years following the Armistice: For example, the steady spread of the city manager form of government, the beginning of zoning and planning movements, and the efforts of the great cities to keep abreast of the transportation revolution then in full swing. Throughout the country the educational and welfare activities of the cities and states steadily increased. Factory legislation matured, while social insurance had its experimental beginnings. Whether such reform impulses were generally weak or stong, one cannot say; but what we do know about developments in cities like Cincinnati and states like New York, Wisconsin, and Louisiana justifies a challenge to the assumption that municipal and state reform energies were dead after 1918 and, incidentally, a plea to young scholars to plow this unworked field of recent American history.

Let us, then, suggest a tentative synthesis as an explanation of what happened to the progressive movement after 1918:

First, the national progressive movement, which had found its most effective embodiment in the coalition of forces that reelected Woodrow Wilson in 1916, was shattered by certain policies that the administration pursued from 1917 to 1920, and by some developments over which the administration had no or only slight control. The collapse that occurred in 1920 was not inevitable and cannot be explained by merely saying that "the war killed the progressive movement."

Second, large and aggressive components of a potential new progressive coalition remained after 1920. These elements never succeeded in uniting effectively before the end of the decade, not because they did not exist, but because they were divided by conflicts among themselves. National leadership, which in any event did not emerge in the 1920's, perhaps could not have succeeded in subduing these tensions and in creating a new common front.

Third, as a result of the foregoing, progressivism as an organized national force suffered a serious decline in the 1920's. This decline was heightened by the defection of large elements among the urban middle classes and the intellectuals, a desertion induced by technological, economic, and demographic changes, and by the outcropping of certain repressive tendencies in progressivism after 1917.

Fourth, in spite of reversals and failures, important components of the national progressive movement survived in considerable vigor and succeeded to a varying degree, not merely in keeping the movement alive, but even in broadening its horizons. This was true particularly of the farm groups and of the coalition concerned with public regulation or ownership of electric power resources. These two groups laid the groundwork in the 1920's for significant new programs in the 1930's and beyond.

Fifth, various progressive coalitions controlled Congress for the greater part of the 1920's and were always a serious threat to the conservative administrations that controlled the executive branch. Because this was true, most of the legislation adopted by Congress during this period, including many measures that historians have inaccurately called reactionary, was progressive in character.

Sixth, the progressive movement in the cities and states was far from dead in the 1920's, although we do not have sufficient evidence to justify any generalizations about the degree of its vigor.

If this tentative and imperfect synthesis has any value, perhaps it is high time that we discard the sweeping generalizations, false hypotheses, and clichés that we have so often used in explaining and characterizing political developments for what they are—the normal and ordinary political behavior of groups and classes caught up in a swirl of social and economic change. When we do this we will no longer ask whether the progressive movement was defunct in the 1920's. We will ask only what happened to it and why.

Chapter 16 PARTIAL SUCCESS

The debate over Progressivism has been a family quarrel. It takes on another dimension when Americans are asked to tell foreigners what the Progressive movement was about. Immediately the context changes, because the audience is suddenly different. Keep that point in mind when reading the lecture below. It is by the editor of this volume, ARTHUR MANN *(1922-), whose special interests, both as teacher and writer, include the history of social movements.*

History is so full of worthy causes that failed that it is particularly pleasant to call your attention to one that succeeded, at least partially.

I have in mind the Progressive movement, which went a long way toward defining the goals of American life during the first two decades of the twentieth century. Itself affected by social reform currents of the 1890s, the Progressive movement for its own part was to influence the New Deal, the New Frontier, and the Great Society. The subject I have chosen to talk with you about today is, in short, a chapter in the ongoing history of American liberalism.

But to talk about the past involves a risk that one will distort it, and the risk is greatest when one tries to relate the past to the present. The great German scientific

Arthur Mann, "The Progressive Movement," a lecture prepared in 1965 for a foreign audience, and subsequently given in altered form in Marajay, Venezuela, 1970.

historian of the last century, Ranke, warned historians of that risk when he urged them to consider every event as unique to itself. Yet even Ranke agreed that things are connected and that we more fully understand them as they are when we know what they once were. He further conceded that a knowledge of the past is indispensable to men who are concerned with social change.

We today are so concerned. Our world is not only seeking change, it is undergoing change at an unprecedented pace and never before has it needed orderly and progressive change on so vast a scale. To such a world, I should like to suggest, the Progressive movement might have lessons to teach. It is an example of how a nation coped with the complex and bewildering and painful problems of modernity through the middle way, within the framework of its own institutions, and on the basis of traditional values.

Let me enlarge and state my point more strongly.

It has often been remarked, and rightly so, that the United States is the sole major country *not* to have had a major Marxist movement. Among the several reasons for that phenomenon, perhaps the most important is that, in the free competition for men's loyalties, Progressivism (or Liberalism, as it is also called) defeated Marxism at the ballot box. Thus,

–In the presidential election of 1912–to cite the most striking example at the height of the Progressive era–the Socialist Party candidate, Eugene Debs, received 6 percent of the popular vote in contrast to the combined 70 percent for Theodore Roosevelt and Woodrow Wilson, his Progressive opponents.

–And during the great Depression of the 1930s when one should have expected Marxism to be especially appealing, the liberal Franklin D. Roosevelt overwhelmed his Socialist and Communist opponents by an even greater margin than Wilson and the first Roosevelt had beaten Debs.

Progressivism contained Marxism in America because it was a more appealing alternative to social action.

I do not mean to suggest that Marxism, or Progressivism for that matter, is of a single piece. Nor would I deny that the two have shared some things in common. Yet, in America, Marxists and Progressives once competed against each other as self-conscious rivals. And they were in rivalry not just because the one proposed a collectivized economy and the other a mixed and regulated capitalism. Like political rivals in general, Progressives and Marxists approached social problems with different assumptions, different aspirations, different methods, and different moods.

Marxism gives priority to the community over the individual, but to Progressivism the paramount task of reform is to satisfy the needs of *both* the community *and* the individual in a formula that will strike a balance between social control and personal liberty. The Marxists divide society into essentially two classes forever antagonistic to each other: the exploited and the exploiters. Progressives, in contrast, view society as pluralistic, consisting of a variety of occupational, sectional, religious, ethnic, political, and other groups, all of whom must learn how to live with each other. The Progressive mood is pragmatic, which is to say that it is tentative and experimental and open ended, whereas orthodox Marxists operate in an intellectual system that is rigid and doctrinaire and closed. Unlike the Marxist aspiration for heaven on earth, Progressivism works within the system for finite goals and expects the struggle for human betterment to continue as long as human beings remain human.

Not that American liberalism has ever rejected the doctrine of progress, or that it is head without heart, lacking compassion, social concern, ethical commitment, or moral fervor. On the contrary.

—To appreciate the capacity for indignation over social injustice that animated the Progressive era, one has only to glance at the titles of such representative books and articles as *Sin and Society; Frenzied Finance; The Shame of the Cities; The Shame of the States; The Bitter Cry of the Children; How the Other Half Lives; Civilization's Inferno; The Negroes' Struggle for Survival. . . .*

—And to appreciate the faith of the generation 1900-1920 that it could create a better future, one has only to skim the pages of *The Old Order Changeth; Drift and Mastery; The Way Out; The Battle of the Slum; The New Democracy; The New Freedom; The New Republic; The Promise of American Life.*

But it was Woodrow Wilson, elected president in 1912 and reelected in 1916, who summed up the activist moralism of his contemporaries when he said in his first inaugural address: "We have made up our minds to square every process of our national life . . . with the standards we so proudly set up at the beginning and have always carried at our hearts."

And it is here that we touch on the essential character of the Progressive movement, which one writer has aptly called "The Revolt of the American Conscience." Properly to deal with that revolt would take more time than I have in this brief talk, and what I should like to do today is to call attention to the relevance of the Progressive movement to our troubled but hopeful world by briefly exploring with you the why, the who, and the what of the movement and to consider how it changed America for the good during a troubled period of transition in its history.

First, the causes.

II

At first glance, one might have expected America to have had an era of self-congratulation, not a revolt of conscience.

From around 1880 to 1920, America was transformed by industrialization, urbanization, and immigration. Those forty years or so were America's take-off point into modernity, and the blessings of an urban, technological, and pluralistic society even then were prodigious. Expansion was so rapid—in investment, production, consumption, land use, urban growth, population, and inventions—that by 1920 America was outproducing every other nation on the globe. And there seemed to be no end to expansion. Capital was plentiful, natural resources were abundant, inventiveness was widespread, and a huge labor force existed not only among natives but also among immigrants who, after 1900, were arriving on average close to a million a year.

But, as we have learned from the experience of new nations today, great social movements are not born when conditions are the most hopeless. They are born when life is changing for the better, during moments of upswing that give people cause to have rising expectations for themselves and their posterity. The Progressive era was one such moment of upswing leading to rising expectations. More specifically,

–In an era of growing abundance, poverty stood out all the more as an indefensible evil.

–At a time when the city was being hailed as a center of civilization, slums were even less supportable than they might otherwise have been.

–To a society of increasing social mobility, the denial of equal opportunity to Negroes was a contradiction so apparent that it couldn't stand without new invention in logic.

–During the decades of America's emergence as a world power, political corruption became even more intolerable than it already was.

–For a nation that had entered a war to save the world for democracy, the granting of the franchise to women was patently long overdue.

–In an economy whose ethos had long been a competitive one, the growth of monopolies (they were called trusts) in banking, manufacturing, and transportation could not be allowed to go unchecked.

I could go on and on with examples, for wherever the Progressives looked they claimed to see an endless number of unhealthy contradictions about them. They contrasted the fact with the ideal–the what-is with the what-ought-to-be-and they found America wanting. But what was the source, we must ask, of the what-ought-to-be?

President Wilson located it for us in his 1913 pledge "to square every process of our national life . . . with the standards we so proudly set up at the beginning and have always carried at our hearts." A college professor and historian of the American people before entering the White House, Wilson meant by standards the principles of the eighteenth-century Enlightenment through which the Americans had justified their War for Independence and on which they had founded a nation state. "Our work," Wilson went on to say, "is a work of restoration."

At first glance, it would seem that Wilson was speaking a strange language for a Progressive reformer. To look to the past for guidelines to the future is a habit of mind we ordinarily associate with conservatives. But we would miss the thrust of American liberalism if we failed to grasp that the American past has been a liberal past and that liberals have sought to preserve it.

Unlike the extreme left, which has rejected traditional values, American liberalism has worked to make a reality of what the Swedish writer, Gunnar Myrdal, has called the American Creed. Formulated by the Revolutionary generation, it has endured for almost two hundred years. According to the testimony of observers from the eighteenth-century Crèvecoeur to the twentieth-century Myrdal, the foundation stone of the Creed is the responsible and self-achieving individual. On him everything else rests: representative government, the secular state, religious pluralism, equality before the law, social mobility, private property, and distribution of public power not only among federal, state, and local governments but also between government and voluntary associations.

On such principles a nation was born. "The American is a new man," Crèvecoeur wrote in 1782, "who acts upon new principles. . . . "

But two other functions of the Creed explain its durability. For one thing, it has enabled Americans, who are of diverse racial, religious, and ethnic origins, to define their identity among the peoples of the world. For another, it has served as an ideological yardstick to measure the difference between the what-is and the what-ought-to-be. If in comparison to other nations America has been barren of ideologies, as some writers have observed, it is because America started out, and in large measure has remained, an ideology in itself.

That is why Wilson could say, without meaning to be sanctimonious, "Sometimes people call me an idealist. Well, that is how I know I am an American."

Call his idealism by whatever name you will—the American Creed, the American Conscience, the American Consensus—it was being tested in Wislon's day, as once it had been tested by the Civil War and later would be tested by the great Depression. The monopoly problem and the poverty problem, the slum problem and the Negro problem, the problem of political corruption and all other problems of early twentieth-century America violated, as Wilson said, the political, economic, and social standards set up at the beginning of the national experiment.

What, then, did Wilson and his generation propose to do about squaring the achievement of American life with the promise of American life?

III

To answer that question, we must first ask still another, namely, who were the Progressives?

Like all successful movements in America, the Progressive movement rested on a broad coalition whose diversity reflected the diversity of the American population itself. For the sake of analysis, however, we might group the Progressives into one of the two following categories:

—On the one hand, a large number of Progressives belonged to groups outside, or not fully inside, the great American bonanza. Their desire for social reform, therefore, derived primarily from the not unworthy motive of self-interest. Here we might single out skilled workers in the trade unions, feminists, middle-class Negroes, and small businessmen who saw in big business a personal threat.

—On the other hand, an even larger number of groups produced Progressives who had nothing materialistic to gain from social reform. They became reformers out of an identification with the underdog, or an opposition to corrupt interests, or a more general desire to promote the public good. These included clergymen, social workers, lawyers, responsible leaders in big business, journalists, college professors, artists and writers, members of old families, and a new breed of liberal politicians.

Some of the Progressives were interested in a single cause, others in many causes, and still others fought fellow Progressives over certain issues, so that one might say, I suppose, that the Progressive movement was several movements. Yet, however varied the movements and the people supporting them, the Progressive movement as a whole pursued four objectives: to expose what was wrong with America, to make government more representative, to regulate big business, and to help the underdog.

A word about each of the four.

A good deal, perhaps most, of the Progressive literature of the first two decades of this century came in the form of social criticism. Gambling, prostitution, slum conditions, bigotry, poverty, concentrated wealth, crime, delinquency, shady business practices, political graft—all these and other social evils attracted the attention of what that day were called muckraking writers. To single out one book or writer would be invidious, but perhaps Lincoln Steffens' *Shame of the Cities* (1904), which first appeared as a serial in a popular magazine, can serve as an example.

Like many other muckrakers, Steffens was a journalist. He wrote a plain but highly idiomatic and realistic prose that has since become characteristic of the best American journalism (the young Walter Lippmann served his apprenticeship under Steffens). Again like other muckrakers, Steffens was unsure of *why* big city politics were so awful, but in his exposé of Chicago, St. Louis, Pittsburgh, Philadelphia, and New York he wrote with authority about the incompetence and dishonesty he uncovered in the political machines of those cities. The solution? Throw out the rascals, Steffens urged, and elect good men in their place.

Other Progressives argued, on the other hand, that the solution lay through institutional reforms. One remedy called for nonpartisanship—nonpartisan elections and nonpartisan government through professional technicians in the form of either a city manager or a city commission. Another remedy demanded that the political parties become more representative of the party rank and file through the direct primary in nominations, the direct election of senators, woman suffrage, and the initiative, referendum, and recall. By 1920 both remedies, as well as Steffens' proposed solution, had been tried on a wide scale.

To some Progressives the purification of politics was an end in itself, but to others it was a means to enable government to cope with other needs of the people. Therein lay the thrust for the welfare state and regulated capitalism. But could a society undergoing industrialization and urbanization achieve those two objectives through political institutions dating from the agricultural eighteenth century?

In answering that question we have to distinguish between the federal government on the one hand and state and local government on the other.

Unlike the federal government, the states and cities had never been restricted by the doctrine of laissez-faire. On the contrary, they had been expected to do a great deal, and throughout the nineteenth century, as Lord Bryce shrewdly observed, they did do a great deal to control areas of the economy judged to have a public character.

Their activities increased between 1900 and 1920. Under Progressive governors and mayors in New York, New Jersey, Wisconsin, Ohio—to cite random examples—laws were passed and commissions were established to regulate insurance companies, the railroads, trolley cars, public utilities, manufacturing. Furthermore, with the help of social workers, Progressives pushed through legislation affecting child labor, industrial accidents, factory conditions, tenement houses, and the like. In short, state and city governments took on even more regulatory and welfare functions during the Progressive era than in the past.

But, with regard to the federal government, there was in 1900 some question as to how far it could go. Actually, from the beginning and through the Civil War, the federal government had involved itself in the economy through a national bank, the tariff, the subsidization of railroads, the disposal of the public domain, and higher education. But at the beginning of the twentieth-century, owing to a two-decade vogue of Social Darwinism, the ruling idea in the nation's capital was laissez-faire.

Accordingly, Progressive intellectuals launched an attack on the conventional wisdom of their day. To reconstruct their argument in entirety would be tedious, and it is enough to say that they succeeded in discrediting the jungle-like ethic of Social Darwinism and also in rediscovering the precedents in the American past for strong federal government. Thus, in his influential *The Promise of American Life* (1909), Herbert Croly, a presidential adviser, wrote that the need of the day was to achieve Thomas Jefferson's democratic objectives through the means of Alexander Hamilton's positive state.

But even if one accepted that formula, as did Theodore Roosevelt and others, the problem remained of what, specifically, the state should do on the federal level. No more than in the drive to purify politics were the Progressives of a single mind. We can best see their most important theoretical differences by examining the contrasting programs of Theodore Roosevelt and Woodrow Wilson, respectively the New Nationalism and the New Freedom, in the 1912 presidential election.

Roosevelt regarded the growth of big business as both historically inevitable and economically beneficial. He was prepared to regulate big business and also to expand the welfare functions of the state in the direction of unemployment insurance, old-age pensions, the abolition of child labor, the protection of women in industry, and minimum-wage and maximum-hours laws. But to Wilson large corporations were inefficient and, what is equally important, a threat to social mobility. He, too, would use the power of the federal government, but to break up big business and return to an older, more competitive, more individualistic economy of small enterprise. In welfare legislation he had little interest.

Wilson won the election, but once in office, he came to understand the futility of turning the hands of the economic clock back and, in his two administrations, enacted the regulatory and welfare policies of Roosevelt's New Nationalism. Ever since Wilson's presidency, for example, the federal government has had a Labor Department headed by a secretary of full cabinet rank.

If one adds up all of the federal legislation between 1900 and 1920, the sum is impressive. It had to do with trade unions (legitimizing them), railroads, food, drugs, natural resources, banking, the telephone, telegraphic cable, wireless, liquor, agriculture, shipping, and the structure of corporations. In none of this did the state go into business for itself, and when it did, as in the case of creating national parks, it already was the owner of the public domain. Its main function was that of umpire. Furthermore, by federal amendment, the Progressives added to the law of the land an income tax, the vote for women, and the popular election of senators.

Thus far, I have been talking about the role of government in the Progressive movement. But there was another side to the movement, involving such voluntary associations as the American Federation of Labor, the American Civil Liberties Union, the National Association for the Advancement of Colored People, the College Settlements Association, the Consumers' League, and many other organizations concerned with education, religion, birth control, and so on, almost indefinitely. Even when pressuring government for legislation—and this was only *one* activity—these organizations took the intitative, formulated goals, and got things done in their respective areas. The good, for example, that Jane Addams did as a settlement house resident in the slums of Chicago in Americanizing the immigrant is incalculable.

And it is here that we can stop and sum up by asking just how much good came out of the Progressive movement.

IV

We might start by saying that it did not create the harm that the standpatters were certain it would. More specifically, the Old Guard was certain that woman suffrage and birth control would destroy the family, but that, of course, is not what happened. They were also certain that the popular election of senators would debase the Senate, but that body has actually had more able men since the first part of this century. Nor did the regulation of the economy and the passage of welfare legislation impede, as the reactionaries predicted, economic growth.

On the contrary, the Progressive movement strengthened historical tendencies and institutions. It saved capitalism from the folly of some capitalists, and by so doing, removed the threat of Marxist collectivism. It enlarged the powers of representative government to deal with the problems created by the forces remaking America. It successfully fought the idea that society is class-ridden and urged that the workingman is not someone to suppress or encourage to revolt but someone who must be drawn into the American dream. The Progressive movement proved that a capitalist democracy can roll with the shocks of social problems and that it contains resources within itself to solve those problems.

In proving that point, the Progressive movement proved, as the New Deal would later prove again, that capitalist democracy is elastic and adaptable. I wish I had the time to show that it further proved the internationalism and eclecticism of such a democracy. More specifically, with an interest in what a journalist called "Foreign Experiment Stations," the Progressives absorbed ideas and institutions from all over the world–from France, postal savings banks; from Switzerland, the referendum and recall; from Germany, workingmen's pensions; from Great Britain, the settlement house; from Australia, the eight-hour day; from New Zealand, public works for the unemployed; from a variety of countries, the scientific management of cities.

In the end, of course, certain problems remained unsolved. Unskilled labor was not to be organized until the 1930s. The current Negro revolt is a sign that the founding of the N.A.A.C.P. in 1910 was but a first step toward achieving equal rights. The secret of how to make the big cities more livable than they are is still elusive. President Johnson's war on poverty is proof that previous efforts had failed to include everyone in America's affluence.

But, a half century and more ago, the Progressives made an important start. The arrogance and the economic power of a J. P. Morgan is unthinkable today. Few persons question the right of the government, on any level, to regulate the economy. Nor is there widespread opposition to the role of the state to achieve social justice. If there is still much to do, that is because American liberalism, like America istelf, is unfinished business. How could it be otherwise? Living up to a Creed infinitely demanding in its democratic idealism engages Americans in a task without end.

Suggestions for Further Reading

The most comprehensive overview of the literature is contained in George E. Mowry's pamphlet, "The Progressive Era, 1900-1920: The Reform Persuasion" (Washington, D.C., 1972). There is also a wealth of bibliographical information in Peter G. Filene's provocatively argued "An Obituary for the 'Progressive Movement,'" *American Quarterly*, XXII (Spring 1970), 20-34. For a survey of the literature that emphasizes the relationship of Progressivism to Populism and the New Deal, see Arthur Mann, "The Progressive Tradition," in John Higham, ed., *The Reconstruction of American History* (New York, 1962), 157-179.

The latest attempt at a synthesis of the Progressive movement is Robert H. Wiebe's *The Search For Order, 1877-1920* (New York, 1967). For the interpretation that Wiebe purports to replace, the status-revolution theory, see Richard Hofstadter's *The Age of Reform: From Bryan to F. D. R.* (New York, 1955). More eclectic in interpretation and much broader in factual coverage than both Wiebe and Hofstadter are three volumes in the New American Nation Series: Harold U.

Faulkner, *Politics, Reform, and Expansion, 1890-1900* (New York, 1959); George E. Mowry, *The Era of Theodore Roosevelt, 1900-1912* (New York, 1958); Arthur S. Link, *Woodrow Wilson and the Progressive Era, 1910-1917* (New York, 1954). For an interpretation that comes close to denying the existence of a distinct Progressive era, see Samuel P. Hays, *The Response to Industrialism, 1885-1914* (Chicago, 1957). The oldest attempt at a synthesis, Benjamin Parke De Witt's *The Progressive Movement* (New York, 1915), is still undated in several ways. There are thoughtful summaries of, and commentaries on, the different schools of interpretation in Dewey D. Grantham, Jr., "The Progressive Era and the Reform Tradition," *Mid-America*, XLVI (October 1964), 227-251; John D. Buenker, "The Progressive Era: A Search for a Synthesis," *Mid-America*, LI (April 1969), 175-193; and Otis L. Graham, Jr., *The Great Campaigns: Reform and War in America, 1900-1928* (Englewood Cliffs, N.J., 1971).

The starting point for an analysis of the relationship between Populism and Progressivism remains John D. Hicks' *The Populist Revolt* (Minneapolis, 1931). Two later works stressing the influence of Populism on subsequent reform movements are Russell B. Nye, *Midwestern Progressive Politics: A Historical Study of Its Origins and Development, 1870-1950* (East Lansing, Mich., 1951), and Theodore Saloutos and John D. Hicks, *Agricultural Discontent in the Middle West, 1900-1939* (Madison, Wis., 1951). In his illuminating monograph on *Populism to Progressivism in Alabama* (Princeton, 1969), Sheldon Hackney shows that, in the state he studied, Populism and Progressivism grew from different social roots. C. Vann Woodward is also excellent on Southern Populism and Progressivism in *The Origins of the New South, 1877-1913* (Baton Rouge, La., 1951). Students who like the biographical approach will profit from C. Vann Woodward, *Tom Watson, Agrarian Rebel* (New York, 1938), and Francis B. Simkins, *Pitchfork Ben Tillman, South Carolinian* (Baton Rouge, La., 1944).

The most influential criticism of Populism is contained in Richard Hofstadter's previously cited *The Age of Reform.* See also Albert D. Kirwin, *Revolt of the Rednecks; Mississippi Politics, 1876-1925* (Lexington, Ky., 1951); Daniel Bell, ed., *The New American Right* (New York, 1955); and Victor C. Ferkiss, "Populist Influences on American Fascism," *Western Political Quarterly*, X (June 1957), 350-373.

Norman Pollack has written two rebuttals in defense of the Populist crusade: "Hofstadter on Populism: A Critique of 'The Age of Reform,' " *Journal of Southern History,* XXVI (November 1970), 478-500, and "The Myth of Populist Anti-Semitism," *American Historical Review* LXVIII (October 1962), 76-80. Also see Pollack's *The Populist Response to Industrial America* (Cambridge, Mass., 1962). There is a further defense of Populism in C. Vann Woodward, "The Populist Heritage and the Intellectual," *American Scholar*, XXIX (Winter 1959-1960), 55-72. For Hicks' justification of his own work, see his "Reform Cycles in Recent American History," *Idaho Yesterdays*, VI (Summer 1962), 11-15, 18-21. The most persuasive refutation of the charge that Populism was bigoted is to be found in Walter T. K. Nugent's *The Tolerant Populists* (Chicago, 1963).

The role of urban reformers in the pre-Progressive era is at the center of Sidney Fine's exhaustive *Laissez Faire and the General-Welfare State: A Study of Conflict in American Thought, 1865-1901* (Ann Arbor, Mich., 1956). Ray Ginger's *Altgeld's America: The Lincoln Ideals Versus Changing Realities* (Chicago, 1958) is good on Chicago, and Arthur Mann's *Yankee Reformers in the Urban Age* (Cambridge, Mass, 1954) is useful for Boston. Howard H. Quint, *The Forging of American Socialism: Origins of the Modern Movement* (Columbia, S. C., 1953) covers more ground than the title indicates. Hans B. Thorelli is competent on the late nineteenth-century roots of *The Federal Antitrust Policy: Organization of an American Tradition* (Baltimore, 1955). For an unsympathetic portrait of elite reformers in the late nineteenth century, see John G. Sproat's *"The Best Men": Liberal Reformers in the Gilded Age* (New York, 1968).

The varied groups that took part in the Progressive movement are the subject of several studies. For the role of businessmen, see Robert H. Wiebe, *Businessmen and Reform: A Study of the Progressive Movement* (Cambridge, Mass., 1962), and the equally sympathetic volume, John A. Garraty, *Right-Hand Man: The Life of George N. Perkins* (New York, 1960). On the elite background of the members of the Progressive party, see Alfred D. Chandler, Jr.'s very important statistical study, "The Origins of Progressive Leadership," in Elting E. Morison, ed., *The Letters of Theodore Roosevelt* (Cambridge, Mass., 1954), vol. VIII, 1462-1465. Progressive journalists are competently handled in C. C. Regier, *The Era of the Muckraker* (Chapel Hill, N. C., 1932), and with greater gusto by Louis Filler in *Crusaders for American Liberalism* (Yellow Springs, Ohio, 1950). The movement of Protestant clergymen to the left is the theme of Charles H. Hopkins' encyclopedic *The Rise of the Social Gospel in American Protestantism, 1860-1915* (New Haven, Conn., 1940), and of Henry F. May's more interpretive *Protestant Churches and Industrial America* (New York, 1949). On the importance of social workers, consult Robert H. Bremner's pioneering volume, *From the Depths: The Discovery of Poverty in the United States* (New York, 1956), together with Allen F. Davis' much more extended treatment in *Spearheads for Reform: The Social Settlements and the Progressive Movement, 1890-1914* (New York, 1967). The best histories on organized labor's relationship to Progressivism include Melvyn Dubofsky, *When Workers Organize: New York City in the Progressive Era* (Amherst, Mass., 1968); Irwin Yellowitz, *Labor and the Progressive Movement in New York State, 1897-1916* (Ithaca, N. Y.,1965); and Marc Karson, *American Labor Unions and Politics, 1900-1918* (Carbondale, Ill., 1958). On the contribution of women and blacks to Progressivism, there are, respectively, Aileen S. Kraditor's insightful *The Ideas of the Woman Suffrage Movement, 1890-1920* (New York, 1965), and August Meier's equally illuminating *Negro Thought in America, 1880-1915* (Ann Arbor, Mich., 1963).

There has been a growing literature about the participation of ethnic groups in the Progressive movement since the publication of J. Joseph Huthmacher's "Urban Liberalism and the Age of Reform," *Mississippi Valley Historical Review* XLIX (September 1962), 231-241. See, for example, Huthmacher's own *Senator Robert F. Wagner and the Rise of Urban Liberalism* (New York, 1968); Nancy J. Weiss, *Charles Francis Murphy, 1858-1924: Respectability and Responsibility in Tammany Politics* (Northampton, Mass., 1968); Philip Gleason, *The Conservative Reformers: German-American Catholics and the Social Order* (Notre Dame, Ind., 1968); Jon Wefald, *A Voice of Protest: Norwegians in American Politics, 1890-1917* (Northfield, Minn., 1971); Victor R. Greene, *The Slavic Community on Strike* (Notre Dame, Ind., 1968).

The literature about the political leaders of the Progressive movement is voluminous, and there are no signs that it is leveling off. For an Easterner who almost became president, see Robert F. Wesser's *Charles Evans Hughes: Politics and Reform in New York, 1905-1910* (Ithaca, N. Y., 1967). Two Midwesterners are the subjects of scrupulously researched biographies: *Albert J. Beveridge: American Nationalist* (Chicago, 1971), by John Braeman; and *George W. Norris*, 2 vols. (Syracuse, N. Y., 1963; Urbana, Ill., 1971), by Richard Lowitt. With regard to big city leaders, in addition to Weiss' *Murphy* and Huthmacher's *Wagner*, both previously cited, see Oscar Handlin, *Al Smith and His America* (Boston, 1958), and Melvin G. Holli, *Reform in Detroit: Hazen S. Pingree and Urban Politics* (New York, 1969). Contrast those volumes with Joel A. Tarr, *A Study in Boss Politics: William Lorimer of Chicago* (Urbana, Ill., 1971). For southern leadership, see Dewey W. Grantham, Jr., *Hoke Smith and the Politics of the New South* (Baton Rouge, La., 1958), and William E. Larsen, *Montague of Virginia: The Making of a Southern Progressive* (Baton Rouge, La., 1965). On the fight over President Wilson's nomination of a welfare-minded Supreme Court justice, see A. L. Todd's *Justice on Trial: The Case of Louis D. Brandeis* (New York, 1964). One of Wilson's attorney generals is the subject of Stanley Coben's thoughtful *A. Mitchell Palmer, Politician* (New York, 1963). James Holt's monograph carefully examines *Congressional Insurgents and the Party System, 1909-1916.* (Cambridge, Mass., 1967). For a superb analysis of the Bull Moose Party and the man who led it, see George E. Mowry's *Theodore Roosevelt and the Progressive Movement* (Madison, Wis., 1946). Contrast Paxton Hibben's debunking biography of *William Jennings Bryan, The Peerless Leader* (New York, 1929), with two recent, sympathetic works: Paul W. Glad's *The Trumpet Soundeth* (Lincoln, Nebr., 1960) and Lawrence W. Levine's *Defender of the Faith* (New York, 1965). Henry F. Pringle's *Theodore Roosevelt* (New York, 1931) is challenged by John M. Blum's more appreciative *The Republican Roosevelt* (Cambridge, Mass., 1954), which, in turn, is challenged by William H. Harbaugh's *Power and Responsibility: The Life and Times of Theodore Roosevelt* (New York, 1961). The best short biography of T. R. is by G. Wallace Chessman, *Theodore Roosevelt and the Politics of Power* (Boston, 1969). As for Woodrow Wilson,

Arthur S. Link's superb, as yet unfinished, ongoing biography of Wilson (5 vols.; Princeton, 1947-1965) have carried the story down to 1916. John M. Blum's *Woodrow Wilson and the Politics of Morality* (Boston, 1956) is a succinct but unflattering account. For the attitudes of post-World War II historians toward Wilson, see the interesting article by Richard L. Watson, Jr., "Woodrow Wilson and His Interpreters, 1947-1957," *Mississippi Valley Historical Review,* LXIV (September 1957), 207-236. In still another excellent review essay, "Seven Progressives," *Business History Review*, XXXV (Winter 1961), 581-592, John Braeman draws an important distinction between modernists and traditionalists among Progressive political leaders. For the image that two political leaders had of themselves, see *La Follette's Autobiography* (Madison, Wis., 1913) and Theodore Roosevelt, *An Autobiography* (New York, 1913).

Beginning with Vernon L. Parrington, *Main Currents in American Thought*, 3 vols.: (New York, 1927, 1930), there has been a rich literature about the intellectual side of Progressivism. Henry Steele Commager, *The American Mind* (New Haven, Conn., 1950) is practically alone in celebrating Progressive ideas. Some writers–among them Daniel Aaron, *Men of Good Hope* (New York, 1951); Arthur A. Ekirch, Jr., *The Decline of American Liberalism* (New York, 1955); and Louis Hartz, *The Liberal Tradition in America* (New York, 1955)–have objected, but for different reasons, to classifying Progressive thinkers as authentic reformers. At the other extreme, David W. Noble, in *The Paradox of Progressive Thought* (Minneapolis, 1958), regards the Progressives as all too typical of the liberal reform mind and dismisses them as fuzzy-minded utopians. More sympathetic are Eric F. Goldman, *Rendezvous With Destiny* (New York, 1952), and Morton G. White, *Social Thought in America* (New York, 1949), who nevertheless find fault with Progressive thinkers for being moral relativists. Richard Hofstadter, on the other hand, censures the Progressive mind for moral absolutism in the previously cited *Age of Reform.* In the *New Radicalism in America*, 1889-1963 (New York, 1965), Christopher Lasch gives the impression that Progressive intellectuals were neurotics all. Daniel Levine is much more sympathetic in *Varieties of Reform Thought* (Madison, Wis., 1964). For a novel approach to the intellectual history of the Progressive era, one that emphasizes a split between generations, see Henry F. May, *The End to American Innocence* (New York, 1959). For two recent, full biographies of Progressive intellectuals, see Jack Tager, *The Intellectual As Urban Reformer: Brand Whitlock and the Progressive Movement* (Cleveland, 1968), and Julius Weinberg, *Edward Alsworth Ross and the Sociology of Progressivism* (Madison, Wis., 1972).

The outstanding primary sources for the intellectual content of the New Nationalism are Herbert Croly, *The Promise of American Life* (New York, 1909); Walter E. Weyl, *The New Democracy* (New York, 1912); Walter Lippmann, *A Preface to Politics* (New York, 1914) and *Drift and Mastery* (New York, 1914). These books and the men who wrote them are the subject of a sympathetic yet severely critical study by Charles Forcey, *The Crossroads of Liberalism* (New York,

1961). For the philosophy that lay behind the New Freedom, the following are essential: Woodrow Wilson's book by that title (New York, 1913); Charles R. Van Hise, *Concentration and Control* (New York, 1912); and Louis D. Brandeis, *Other People's Money and How the Bankers Use It* (New York, 1914). William Diamond, in *The Economic Thought of Woodrow Wilson* (Baltimore, 1943), is as critical of the New Freedom as Forcey is of the New Nationalism.

For the local and regional variations and similarities of Progressivism, the student would do well to start with *The Autobiography of Lincoln Steffens* (New York, 1931), a classic by a muckraker whose investigation led him to many states and cities. On the question of why an old center of reform lagged behind the Progressive movement, see Richard M. Abrams' intriguingly argued *Conservatism in a Progressive Era: Massachusetts Politics, 1900-1912* (Cambridge, Mass., 1964). Winston A. Flint's *The Progressive Movement in Vermont* (Washington, D. C., 1941) is pedestrian in comparison to Ransome E. Noble, Jr.'s *New Jersey Progressivism Before Wilson* (Princeton, N.J., 1946). There is a useful and long-needed monograph by Jane S. Dahlberg on *The New York Bureau of Research: Pioneer in Government Administration* (New York, 1966). Walton Bean's *Boss Reuf's San Francisco* (Berkeley, Calif., 1952) is a splendid companion piece to George E. Mowry's *The California Progressives* (Berkeley, Calif., 1951), but both are challenged by Michael Paul Rogin and John L. Shover, *Political Change in California: Critical Elections and Social Movements, 1890-1966* (Westport, Conn., 1970). The role of the South is amply covered in Woodward's *Origins of the New South*; Hackney's *Populism to Progressivism in Alabama*; Hugh C. Bailey, *Liberalism in the New South: Southern Social Reformers and the Progressive Movement* (Coral Gables, Fla., 1969); William D. Miller, *Memphis During the Progressive Era, 1900-1917* (Memphis, 1957). For an insightful history of a border-state city, see James B. Crooks, *Politics and Progress: The Rise of Urban Progressivism in Baltimore, 1895-1911* (Baton Rouge, La., 1968). Since the publication of Nye's already mentioned *Midwestern Progressive Politics* in 1951, the following important monographs have been published: Carl H. Chrislock, *The Progressive Era in Minnesota, 1899-1918* (St. Paul, 1971); Lyle W. Dorsett, *The Pendergast Machine* (New York, 1968); Holli's previously cited *Reform in Detroit*; Zane L. Miller, *Boss Cox's Cincinnati: Urban Politics in the Progressive Era* (New York, 1968); Hoyt L. Warner, *Progressivism in Ohio, 1897-1917* (Columbus, Ohio, 1964). Compare Robert S. Maxwell's *La Follette and the Rise of the Progressives in Wisconsin* (Madison, Wis., 1956) with the two following later studies: Herbert F. Marguiles, *The Decline of the Progressive Movement in Wisconsin, 1890-1920* (Madison, Wis., 1968), and David P. Thelen, *The New Citizenship: Origins of Progressivism in Wisconsin, 1885-1900* (Columbia, Mo., 1972).

The most useful starting point for the regulation of the economy is James E. Anderson, *The Emergence of the Modern Regulatory State* (Washington, D. C., 1962). In the previously cited *Businessmen and Reform*, Robert H. Wiebe shows the extent to which different kinds of businessmen shaped the regulatory state during the Progressive era, but he stops short of saying that the regulatory state was wholly the creature of big business. For that extreme interpretation, see, in addition to Gabriel Kolko's *The Triumph of Conservatism: A Reinterpretation of American History, 1900-1916* (Glencoe, Ill., 1963), and his *Railroads and Regulations, 1877-1916* (Princeton, N.J., 1965). Stanley P. Caine argues much the same point in *The Myth of Progressive Reform: Railroad Regulation in Wisconsin, 1903-1910* (Madison, Wis., 1970). For an opposite interpretation, turn to Martin Albro, *Enterprise Denied: Origins of the Decline of American Railroads, 1897-1917* (New York, 1971). In *Law and Economic Policy in America: The Evolution of the Sherman Antitrust Act* (New York, 1965), William Letwin calls attention to the confusions and contradictions of Progressive regulatory policy. There is a revealing case study of the relationship of the federal government to one industry in Melvin I. Urofsky's thoughtful *Big Steel and the Wilson Administration: A Study of Business-Government Relations* (Columbus, Ohio, 1969). A good primary source on the regulation of the economy by state government is Charles McCarthy, introduction by Theodore Roosevelt, *The Wisconsin Idea* (New York, 1912).

The most readable history of the political reforms that originated in the Progressive era is Lorin Peterson's sprightly written *The Day of the Mugwump* (New York, 1961). For a superb review of the literature in the field, see Lyle W. Dorsett, "The City Boss and the Reformer: A Reappraisal," *Pacific Northwest Quarterly*, LXIII (October 1972), 150-154. Also see two excellent books of readings, Blaine A. Brownell and Warren E. Stickle, eds., *Bosses and Reformers* (Boston, 1973), and Bruce M. Stave, ed., *Urban Bosses, Machines, and Progressive Reformers* (Lexington, Mass., 1972). There is also a wealth of information in John P. East's *Council-Manager Government: The Political Thought of Its Founder, Richard S. Childs* (Chapel Hill., N. C., 1965), a monograph that covers more ground than its title implies. Contrast East's eclectic interpretation with James W. Weinstein's single-factor analysis, "Organized Business and the Commission and Manager Movements," *Journal of Southern History*, XXVIII (May 1962), 166-182. For accounts of how an old reform movement merged with the Progressive movement, see Kraditor, *Ideas of the Woman Suffrage Movement*, and the appropriate chapters in Eleanor Flexner, *Century of Struggle: The Woman's Rights Movement in the United States* (Cambridge, Mass., 1959); Andrew Sinclair, *The Better Half: The Emancipation of the American Woman* (New York, 1965); Anne F. Scott, *The Southern Lady: From Pedestal to Politics, 1830-1930* (Chicago, 1970). In *The Puritan Ethic* and *Woman Suffrage* (New York, 1967), Alan P. Grimes emphasizes nativist reasons in giving women the vote in western states.

There is as yet no published synthesis on the foundations of the welfare state during the Progressive era. However, in his previously mentioned *Spearheads for Reform*, Allen F. Davis amply covers the welfare proposals of the Progressive movement. There is also an accumulating literature on child welfare. See, for example, Jeremy P. Felt, *Hostages of Fortune: Child Labor Reform in New York State*

(Syracuse, N. Y., 1965); Walter I. Trattner, *Crusade for the Children: A History of the National Child Labor Committee and Child Labor Reform in America* (Chicago, 1970); Stephen B. Wood, *Constitutional Politics in the Progressive Era: Child Labor and the Law* (Chicago, 1968). Contrast the jaundiced approach that Anthony M. Platt takes in *The Child Savers: The Invention of Delinquency* (Chicago, 1969), with the sympathetic point of view in the concluding chapters in Joseph M. Hawes' *Children in Urban Society: Juvenile Delinquency in Nineteenth-Century America* (New York, 1971). No scholar of the history of welfare has made greater contributions than Roy Lubove. See, for example, his *The Progressives and the Slums: Tenement House Reform in New York City, 1890-1917* (Pittsburgh, 1962); *The Professional Altruist: The Emergence of Social Work as a Career, 1880-1930* (Cambridge, Mass., 1965); and *The Struggle for Social Security, 1900-1935* (Cambridge, Mass., 1968). Of the many fine biographies of welfare reformers, students might want to start with Louise C. Wade's *Graham Taylor: Pioneer for Social Justice, 1851-1938* (Chicago, 1964); Walter I. Trattner's *Homer Folks, Pioneer in Social Welfare* (New York, 1968); John C. Farrell's *Beloved Lady: A History of Jane Addams' Ideas on Reform and Peace* (Baltimore, 1967); Clarke A. Chambers' *Paul U. Kellogg and the Survey: Voices for Social Welfare and Social Justice* (Minneapolis, 1971). The indispensable primary source for the welfare side of Progressivism is Isaac M. Rubinow, *Social Insurance, with Special Reference to American Conditions* (New York, 1913). Contrast Rubinow's large hopes with the failure that Forrest A. Walker reports in "Compulsory Health Insurance: The Next Great Step in Social Legislation," *Journal of American History*, LVI (September 1969), 290-304.

There is a need for someone to pull together, in a single volume, Progressivism's mixed legacy with regard to race and immigration. For the latter subject, see the appropriate chapters in Oscar Handlin's *The Uprooted*, 2d ed. (Boston, 1973); John Higham's *Strangers in the Land* (New Brunswick, N. J., 1955); and Barbara M. Solomon's *Ancestors and Immigrants* (Cambridge, Mass., 1956). As for race, an important primary source is Ray Stannard Baker's *Following the Color Line* (New York, 1908), which has been reprinted in paperback (New York, 1964), with an illuminating introduction by Dewey W. Grantham, Jr., and subtitled: *American Negro Citizenship in the Progressive Era.* For an excellent biography of Baker, see Robert C. Bannister, *Ray Stannard Baker: The Mind and Thought of a Progressive* (New Haven, Conn., 1966). For other non-bigoted Progressives, see Davis' *Spearheads for Reform*, Chapter 5, and Steven J. Diner, "Chicago Social Workers and Blacks in the Progressive Era," *Social Service Review*, XLIV (December 1970), 393-410. Much less favorable to Progressives on the race question are Dewey W. Grantham, Jr., "The Progressive Movement and the Negro," *South Atlantic Quarterly*, LIV (October 1955), 461-477, and David W. Southern, *The Malignant Heritage: Yankee Progressives and the Negro Question, 1901-1914* (Chicago, 1968). For lily-white Southern Progressivism, see Woodward's *Origins of the New South* and

Hackney's *Populism to Progressivism in Alabama*. As for black efforts toward racial justice, the best work is Meier's *Negro Thought in America, 1880-1915*; Charles F. Kellogg, *NAACP: A History of the National Association for the Advancement of Colored People, Volume I: 1909-1920* (Baltimore, 1967); Nancy J. Weiss, "From Black Separatism to Interracial Cooperation: The Origins of Organized Efforts for Racial Advancement, 1890-1920," in Barton J. Bernstein and Allen J. Matusow, eds., *Twentieth Century America: Recent Interpretations* (New York, 1972), 52-87; Stephen R. Fox, *The Guardian of Boston: William Monroe Trotter* (New York, 1970); Elliot M. Rudwick, *W. E. B. Du Bois: A Study in Minority Group Leadership* (Philadelphia, 1960); Arvah E. Strickland, *History of the Chicago Urban League* (Urbana, Ill., 1966). For guides to further reading on the race question, see the appropriate sections in James M. McPherson, et. al., *Blacks in America: Bibliographical Essays* (New York, 1971), an extraordinarily useful work of careful and thoughtful scholarship.

Progressives took positions on other issues besides race, welfare, political reform, and economic regulation. On conflicting interpretations of the relationship of Progressivism to prohibition, see Andrew Sinclair, *Prohibition: The Era of Excess* (Boston, 1962); Joseph R. Gusfield, *Symbolic Crusade: Status Politics and the American Temperance Movement* (Urbana, Ill., 1963); James H. Timberlake, *Prohibition and the Progressive Movement 1900-1920* (Cambridge, Mass., 1963). The relationship of Progressivism to still other concerns is suggested by the titles of the following works: Samuel P. Hays, *Conservation and the Gospel of Efficiency: The Progressive Conservation Movement, 1890-1920* (Cambridge, Mass., 1959); James Penick, Jr., *Progressive Politics and Conservation: The Ballinger-Pinchot Affair* (Chicago, 1968); Samuel Haber, *Efficiency and Uplift: Scientific Management in the Progressive Era, 1890-1912* (Chicago, 1964); Sol Cohen, *Progressives and Urban School Reform: The Public Education Association of New York City, 1895-1954* (New York, 1964); Donald K. Pickens, *Eugenics and the Progressives* (Nashville, Tenn., 1968); Egal Feldman, "Prostitution, The Alien Woman, and the Progressive Imagination, 1910-1915," *American Quarterly*, XIX (Summer 1967), 192-206; John C. Burnham, "The Progressive Era Revolution in American Attitudes Toward Sex," *Journal of American History*, LIX (March 1973), 885-908; William L. O'Neill, *Divorce in the Progressive Era* (New Haven, Conn., 1967); O'Neill, *Everyone Was Brave: The Rise and Fall of Feminism in America* (Chicago, 1969); David M. Kennedy, *Birth Control in America: The Career of Margaret Sanger* (New Haven, Conn., 1970).

Despite the importance of World War I for the Progressive movement, there is still no full-length, overall examination of that disputed subject. Various aspects of it are treated in Seward W. Livermore, *Politics Is Adjourned: Woodrow Wilson and the War Congress, 1916-1918* (Middletown, Conn., 1966); Robert K. Murray, *Red Scare: A Study in National Hysteria, 1919-1920* (New York, 1955); Charles Hirschfeld, "Nationalist Progressivism and World War I," *Mid-America*, XLV (July 1963),

139-156; Neil Thorburn, "A Progressive and the First World War: Frederic C. Howe," *Mid-America*, LI (April 1969), 108-118; Robert F. Himmelberg, "The War Industries Board and the Anti-Trust Question in November, 1918," *Journal of American History*, LI (June 1965), 59-74; Arthur M. Schlesinger, Jr., *The Crisis of the Old Order, 1919-1933* (Boston, Mass., 1957), 37-45. For still further titles, see Herbert F. Marguiles' sensible handling of a very hard subject, "Recent Opinion on the Decline of the Progressive Movement," *Mid-America*, XLV (October 1963), 250-268.

The debate on the continuity of the Progressive impulse after 1920 is still unresolved. For historians who emphasize the discontinuity, see Hofstadter's *The Age of Reform*; William E. Leuchtenburg, *The Perils of Prosperity, 1914-1932* (Chicago, 1958); Otis L. Graham, Jr., *An Encore for Reform: The Old Progressives and the New Deal* (New York, 1967). For evidence that stresses the continuity, see Schlesinger's *Crisis of the Old Order*, 111 ff; Kenneth C. Mackay, *The Progressive Movement of 1924* (New York, 1947); J. Joseph Huthmacher, *Massachusetts People and Politics, 1919-1933* (Cambridge, Mass., 1959); Arthur Mann, *La Guardia: A Fighter Against His Times, 1882-1933* (Philadelphia, 1959) and *La Guardia Comes to Power: 1933* (Philadelphia, 1965); Clarke A. Chambers, *Seedtime of Reform: American Social Service and Social Action, 1918-1933* (Minneapolis, 1963); Robert S. Maxwell, "The Progressive Bridge: Reform Sentiment in the United States Between the New Freedom and the New Deal," *Indiana Magazine of History*, LXIII (June 1967), 83-102; William E. Leuchtenburg, "The New Deal and the Analogue of War," in John Braeman and Robert H. Bremner, eds., *Change and Continuity in Twentieth-Century America* (Columbus, Ohio, 1964), 81 ff. For further reading on the subject, see Burl Noggle, "The Twenties: A New Historiographical Frontier," *Journal of American History*, LIII (September 1966), 299-314.